UNION

HISTORY

SERVITUDE, METAYAGE AND

CIVILIZATION

The Belmont Salt-Pond, Union Island

Sea Salt -Union Island's treasure & natural resource.   Photo: Don Wiss.

You are about to embark on an exciting journey!

UNION ISLAND'S HISTORY

UNADULTERATED

Copyright © 2012 by Joseph Stewart
Edited and Published by Josiah Stewart (2018)
Front covers photograph by Josiah Stewart
Book Interior designed by Josiah Stewart
Book cover made by CreateSpace
LIBRARY OF CONGRESS TXU 1-797-154

ISBN: 978-0-9913374-1-5

My Friend & Coworker

Coretta. Enjoy!

6/25/'18

Josiah .

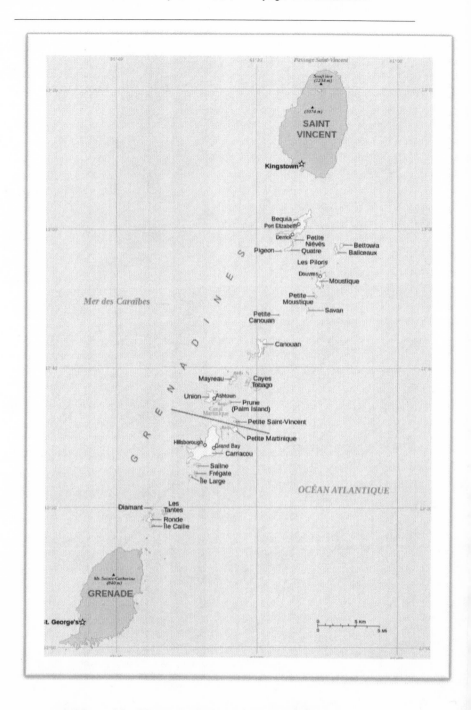

A Map of St. Vincent, Grenada, & the Grenadines.

Table of Contents

Opinions, Accolades & Gratitude On Union Island History, From Servitude to Civilization.

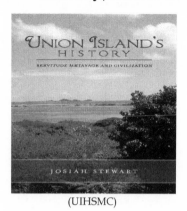

(UIHSMC)

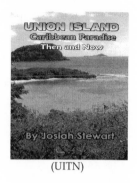

(UITN)

In the month of January 2014 when this book (UIHSMC) was introduced in its raw form, everyone was exquisitely excited about the preservation of Union Island history. In only a few weeks of its publication, the office phones were ringing incessantly. They were avalanched by myriads of love and gratitude from folks whom I had never heard of, or seen before. Diurnally, a multitude of phone calls were coming in from the United Kingdom, France, Canada, Kenya, Ghana, Nigeria, Curacao, Aruba, Trinidad & Tobago, Barbados, Grenada, Carriacou, St. Vincent, Mustique, Bequia, Canouan, Mayreau, Union Island, and right here in the United States of America. Among the many whom I have spoken to from the comfort of my office, three people stand out predominantly. The names of these people are Ms. Eastlyn Alexander, Pastor Edwin V. Richards, and Raleigh Raymond; they reside in the United States of America and Canada respectively. Later that year, I had the opportunity to meet and greet these folks for the first time. Their words of advice and encouragement were tremendous; I cannot explain how much I remained inspired since then. Several other telephone conversations with friends and fans were also very stimulating. Startlingly, their thoughts were almost identical. They wrote: "The hardest thing to do was to put down this book once I began to read it." "That book had all of my attention Josiah! I have never read any book like it before." "I can identify fully with this one; you touched on everything Joe." "This book is amazing, inside out." "This is my favorite book –may be the best Caribbean book that I have ever read." "On my way home on the train, I started to read this book, but…O my God, I got carried away so quickly that I literally missed my stop for the second time in a week." "This book had me zone-coasted Joe." They went on and on. On a one-to-one basis, many of my compatriots have said to me: "Thanks for your research and the many years that you have taken to document our history. Without this book, we believe that the history of this little island would have gone down the tubes. Luckily, what we have here now will last for centuries to come." Many others, within their calm, unflustered lifestyles have chosen the pen and the keypads instead. Below are the voices of a selected few –the written words.

"Union Island! Where is that?" I asked Mr. Stewart when I met him for the first time. He mentioned that he was born on a tiny island called Union Island. "Never heard about that island before!" I responded in amazement. Then he told me that I could learn about Union Island if I read his book, *Union Island Caribbean Paradise Then & Now* -his first publication as a writer. In 2014 I purchased this book at a reasonable cost, and the rest was his-to-ry."

"It is now 2018, and I still haven't been to Union Island; but after reading his book, I feel as if I had visited that island several times before. Mr. Stewart's description of his birthplace is outstanding and phenomenal. His book is informative and exciting; I learned quite a lot about the culture of that island and its people. I am also from the Caribbean; I was born in the beautiful *Land of the Humming Bird* -Trinidad & Tobago, and I can tell you that the culture of Union Island is similar to that of Trinidad & Tobago."

Union Island "Caribbean Paradise" is very interesting, and arguable the best books that I have ever read regarding Caribbean's history. I enjoyed this book tremendously. If anyone wants to learn about Union Island, its people, and culture, I request that they invest in a copy of Union Island *Caribbean Paradise* Then and Now and the new publication Union Island History –Servitude, Metayage and Civilization. These are excellent reads folks, and I guarantee that you won't have any regrets after reading these books.

Veronica Jobe –
Healthcare provider, U.S.A.

Josiah, congratulations to you with the publication of "*Union Island's History.* This work is undoubtedly the most definitive account that I've ever read that details the history, life and culture on this small island in the Grenadines. Union Island is the same Caribbean island that I grew up learning and knowing to be the erstwhile home of my family and that of my ancestors. Your meticulously researched work has provided me with a wealth of information, which supports, amends, and corrects long-accepted notions about the origins of the Mulzac/Malzac family. I learned that they were actually French Huguenot Émigrés who evolved over time, from the spelling of their surname to the colors of their skin. Thanks again.

Henry Mulzac -
Entomologist, Former Detective,
Criminalist and Intelligence Officer, USA.

Henry Mulzac, a Third-generation immigrant from Union Island in the Caribbean, is one of the grandsons of James "Jim" Mulzac and wife Mary Ramage of Ashton, Union Island, St. Vincent. James is the younger brother of the famed Captain, Hugh Nathaniel Mulzac.

I started to read your masterpiece last night but couldn't put it down for a long while. Nice job! You have covered a lot of grounds Josiah? Today, I resumed my reading and found myself choosing specific chapters to read. I learned so much…. e.g., although I knew the story of Bine, my uncle, I did not know that he met such a tragic death in the city of New Orleans. I particularly like your writing style. Congratulations once again on a job well done. I am looking forward to your next book.

Gloria Stewart-Ambrose –
Former Educator, McGill University, Canada
The Author of *Union Island Revisited.*

Good read Mr. Stewart! My husband and I (both in our 60s) have read your book in January, and then in June 2014 -six months later. We just wanted a refreshment of the Caribbean flavor. We looked up St. Vincent & the Grenadines and saw Union Island -the little paradise among a chain of other small islands. We hope to visit your neck of the woods soon.

Janice G. -
Maryland, U.S.A.

In this book, the history of Union Island is well researched; it is a well thought about publication. It was written with much love for the island and its people. The author captured the essence of the island, the "Then and now." He brought back some long-forgotten memories of how things were in the past; how far the island has progressed in regards to modernization, and undesirably its distasteful regression of love and unity for one's fellowman. Good going, Josiah.

Ann Adams-Hendricks –
School Guidance Counselor,
Department of Education, U.S.A.

Yes, Joe, God has enabled you to perform so great a feat in writing such an excellent book. This book is really food for thought. You do know that there was a guiding hand in all of this, don't you? Give the praise and the glory to him (Jesus Christ) who gives all good and perfect gifts. I pray that "His" will be done in all of your future endeavors and that you will be careful to recognize it and thank him for his loving kindness to you. Bless his name.

Caroline Delancy -
Former Respiratory Therapist,
New York, U.S.A.

Wow! The story of Union Island is finally out. Now, it is the time for everyone to become apprised of the history of this practically unknown island. I do believe that this fine literary work of art will last a lifetime. The great effort, dedication, and determination that you put into this single project qualify it to become the magnum opus of your literary career. I Love you Dad.

Khalid Josiah Stewart Jr. -
Student, U.S.A.

Let me start by saying that this book is a Must Read, and by far, the best one that is written on Union Island's history. As a young girl growing up on this tiny island, I had my fair share of Roast Bakes and Cattle-Milk Butter, but strangely, I never knew how this fine butter was made. You documented some amazing stuff here Josiah! Thank very much for sharing.

Gracita Wilson-Alert –
Resident, United Kingdom.

I love this book! Not withstanding the author's personal experience. I admire the systematic exploration of the historical studies and references that have been done to establish the facts of this beautiful, yet virtually unknown island. His hard work and perseverance have certainly done its part in regards to keeping the history of Union Island alive. Great Job!

Khadijah Stewart –
MSc Human Resource Management
Trinidad W.I

Great book Josiah! Accurate, interesting, but most importantly, it is a superb read. I truly enjoyed it. Once I started reading this book on *Union Island's history,* I just could not put it down for a minute. You did Justice to Union Island.

Sincere Morgan-Noel –
RNC, BSN Nursing MSc. U.S.A.

Reading the history of Union island stirs my patriotism and revived my loyalty to the teaching profession; it restores trust in the development of the students and triggers creativity for my next visit to Union Island. The last chapter, I must admit, was a bit too real for me – so many of our elders have been laid to rest. Thank you, Joe, for sharing the stories of Union Island Then.

Mickey Hutchinson –
Former High school teacher,
Union Island, St. Vincent.

The research done to make Union Island History –Servitude Metayage and Civilization a reality is admirable. The content of this encyclopedia is second only to none. It has been meticulously written with unusual but informative facts; it unveils the history of a tiny Caribbean paradise that is situated among some dense coral reefs of the Caribbean. It speaks about the African Diaspora that was ushered in during the 18th century to become the burden bearers for the Europeans in their quest for wealth and power. This was the untold story of a people, a time, a culture. It needs to be in the classroom. Thank you. Your effort falls not on stony ground.

Kwame Stewart –
Entrepreneur & Building Contractor
New York, U.S.A.

Union Island, from its early stages to its present state, was depicted here in a logical sequence and classical form. Reflecting on the Island's growth and development while reading, this book outlined the intricate route and transformations that she has experienced on her journey to this present economic and social state. The author researched all the important areas obtained from documented literary assistance, personal experiences and most importantly, the incalculable information that he culled from the elders. Certainly, it was a pleasure to read *the history of Union island*. It reflects the struggle and pride of the past generations –A job well done.

Unquestionably, this book should occupy a special spot in one's personal literary collection on Union Island. Thank you, Josiah.

Raleigh Raymond -
Mechanical Engineer &
Former High school teacher-Canada.

As a second-generation Stewart/Mulzac, I had the privilege of traveling to Union Island at a young age. There I learned about my culture and heritage. However, this book has allowed me to obtain a fuller picture of *the how* Union Island came to be. The research done to write this book is commendable. I am almost halfway through the book, and I can't wait to read what is next. Thanks once again!

Dr. Ken Stewart -
Ph.D. Public Health, U.S.A.

I compared the complete story of UIHSMC to a series of books that are written about the Caribbean. This book by far exceeded them all. I love your writing style Josiah; it is freakishly inviting and impels the reader to explore deeper from paragraph to paragraph, page to page, and chapter to chapter into the island's history. I can imagine the great effort you took to align all of the elements into this single project. It is truly an expression of hard work, dedication, and purpose. I also thought that the price of this book is exceptionally reasonable too; it winds up being a lot cheaper than if I were to buy several books to attain the core essence of this single text. I gave *Union Island History Servitude & Civilization* 5 stars.

Barbara N. -
Durham, South Carolina -U.S.A.

Needless to say, this is a job well done, Josiah! I must admit that this is an outstanding piece of work here! People like you will continue to make us (Unionites) feel proud of Union Island and its rich history. Thank You.

Aldon Ambrose –
Minister of Religion (SDA)
St. Vincent & the Grenadines

Union Island History –Servitude, Metayage and Civilization is a great read for the African Diaspora, especially natives of the Caribbean; it has exposed just how pervasive the Europeans explorers were to the Amerindian and African societies of Union Island during the earlier years. And so, we must act and perform in schools and colleges, community centers, and seminaries, the stories, as a reminder of yesterday's events – simply raising awareness is not enough – in fact, it's not even close to enough.

Colin Roache -
Cleveland, OH. U.S.A.

This book is an encyclopedia that is laced with memorable anecdotes. It is also infused with some of the most glowing tributes to our indigenous builders of Union Island -those remarkable, splendid, and dedicated ancestors.

I, therefore, recommend that all Unionites, at home, and in the diaspora should own a personal copy of this book, and ensure that it is carefully preserved in each home for the interest of posterity.

Leroy G. Thomas –
Minister of Religion (Ashton, Gospel Hall)
Union Island, St. Vincent.

Below are the views of others with seemingly greater ambitions for this book (Union Island History –Servitude, Metayage & Civilization); they have taken their views a bit further by appealing to the Ministry of Education in St. Vincent & the Grenadines. Their ultimate desire is that the history of Union Island should be embraced and incorporated into the School's Curriculum. Read on.

For decades, I have resisted reading many books that speak sparingly of the Grenadines and the history of its people. I was of the opinion that these little islands do not have a documented cultural past or a history of their own. Amazingly, the title of this book speaks volume (*Union Island's History*), and indeed, the author has done a tremendous job; he dug up the past, condensed it, and now, it is available to humanity. In his book, he made multiple comparisons of the good old days of yesterday, and the customs of the people then as it relates to the contemporary lifestyle on the island.

With the above being said, this timely manuscript, which outlined the history of Union Island, has never been documented or made available in such a lucid and compelling manner. This book speaks of the indigenous natives -the Amerindians that once inhabited the region for centuries, and the emergent of two Frenchmen, Antoine Rigaud, and Jean Augier during the 1750's. These two French settlers, on their arrival, initiated the institution of slavery and the lucrative cotton cultivation on the island. Their presence though, represented the demise of the Amerindians as he carefully outlined in his text. Then came the Treaty of Paris in 1763, which give way to the dominance of the British Empire, and Samuel Spann, a wealthy merchant that immediately assumed the role as the patriot of the island. This island, which belonged to a chain of islands that were once referred to as Los Pajoros (flock of birds), was later given the name *Union Island* by Mr. Spann. He also named the two small villages that comprised the island; these villages are Ashton and Clifton -names that derived from two suburbs in England.

The author further outlined the arrival of Charles Mulzac's in 1863 (my great-great-grandfather). Charles initiated a system of sharecropping that was a travesty to the newly emancipated slaves. His eldest son Richard, a witty young man, supplanted him in his later years to become the entrepreneurial mastermind of the island. Richard, the father of the famous Captain Hugh Mulzac -the first black sailor to captain a US Merchant Marine, was a shipwright and the owner of several ships that conducted interisland trade in the Caribbean. He also did fishing and whaling extensively and reared a tremendous amount of livestock –an art that is still practiced on the island today.

The author made mention of the Maroon, Salt Picking, Boat Launching and a myriad of other customs that brought the salient memory of the early 20th century alive. The inclusion of the local dialect, in my assessment, is a critical point in this book and unquestionably a treat, especially for older folks. Surely, one may never know what this can conjure up. But, in my estimation, it was intended to evoke passion and emotion that will bring about many, many purposeful discussions.

Evidently, this book should be inducted into the school curriculum, for it is the most inspiring, informative and educational book that is written on Union Island by any Vincentian author in recent times. Undoubtedly, this is a book for the past, the present, and the future. Folks, this is a must read!

Dr. Kendall B. Stewart DPM. -
Podiatrist, Brooklyn, New York.
Former City Councilman, New York.

Dr. Kendall Stewart is the Great-great-great-great-grandson of Admiral Oliver Samuel Spann, the first owner of the island. And as mentioned above, he is also the Great-great-great-grandson of Charles Henry Mulzac. These gentlemen were two of the earliest European descendants to lay foot on the little paradise -Union Island.

Many years ago, (1948-1963) I have taught at primary schools in St. Vincent and Union Island respectively. As a former schoolteacher, I have always been interested in the educational well being of children of all ages and walks of life. Recently, I have read the history of Union Island, written by Mr. Josiah Stewart, a native son of Union Island. I was captivated with the authenticity and the fervent manner that he used to outline and express the history of the little island. The information is in accord with what my grandmother Adriana Ambrose had told me about my ancestors during my teenage years. I was awestruck to read about my great grandparents Oliver and Mariana Spann; they were buried at Garden Field Cemetery –a forgotten private burial ground that is located in the bushes of Ashton. I am equally surprised to be reminded of local customs, traditions, Idioms, and dialects that are mentioned -they once were an essential part of the island's culture. With absolute certainty, I can state with authority that no such history of our island can be found in the school's curriculum of St. Vincent & the Grenadines, or in any other literature for that matter. Thus, I am appealing to the Ministry of Education of St. Vincent & the Grenadines that such outstanding work should be acknowledged, embraced, and incorporated into the curriculum of the schools of St. Vincent & the Grenadines.

It is in my opinion and reason that the youth of today must be educated, informed, enlightened, and to a greater extent, conversant of the history of our ancestors. This book will award them for the first time with a history of their own; a history that will tremendously expand their knowledge and self-worth. With that being said, I must now say congratulations again to you Josiah, and thanks for writing and explaining in such an eloquent manner about our history. I am looking forward to your next book, lots more about Union Island. Keep up the good work.

Eastlyn Alexander -
Former Healthcare provider, U.S.A.
Former Schoolteacher/Head Mistress, SVG.

Ms. Eastlyn Alexander, an octogenarian who resides in the heart of New York City; she is the great-great-great granddaughter of Admiral Samuel Oliver Spann -the wealthy British merchant and first European that owned Union Island.

The stories of Union Island were passed on through the oral tradition for over 200 hundred years. Recently one writer authored three books: (I) On the life of the writer's father (ii) Entrepreneurship on Union Island and (iii) Union Island Revisited– this was an attempt to capture and preserve in writing some of Union Island's cultural past.

In this book, the author provided an in-depth view of the history of the island, its business development and the peoples' way of life. The stories are told from research, testimonials, and personal experiences. The personal approach of the Impetus (Stimulus) and Introduction to the Book sets the tone for the reader. Everyone likes a story, and in this case, a story laced with the common vernacular of the island keeps the readers' interest, even laughing out loud at times. The ah-ah moments are frequent. The No-o-o-o's, the surprises – Is that so? And the exclamations – Didn't know that! Or how did he come about such information?

The writer demonstrated excellent listening, recording, and recall skills. Displayed solid research abilities and the kind of tenacity seen only in bulldogs. This book fills the gaps in the reader's mind of the history and culture of the island. It compels the reader to reflect, reminisce, and stirs up a desire to restore and preserve the history and culture of Union Island.

For readers, particularly in the Diaspora, they are beset with laughter, recall some scenarios with trepidation, awareness of the ever-crossing bloodline and begin to put the long-lost pieces in place. The stories are sobering and compelling. The author has taken me by surprise – he was my student at the Union Island Secondary School. This book is highly recommended as a text for all students at St. Vincent & the Grenadines Secondary Schools.

Mickey Hutchinson –
MA. Community Counseling, Canada,
DIRECTOR -RITE OF PASSAGE EXPERIENCE PROGRAM, CANADA.

The author is a Caribbean middle-aged male, whom one can classically call "A student of life." Despite having limited resources available to him throughout his youthful years, he has always found a way to attain knowledge via creative utilization of every opportunity and challenges he has encountered. Working his way up, he has self-taught and mastered the discipline of woodworking before eventually preparing himself for a career in the medical field as a HealthCare Provider -a passion he has long harbored since he was a young boy. Observing the phenomenon of Caribbean immigrants that have left their homes each year in search of a better life in America has prompted him to examine the trend of relocation, and the impact that it has on them. Armed with the knowledge that had been passed down to him from elders, coupled with his youthful experiences, assertiveness, and unwavering tenacity for knowledge, he set out to archive his valued collection - history rather. Over the span of a decade, he has amassed a wide array of information by way of interviews, books, and an extensive range of Internet researches. Steadily piecing together an accurate and intricate story-like narrative of his birthplace, this erudite has expressed it superbly in his second book, Union Island's History – Servitude, Metayage & Civilization. His work is surely a Classic.

Terri Janelle –
City University of New York, U.S.A.

Union Island Servitude, Metayage, and Civilization provides much-needed insight of a tiny island that often goes unnoticed amidst the commotion and attractions of the larger Caribbean islands. This island is a part of Saint Vincent & the Grenadines and has a very rich history and traditions that to this day still permeate the island's culture. However, most of this is unknown to the rest of the world, I reiterate. The author does a fantastic job of shedding light on this island in the shadows. Easy to understand, skillfully descriptive, and illustrated with a multitude of beautiful images, this book provides the reader with vivid imagery that transports him to Union. The author both incorporates and deciphers common lingo of the island, making it easily accessible to all. This book is a must-read for those unfamiliar with the Caribbean Islands, and more importantly, for all those who have lost touch with their ancestry and history through the generational gap and immigration.

Shaniah J. –
New York University, U.S.A.

I migrated to Union Island in 2007, and quickly fell in love with the people and their culture; I became very excited, and inevitably got involved in the many cultural activities on the island. Observing that no entities were covering these events, I quickly, started a non-profit media outlet -Radio Grenadines; with that, it enabled me to cover the many cultural activities of the Island. I utilized many written articles with videos, photos, etc. to make it possible. Then in 2013, I was introduced to Josiah Stewart; he was collecting pictures for his book -*Union Island, Caribbean Paradise, Then and Now,* and I was willing and excited to share whatever media I had to make this a success.

The Author told me that at the age of 19 he had a dream, and was passionate about documenting the things that he had seen as a young boy, and also stories that were told to him, (Then and Now). Today, being much older, he has fulfilled that lifelong dream to make his contribution to Union Island.

My first impression of the book was "Wow!" Josiah captured all the stories that I have heard about over the years; he did it in a well documented easy to read fashion. I read the book myself -the entire book! And it literally helped me put a lot of things into perspective. I have also learned that over the past century, Unionites, as they are affectionately called, have been migrating from Union Island to greener pastures; that exodus ultimately shaped the culture of Union Island. The author, with a heavy heart, referred to it as the "Exodus Factor."

Reading about the "Things We Used to Do" gave me an understanding of what Union Island was like before electricity was introduced on the island. Surprisingly, some of these customs are still practiced today while others can only be imagined or dreamed of. Union Island Then & Now captured an illustrious past that anyone can tap into.

For the cultural activities that are written in this book, again, some are still practiced up until today. Reading about them can leave you excited and craving to witness them. For me, learning about these activities has given me a more detailed understanding of the projects that I cover each year.

The Table of Contents is easy to navigate; the author makes it easy for quick referencing. Overall, this book is both a history lesson for me as well as a critical referencing tool; it helps me considerably while covering multiple stories for Radio Grenadines.

Stanton R. Gomes –
Director, Radio Grenadines Inc.

I have read many books written about Union Island, but this book on *Union Island's history* has surpassed them all. Josiah has covered a vast array of subjects: from crabs to cattle, bees to birds, fishermen to firefighters and plants to people. He has now immortalized its Traditions, Idioms, and Cultures. This book is a pocket-sized encyclopedia. It should be recommended reading for students in St. Vincent & Grenadines. I eagerly await the Revised Edition –Union Island's History Servitude, Metayage, and Civilization.

Pastor Edwin V Richards. –
Florida, U.S.A.

Pastor Edwin V. Richards, a Floridian resident, is the grandson of the last owner and landlord of Union Island, the late Mr. E. Richards of St. Vincent, West Indies.

GRATITUDE

Thank you everyone! It is largely because of your appreciation, love, gratitude, and candor for UITN why I am enthused to delve a little deeper to give you this unabridged version (UIHSMC). My only legitimate fear is the ever-present thought of being goaded into a catch 22 by many readers. Presumably, YOU might still find a way to ask for an extended edition after you have read the final paragraph of this book. And although I cannot promise satiety to everyone, I can guarantee one thing for sure. That one thing is a complete comprehensive view of Union Island's History, straightforward and unadulterated. Below is a sneak peek!

This revised edition of Union Island's history reflects on a detailed account on some subjects that I had scratched the surface in my previous publication. Some of these key examples include but are not limited to: The Exodus Factor, Captain Hugh Nathaniel Mulzac, The Stewart Family, Maroon Festival, Education & Homes, The Introduction of Religion, Landmarks & the Gospel Hall Church, The Revered Elders & A Woman's Role Yesterday. Some of these are worthwhile subjects that needed inclusion, for they complement the island's history considerably. And lastly, but certainly not the tiniest among these intriguing subjects is, The Stimulus. The Stimulus injects curiosity and zealousness into the reader's mind. As one reader in his perspective superbly expressed: "The personal approach of The Impetus (now, The Stimulus) and The Introduction in UITN set the tone for the reader." The Stimulus in this book compels the reader to put himself/herself in the author's shoes for a fine takeoff; what an intriguing journey that is! Oops! That still isn't the end, for I also have another fascinating subject that will captivate your attention. And although this event occurred on the soil of Union island some 38 years ago, no effort was ever made to document the detail of this occurrence. Sad, isn't it? Sure. Well, this intriguing subject is The Union Island Uprising. With the inclusion of this topic, readers are now opportune to read and understand for the first time, some of the principal ingredients and activities that led up to, and what transpired throughout that day - Friday, November 7th, 1979. Amazingly, UIHSMC comprises of all of the above and then some. Please buckle up your seatbelts.

To further pique the reader's interest on some of the above-mentioned subjects, a plethora of relevant pictures were interpolated throughout this book, and also on the URL (*unionislandhistory.website*) where you can get a better view of all the pictures that are listed in this text (*please visit*). These photos bring out character and authenticity, and to some, it evokes a numbing feeling of nostalgia. But I must inform you that after you have read the Stimulus and the Introduction in this book, you will recognize immediately that you have already gotten what you paid for this book. The rest is a bonus to you.

Folks, since I began to document Union Island's history, you have communicated with me via Email, Skype, Viber, WhatsApp, Facebook, Instagram, Tweet, IMO, texted, etc., and I have taken the time to listen, read, ponder, and now, to fill in the gaps, make the necessary emendations and relevant interpolations in areas that inevitably needed some work. I also responded in harmony with what you have expressed and requested. And so, I do hope that the demographics of today and tomorrow, like you, can find the time to read, study, deliberate, and to a larger extent, understand the long, difficult journey that our parents and fore parents have trodden. It was by no means an easy voyage. Colleagues, when it comes to the history of Union Island, I have to admit that there wasn't anything available to us for the last century. Absolutely nothing was in store for the native sons and daughters of this little island. And for that reason, I had been saddened for several decades. Saddened by not having a rudimental knowledge of our history, but I remained fervently hopeful and passionate that someday, something good will happen. And it did! But I never knew that that critical moment or period of decisive action and responsibility would have been mine –a commitment that is squarely assigned to my delicate and fragile shoulders. Many will agree that nothing comes easy. Yes, indeed. Well, the toughest thing that I had to tussle with was putting my hands on our history –a fragmented history that never made its way to a history book. Hence, we had nothing to call our own. As a result, I had to visit the bushes and cemeteries, and in some cases, the cemeteries in the bushes. There I partially dig up numerous tombstones to obtain their defaced epitaphs. Then after all of that, I had to comb the Registry of St. Vincent & the Grenadines in order to substantiate some of that information. Was it daunting and tedious? Absolutely! But was that the end of my harrowing work? Certainly, not! To complete my project, I also had to visit the homes of many elders to obtain supplemental and complementary information; sadly, 99.9 % of those the Silent Generation and Traditionalists are now deceased. And so, through hard work, struggles, successes, ideas, and energy I have been able to scratch the surface of achievement. Well...almost. And with the compilation of this data, you the reader will be hard-pressed to find this quality of information in any single text that is written about Union Island, or St. Vincent & the Grenadines, for that matter. Nevertheless, I feel energized and greatly delighted to do it, all for, and in the best interest of Union Island.

By scratching the surface of Union Island's history, and her-story, if you will. Hopefully, someone in the future will take it a bit further. As it stands today with this work, I do agree with many of you, that this book can serve well in the schools and libraries of St. Vincent & the Grenadines, and by extension, the Caribbean as a whole. Why? This book speaks about the African diaspora and culture that exited the motherland and startlingly made its way through the many waters to the Caribbean, the archipelago of 32 islands, the multiple coral reefs, and finally to the shores of an arid 3.5 SQ. Miles' landmass via the institution of slavery. And despite the constant cultural evolution and challenges, remarkably, many facets of the African culture are still alive today.

For this modest contribution of literary work to Union Island, I felt as though some of my social and patriotic responsibilities to her have been defrayed. Most importantly, I am blissfully in love with the affection, gratitude, and receptiveness from the many who have expressed their heartfelt thanks for my literary service to this little Island. Folks, you have fortified me with the subtle, but valuable information that has enabled me to reinforce my work.

Today, with many that are destined to read this book, evidently, the futures of our youths will be much more secure. And so, I do believe that every demographic has now been given the tools with which they can work effectively and with great facility. And so, it is out of humility that I chose to remain a servant to Union Island.

DEDICATION

To my Great Granny **Isabella Roache** of Point Lookout, Clifton. This lady was a vivacious nonagenarian of the 20th century; the sole individual whom I accredited greatly for discovering, or giving birth to a historical passion in me during my tender age of six. This passion has since morphed into an uncontrollable addiction -the kind of obsession that keeps my sanity fully intact and alive while I remained grounded. To the esteemed **Mr. William McDowell Stewart**, and his wife, **Mrs. Louisiana Stewart née Wilson** (My great, great grandparents), they are the root and sole ancestors of the entire Stewart family, which at one point made up the largest segment and core of Union island's population. And the final honor goes to **Mrs. Sheila Roache/Stewart** -my mother. She is the Encyclopedia, the Information Repository, the Google, the Databank, the Search Engine, and Stem Wall that enabled my vertical growth for well over five decades of existence on planet Earth; she is the single person whom I accredited with the greatest memory bank that I have known throughout my entire life. **Sheila** once lived with her grandmother, **Isabella Roache** at Point Lookout, from childhood to adolescent.

FOREWORD

There is a proverb that goes somewhere along the lines of, "We must first learn our history if we want to change our future." For countless years, as well as most of our lives, history told by the victors -those who have benefitted immensely from the labor, sweat, and tears of the African people and several other minorities across the globe has skewed our perception, lessened our self-value, and still inspire self-hatred.

It is essential that we reclaim ourselves and develops an understanding of our culture -one made rich through the lineage of powerful and effective kings and queens. We must remember that progress may be slow and steady, and change certainly does not take place overnight.

Since I have read "*UITN, and then the unabridged, Union Island's History, From Servitude, Metayage To Civilization.*" I must say that I have been enlightened tremendously. I strongly urge you to immerse yourselves in the pages ahead. They illustrate a rich and accurate history but also empower you to reclaim your heritage. As you relearn the beauty of the community, family, and honest hard work, all efforts to establish and maintain a solid foundation, make a promise to yourself to utilize your newfound knowledge of our ancestors and incorporate it into your daily lives.

It is crucial now for us to reverse the roles that we have been long cast into for the sole purpose of regaining our identity for future generations. We chose education over freedom knowing that when the mind is free, so is the spirit; and for the shackles that bind our physical beings, they too begin to mean very little.

Enjoy this journey through time and pay the knowledge forward always.

--

Shaniah Stewart

A World at School | Global Youth Ambassador
CAS | Environmental Studies
New York University | Class of 2017

Acknowledgement.

As stated before, this literary assignment -*Union Island's History –Servitude, Metayage, and Civilization* is an expansion of its predecessor, UITN. Therefore, my gratitude has no boundaries. Once again, I have been blessed to remain in the esteem company of enthusiastic individuals who have rendered support to me throughout my tedious journeys. With that added energy, my literary work seems to have no end. My strength cometh from my immediate support structure, which comprises of: **Sheila**, Khalid, Khadijah, Niael, Anesia Belgrove, Evelyn Lucas, Carol Simmons, Solomon Adu, Andy Stewart (my brother), and Ruth John (my cousin, and great-granddaughter of *Isabella Roache*). Thanks again to Carol Simmons for assuming the status as my *Help Meet*, as Eve in the great book of Genesis, was to Adam, the father of civilization. To my former classmates of Swedish Institute, College of Health Science who were energized to hear me speak passionately about Union Island, an Island that they have never heard about. They are: Adriana Almanzar, Tinean Livingston, Cassandra Fleurimond, Ann Marie Turner, Cindy Rodriguez, Mallorie Guevarez, Naiyma Livingston, Gabriel Poonce, and Alice Lock. May your various careers be bright. To my instructors: Ms. Shoba Parasram, Cindya Coffey, Hazel Bernardino, Giselle Peralta, Dr. Sherman, Dr. Nihad Atlic, Dr. Fredric Cohen, Dr. Jeremy Moss, Raul Castillo, and Juan Pilarte. Your vast knowledge has permanently transformed our lives; fortunately, we cannot return to our former selves. To you guys, I am very thankful. I love you all.

Special appreciation also goes to the following individuals who gave freely of themselves, their time and energy to help make *"Union Island's History –Servitude, Metayage and Civilization (UIHSMC)* a reality. Among this invaluable group are: Mr. Mills McIntosh, Pastor Edwin V. Richards, Minister Leroy Thomas, Raleigh Raymond, Pamela Grant, Glenford Stewart, Norma Thomas, Tyler Thomas, Kay Thomas, Junior Coy, Carlton Stewart, Maria Alexander, Lennox Charles, Annette & Stephen Thomas, Junior Polson, Holden Regis, Keith Stewart, Jenny Charles, Harold

Daniel, Caroline Delancy, Millicent Alcide (Liz), Marjorie Roache, Annie John, Henry Mulzac, Pete Ahern –son of late Elaine Mulzac, and most importantly, the ever-present **Sheila Stewart** who never ceases to amaze me. From those who are now deceased, their information remains priceless. They are: Charles Stephen Stewart "Ba Mindo" (my grandfather), Mr. Alfred Cox, Martha Edwards, Patience (Ma-paysh), Ma Julies, Janey Stewart, Janey Roache, Ethneil Mitchell, Caroline Telina Roache "Tan Tillix" (my grandmother), August "King" Mitchell, Leonard Scrubb, and my dad Charles Garfield Stewart. And most importantly, I owed an incredible amount of thanks to my great granny, *Isabella Roache* (Ta Muggy), the old lady who discovered me, and aroused/evoked that never-ending historical passion of Union Island that I now hold on to doggedly. For their immeasurable contributions, inputs, and blessings, I owe a tremendous amount of gratitude and incomparable thankfulness.

Special recognition again goes to my daughters Khadijah and Shaniah, who has been my inspiration since their births in 1988 and 1994 respectively; and now, Khalid Josiah Stewart Jr., my last son who was born in 2005. They all have helped to put my life on an even keel during my sojourn away from my natural habitat. Once again, I express my sincere gratitude and love to Mrs. Eileen Stewart, for her priceless interventions during the many demanding years of my life; I must say categorically that I am eternally grateful.

To the many, whose names are too numerous to mention, but whose love, support, respect, help, inspirations, and encouragements are incredible, I thank you. And to you, *The Thousands* whose lives have been touched after reading UITN, I have valued, recognized, savored and appreciated greatly your abundant love and contributions. And yes, the last word belongs to my mother **Sheila E. Roache-Stewart**. For all that I am and hope to be, I owe it to her indelibly.

For your collective help and intervention into my space, I feel loved, honored, and greatly inspired to continue my literary work with celerity, renewed energy, and cheerful readiness. Once again, I thank everyone.

From my roots, which derived from the west coast of Africa, I speak loudly from the mother tongue. In the Yoruba language, I utter with dignity, the word of my ancestors, *"Ase!*

AUTHOR'S NOTE

I have realized that every household in Union Island has at least one member of its family that is living abroad. Yes, indeed! And the countries that these Unionites have emigrated to, are: England, Canada, USA, Trinidad & Tobago, Aruba, Curacao, Panama, Martinique, Antigua, St. Martin, Nevis, Anguilla, Tortola, Barbados, and even in the sister island of St. Vincent. Youngsters are always the first to venture abroad; their parents, while still in Union Island, are always excited to speak passionately of their children's accomplishments and good deeds. *"Jenny is in Canada yo know,"* Miss Elma said. *"She working in ah hospital in Toronto; she is meh first daughter. Marva is studying Law in England; she say she want to be ah lawyer and have she own company when the time come. Emris, yo know Brent married? Yes...meh last son; he married ah nice English girl; she mother is ah Jamaican, and she father is from Italy. And they go to the same church way the senator go to. So, yo see meh three pickney doing good."* (By derivation, the word *Pickney* came from the word *Pickaninny* that means small black child). They go on and on. On seeing the excitements on the faces of these neighbors, I too was elated, and had high hopes of traveling abroad, and so were the many young chaps and contemporaries like myself. They also were equally excited to visit England, Canada, and the United States of America, etc. It was a status symbol then and still is today for anyone at home to have a relative that lives in those parts of the world. And obviously, it was every youngster's hope and dream to travel abroad at some point in his life.

For several decades, I have studied and analyzed the history of the people of Union Island and observed that there is a trend that was born during the early 20th century. This inexorable development has resulted from the sharecropping or Metayage era, another reprehensible period that superseded the malignant institution of slavery in Union Island. Regrettably, this trend has escalated during the 1930's and had yet to show any signs of decline. It is there to stay! But what is that trend? And why? Well, as you the readers carefully delve deeper into the contents of "*Union Island's History –Servitude, Metayage, And Civilization,*" your understandings will be substantially enhanced in the socioeconomic life of Union Island. You will also be apprised of the salient factors and influences that necessitate that trend. These factors are largely/primarily responsible for the molding and shaping of the island's culture.

In a lengthy interview/discussion with the late Ethneil Mitchell on Sunday, December 26th, 2010, she had quite a bit to say. This noble lady was a respectable citizen, and former schoolteacher of the first government primary school on the island (still referred to as Small School). We deliberate on several issues that are affecting the island as a whole. Most importantly, we spoke extensively, but passionately on a trend that we believed is most impactful on the island's culture. We later deemed it as The Exodus Factor. But why does this trend exist in such a physically beautiful island that possesses white sandy beaches, and hospitable people, all in a pristine tropical environment? The details of The Exodus Factor you will read in a subsequent chapter.

To complete this book, one of the mandates was to locate the burial site of Captain Hugh Nathanial Mulzac -the first black man to captain a Navy Ship in the U.S.A. Merchant Marine. His tombstone is located in Queens, New York -a site that Vincentians at home and abroad have never seen. Well, it took me two years of intense search to find that huge cemetery, and then to locate the gravesite. On a Sunday morning, I took with me, my brother Kwame, my daughter Shaniah and son, Khalid Josiah Jr. to the cemetery at Queen, New York. We were in the cemetery for approximately 45 minutes, looking frantically on some old tombstones for the caption "Hugh Mulzac." Then, I heard Kwame and Shaniah shouted in unison, "Look it here!" It was his tombstone which lies insignificantly like a needle in a haystack. Immediately, I became at peace with myself. We finally found the captain's grave –a job well done. Pensively pondering while we stand over this giant's grave and daydream, I placed my hands on my head. By then, I was experienced enough to know that it was safe to do so, even though my great granny had admonished me on a January afternoon some 50 years earlier (mentioned in *The Stimulus*). I closed my eyes in fear, and mentally journeyed to Union Island, then to Ashton Village where this man once lived. I realized one thing for certain. This man, when he left Union Island on Tuesday, March 12 of 1907, he thought that his stay abroad would have been for a few years, and a few years only. How wrong he was. Like many others, he too was totally unaware of the formidable might of The Exodus Factor. Unrelated, he indicated in his book, *A Star to Steer By*, "No matter how well one prepares oneself for life, the future is always in others hands!" Indeed, he is right! I also believe with all of my heart and being that even when planned activities are conducted with the best intentions and skills, they don't always turn out as expected. This is a condition that most Unionites (males) become aware of, especially during their unproductive latter years. Regrettably!

And with that, I came to realize that the lives of Unionites were never without challenges; but amidst those trying times, there was always laughter that derived from a type of humor that is unique to this little island. With that in mind, I felt obligated to incorporate that kind of humor with real life's experiences –the type that was native to our ancestors and remained as current as the air we breathe.

The tasty dialect of Union Island has always been integral to the island's culture. Hence, it has been sprinkled, pasted, mixed and massaged throughout this book to enhance flavor. For the entire Caribbean community, this old-fashioned dialect evokes a feeling of homeliness among the Silent Generation, Traditionalists, Baby Boomers, and even Generation X. To omit this Kalalloo flavor will be a blatant act of dereliction.

Attention! To the above-mentioned demographics that have spent some part of their lives on Union Island, what you read here will evoke passion and emotion that can engender a mirage of wistfulness. In other words, after you read this book, the yoke of nostalgia will be at your doorsteps. A relevant subject in this book is *The Stimulus*, which begins on page 1. The Stimulus is an intriguing story -an appetizer; it tells quite a bit about my personal experience on Union island during my formative years. It also creates a pathway to clearly understand this entire manuscript.

I do believe that this work, the compilation of the history and her-story of Union Island in "*Union Island's History –Servitude, Metayage, And Civilization,*" should be oriented towards the classrooms. It will inform, engage, enlighten and excite many on the story of Union Island's past -a unique one indeed. I further advise that every Caribbean household should own a copy of this book; not just having one for the sake of it, or to be placed on a shelf to accumulate dust. Instead, this book should serve as a clear reminder of our past, an African-Caribbean past.

"Immerse yourselves now, and enjoy the compilation of the history of Union Island and its people, the UNION-ITES. These people may be the only in the West that bears the ancient suffix *ITE*."

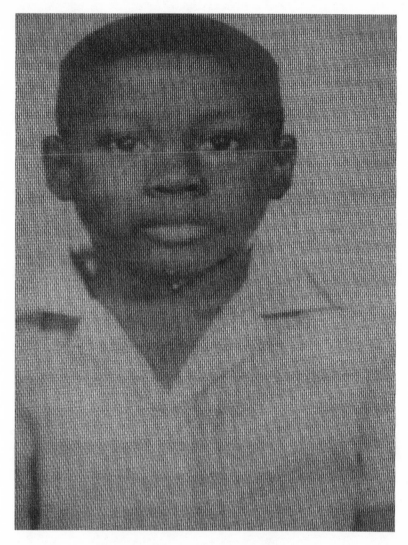

A Picture of Josiah Stewart, taken only two weeks prior to his departure from Port of Spain, Trinidad on January 15th, 1968.

THE STIMULUS

"Take yo hands off yo head; you want to kill yo modder?"

Port of Spain, Trinidad, once deemed the Refuge-Capital of the Caribbean for poorer islands like Vincent & the Grenadines, Grenada, St. Lucia, Dominica, Guyana, Barbados, Jamaica, Antigua, St. Kitts, Nevis, Anguilla, and other regional islands. During the turn of the 20th century, tough times were felt everywhere, but for the Grenadines that had little to do in the way of industries to enhance an already fragile economy, the region was scarred, Badly! Thus, many Unionites left their place of birth, visited this southerly haven in the Caribbean (Trinidad) and quickly make it their homes. My family too, they lived in the capital city, Port of Spain; we had a house there, and my father, Garfield, was a stevedore at the docks. He worked very hard to make ends meet, while my mother, **Sheila**, (a typical housewife) took great care of the household. At home, my parents always use the phrasal expression *Life is not* a *bed-of-roses;* in ignorance, I thought that they were referring to the bed in our room; little did I know that it had to do with the strains of everyday life in Trinidad. Rough times!

On a sunny Monday morning, January 1, 1968, I just had my sixth birthday when my mother told my sister Lyris and me that we were going to Union Island to live. At six, I did not know what she meant and had never heard of Union Island before. To be frank, I was quite innocent and hence did not know what an island was. A couple of weeks later, I learned that the beautiful little island, which is situated some 180 miles North of Trinidad, was the place of my birth. My parents told me that they had taken me to Trinidad when I was only three months old.

My sister and I were extremely excited about our intended travel to Union Island, and we spoke passionately about it each day with every ounce of energy we had. My mother and father, too, they were preparing tediously each day for that long journey at sea. "We have to get a bigger Grip (suitcase) for them children; that brown one too small to hold all da clothes," Mom said to dad as she looked through the kitchen window, *winding* a hot cup of Milo; she was preparing breakfast for us that early morning. We sat around the dining table and devoured our cups of milo and Hops bread. "We have to get a bigger Grip for them children" Mom uttered again. And sure, enough, she got us another brown suitcase, but that one was huge. All of our clothes and shoes fit perfectly inside of it. Exactly two days before our departure from Trinidad, I dreamt of my grandmother (Telina Roache), a woman whom I had never seen before. On Monday, January 15, 1968, we left the city of Port of Spain on a vessel bound for Union Island; waterway was the only viable means to gain access to the island. That vessel's name was Speedy Queen. Two days later, about midday, we arrived at Clifton Harbor, our destination. With my sister Lyris standing next to me, our father lifted us off the craft onto the jetty. While standing on the little pier, a strange feeling inundated my frail body. It was the beginning of a new phase of my life. I was a very curious child back then; always want to know why things were done a certain way. But I learned quickly that asking a lot of questions were not in keeping with the culture and tradition of Union Island; it is considered *out of place* for a child to ask an adult too many poignant questions. Because of that, I seldom asked any question in class for I just did not know which of my question might be considered out of place or rude. Eventually, I became a recluse in class and was uncharacteristically quiet. Nevertheless, I grew to love Union Island tremendously, but I also grew to understand that I was in a land of sparse opportunities.

At Clifton Harbor, we met with two other siblings, Urias, and Ezrard. They were equally excited to see us, as we were to see them. The landscape was very flat I observed; the sun was beaming down on us. It was a very hot day too. It was incredible to see the sandy surrounding; I was fascinated when I saw goats and cows tied to their stakes. I had never seen that before. I thought they were very close to the sandy road and I wanted to touch them. That day, I saw my grandmother, Telina Roache, for the first time; her head was wrapped in a red bandana, which she called a *head-tie*, and her face was a replica of the person that I had dreamed about a few nights earlier. I later learned that the bandana that Grandma had wrapped around her head was one of the customs of the female slaves on the cotton plantations of Union Island. The slaves were given head scarfs by the slave masters and commanded to keep their heads tied at all time. The reason for this was because the slave master thought that the hairs on the head of most female slaves on the plantations were unkempt or disheveled. Grandma took us from the jetty at Clifton Harbor and walked us all the way to Point Lookout to meet our great-grandmother, *Isabella Roache* (her mother). Unlike my siblings, that walk was the beginning of a life-changing journey for me.

In that community, everyone calls **Isabella** "Ta Muggy," but we, her immediate relatives, call her "Ma." Grandma took us to the little house to meet Ma, an old woman with a head of silvery-white hair. Then, a few minutes later she (grandma) went approximately two hundred feet away to her little house. Ma held me and kissed me, then later seated me on a wooden bench. I thought that I could have touched the other side of the house; it looked very tiny.

That evening I remember seeing a Bumblebee trapped in her curtain, and as I rose to catch it, I was stung and in pain. Almost immediately, my index finger began to swell. Instantly I placed my hands on my head and screamed as loud as I can. Ma looked at me in amazement and shouted, "Take yo hands off yo head lil boy; you want to kill yo modder?" With tears in my eyes, I quickly remove my hands from my head and stared at the old woman, and instantly she came to my rescue. She tore a piece of cloth from an old brown dress that she had, and with some Canadian Healing Oil, she dressed and tied my little finger firmly. "Felix, don't worry," she exclaimed in a gentle voice. She then opened a jar of Paradise Plums and Kaiser ball (candies), and with a soft smile, she placed one of those huge candies into my mouth. Instantly I smiled but was quite baffled; I did not understand what she meant when she asked if I wanted to kill my mother. A few years later, I learned that she was referring to one of the superstitious beliefs that are native to Union Island. According to that superstition, if any youngster puts his/her hands on their head, their mother will die soon after.

I stared at my great-granny while observing the distinct difference in her dialect but remained intensively perceptive to everything she had to say. She proceeded to place me on her lap to assuage the pain of my swollen finger. It was during my short stay on her lap that I received my first lesson on the history of Union Island. Ma told me about a slave on a Union Island plantation that refused to work and was subsequently buried alive. She also referred to another who had the roof of his little house yanked off; as she told the story, she pointed in the direction where his little shack was situated. She mentioned that she already had a daughter named Clouden and a son named James when the incidents had happened. My granny also told me about her years as a child growing up in Clifton and also her involvement in the Maroon Festival, Big Drum Dance, catching turtles, picking salt and doing other activities on the island. She said to me in a gentle voice, "Boy, when yo get bigger, yo will bring me some turtle eggs and crabs, yo hear?" Later, my Mom told me that she loves crabs.

Although I did not understand clearly what she was saying, I smiled and nodded affirmatively. I guess that's what she expected me to do. One thing for sure, I remembered vividly most of the words that she used.

Seeing how attentive I was, my mother, **Sheila**, laughed when my great granny mentioned the Maroon Festival, and she teased her about her dancing during the festivals. "You always jump and hold yo frack (frock) during the Maroon Dance," Mom exclaimed. "Less yo noise, **Sheila**!" Ma retorted. "What you know about Maroon dance? You don't know that I was one ah the best dancers in Clifton?" Immediately, Mom burst out in laughter. But before we could settle on who was right, we left Point Lookout in a grey jeep that was driven by Peter Wilson, a resident of Ashton Village. Our destination was Campbell Village, a small district of Ashton where my parents had a tiny wooden house.

On our journey to Campbell Village, via the main road, the route took us directly into Ashton Harbor, an area that was called Pauper Land at that time. There, we observed that the coastline of this little harbor was lined with thousands of conch shells; they were all heaped into several small hills. I was greatly astounded to see so many beautiful pinkish shells at one place. What a huge quantity at this single location? I questioned myself. Then I asked my mother. "How did they all get at that location?" She laughed as she looked at my perplexed facial expression. I was in awe. I thought that they were brought there from several locations to be used for some unknown purpose. Little did I know that this enormous quantity of shells had accumulated over a period of approximately 210 years? The conch that is native to the local reefs was an important part of the slave and sharecropper's diets. And with a scarcity of food on the little arid landmass, they eat it bountifully. Ashton Harbor, which was once called Frigate, was the home of the ancestors –the Africans that were brought and enslaved. They had been placed at that site since their arrival from Africa during the mid 18th century. Unaware why so many shells were at this harbor, I remained baffled for well over thirty years.

Approximately eight minutes later on our journey, we arrived at the little wooden house in Campbell. There we settled in nicely, and it became our home for the next twelve years. At Campbell, I observed that the houses were situated far apart from each other, but at Point Lookout, there was no difference. My grandfather, Charles Stephen Stewart, also had a small house several yards from our house; the neighbors called him Ba Mindo, but all of his grandchildren called him *Dada*. He had loved me very much; one afternoon, he looked at me and said to my father Garfield, "Gaf, this is one of us." He meant that I resembled his side of the family very much, and he was pleased about that. Amazingly, some forty years later in Brooklyn, New York, my father looked at one of my daughters and said to me calmly, "Felix, this is one of us." I was speechless, but we had a hearty laugh. I think that the onus might be on me now to perpetuate that legacy. I guess it is a *Stewart Thing.*

Meanwhile, my sister Lyris and I were bored to death in that little district of Campbell because we did not have any TV to look at; there was no electricity on the island. No one had TV's on the island, period, but some homes had huge battery operated brown radios; it was the only device that was used to access news and the outside world. We did not play with other children as we did in Laventille, Trinidad. Urias and Ezrard had already adjusted to the ways of life in Union Island, having lived there for six months before our arrival. At Campbell, each of us had our chores around the house. But one thing that amazed me greatly was the method that my mother used to keep our yard clean. For the first week in our new home, she cut shrubs early each morning, tied them together tightly and used it as a broom to sweep our yard. It was unbelievable how clean our yard looked each morning after being swept with those bush-brooms. My siblings and I immediately grasp the art of making those brooms and later took over the task of cleaning the yard each morning. That was one of our first chores.

The nights at Campbell were very dark, but the darkness was driven away by a kerosene lamp, which was our only source of light. I can still remember clearly, our first lampshade, with the words "Home Sweet Home" on it before my sister caused it to fall and break. The crystal-like lampshade broke on a late Friday evening, and all through that night, our little lamp remained lit without a shade.

It was several weeks now since my sister and I had been taken out of Piccadilly Government School in Trinidad, and we needed to resume our schooling in Union Island. So early that year, I was enrolled at the Ashton Primary School, referred to as "Small School." Lyris and Urias, my two elder siblings, were enrolled at another primary school. Ezrard was too young to attend school.

My first day at school was very intriguing. The experience of being a student of Small School just held on to my memory doggedly. That morning, my mother and I left home very early and were the first at the schoolyard. We stood on the front steps and waited for the school to be opened. About fifteen minutes later, almost everyone was at school. That day, I saw the smallest of children walking bare feet to school all by themselves. I was in awe. A few minutes later, each teacher took his or her class outside into the schoolyard for inspection. My teacher was Ms. Sincere Alexander, she asked us, the students, to form a single line. The sun was shining down bright on us, and we were sweating profusely. Sincere asked us to put our hands together with our palms facing downward and held it up in front of us. *"I want to see All-yo fingernails."* She said sternly. Our hands were all pronated and stretched out, waiting to be inspected. Sincere went to the front of the line and started to examine each student's fingernails. And as she examines each student's nails, she uttered: *"Yo fingernail ain't clean at-tal, all yo too nasty, you didn't clean yo fingernail this marning, your fingernail always nasty, lay me see yo big finger?"* She continued. Finally, she came to me, checked my stubby fingers, look me in the eyes, then uttered in a commanding voice, *"Yo have to keep yo fingernail clean eh. Way yo name?"* I just stared at her nervously as someone in the line voiced, "He name Felix." Then another shouted, "No, dat nat he name, he name Jovez." I remained quiet in line and did not utter a sound.

In class, whenever a student wants to communicate with Sincere, they called her Teach-ar. This was not exclusive to our class, for each class in the entire school referred to their teacher as Teach-ar. That day, like most days, there was always a cacophony of noise at the school. But on that Monday, it appeared more alarming to me because it was my first day at school. Almost every few minutes someone at the school wanted their teacher's attention; and to get that attention from their respective teachers, they yelled at the top of their voices: Teach-arr, Teach-arr, Teach-arr. Most times, it was annoying, but I had no choice but to adjust quickly. I did just that.

At one particular time, I too needed the attention of Sincere, and unlike my classmates, I reluctantly uttered the word *Teacher*, but because the surrounding noise was quite overwhelming, it was difficult for her to hear my soft voice. Well, that was the first and last time I ever used the word *Teacher* whenever I wanted to communicate. I wasn't excited to say *Teacher* anyway, for I was used to saying Sir and Miss at my former school. Months went on, and at the end of the term and subsequent terms, I was labeled as reclusive or very quiet in class. Throughout my entire attendance at the primary schools of Union Island, I never initiate a conversation with the faculty in, or out of the schools.

My class had five long wooden benches. Each of them seats six students apiece. The students that sat on our bench were Elvis Allot, Junior Polson, Joel Bartholomew, Godfrey DeRoache, Sharon Simmons and me; everyone wanted to be my friend. Amazingly, during my first school term, I saw two students with writing slates in the classroom but never seen one afterward. Unfortunate for us, the people who were our educators were senior students 14 and 15 years of age, who had just left school after attaining a School Leaving Certificate. Sincere too was in that age group. This issue of having inexperienced teenagers as educators during my formative years will be expanded in another book. Unluckily, I never was able to assimilate fully into the entire school system of Union Island.

On my second day at school, my mother bought me The West Indian Reader. It was the sole textbook used in my class, and we, the students, were committed to memorizing many parts of this book rather than comprehending them. In retrospect, many past students of this school will agree that the contents of this textbook were pro-Europe; we were daily fed this menu as part of our intellectual diets. Whenever a book with pictures was brought to the classroom, my classmates and I become particularly excited. Immediately we will use that book to play games rather than reading it. One of the games that were played was called "Picture-Picture." With that game, a central person will hold the book in a closed position, and that person will then ask the question,

"Picture, picture?" Then one of us (classmates) will answer, "Yes picture or No picture." Then that central person will randomly open the book on any page, and if there is an image on either page, that student who answered "Yes Picture," won. That same student is permitted to remain in the game until he/she gives a wrong answer. Then, the central person will close the book, turn to another student and ask the question, "Picture, picture?" The game continued until the entire class has partaken of this game.

My class was Standard 2, and most of my classmates did not have a book of their own (The West Indian Reader), so Sincere thought sharing was the logical thing to do. One Wednesday afternoon, without alerting anyone, Sincere took our textbooks, divide the class into small groups, and appointed the person at the center to hold the book while the rest of us took a peek and read along. Later that afternoon, I discussed this with my mother who jokingly said to me, "The next time the teacher takes your book, you must say to her, "Dis nor fah-we, dis ah fo-meh." On hearing that, from my mother, I was bent on saying these words to any teacher who dared to take my book in the manner Sincere had. The following day, my book was again taken. Instantly I opened my mouth to recite the words that were given to me by my mom. I started out briskly, "Dis nor." but froze almost immediately and could not utter the remainder of the phrase. I realized that these words were foreign to my mouth and that I should have rehearsed them ahead of time. What the phrase *dis nor fah-we, dis ah fo-meh* means is "This doesn't belong to us; it belongs to me."

The above dialect is what was prevalent in Union Island many years ago; it was what I had to assimilate quickly into, and I had loved every ounce of it. It was an intriguing journey indeed, one that was worth every minute of my time spent on the little rock.

At our home in Campbell, boredom was stepping in. Days turned into weeks, and weeks into months, but eventually we were able to cope with our new environment. Then unexpectedly we lost our grandfather who died suddenly. He was only 84 years old.

It was on a Thursday afternoon, May 24, 1968; my mother was attending a meeting at her church. My father, on the other hand, had visited St. Vincent earlier that week and was expected back in a week's time. My siblings and I were all alone at home when my brother Urias and I decided to pay Dada a visit. It was approximately 4:00 P.M. We went right into the old man's house, for his doors were never locked. Urias trotted straight into his bedroom, while I remained in the living room. It wasn't even a minute later when Urias ran back out of the bedroom and quietly whispered to me, "Come, ah think Dada dead." I was unmoved. Then immediately, we went into our grandfather's bedroom and there, the old man was, lying motionlessly. Urias took his fingers and opened Dada's eyes to assert that he was lifeless. The blank stare I saw in his eyes made me shiver to my bones. My brother was right; the old man was dead indeed. Unlike my brother, I was in haste to leave the house. And instantly I was out of the door. That night, many people came by to pay their respects; I thought I saw the entire village of Ashton at his home. Most women in attendance had their heads nicely tied with *head-ties* like the one my grandmother wore that January afternoon when we arrived at Clifton Harbor. It was one of the customs of the natives. In the huge crowd, an old lady gazed at me and said to her husband, "O Gad, this lil boy favor Garfield eh?" (Oh my God, this little boy resembles Garfield, don't you think?). She looked at my sister Lyris, and said, "I could see this one is **Sheila** self; Lil ghal, come ya ley meh fix yo bodaze (bodice)." My sister, who was standing next to me, instantly stared at the old lady before going to her to have her sleeveless blue shirt adjusted. "But **Sheila** ain't see yo frack (frock) too long?" the old lady questioned my sister; Lyris, without a response, continued her stare at the old lady. "Nah watch meh bad-eye eh noh," the old lady said to me with a friendly smile, then she hugged me and asked if I wanted a sweetie. I nodded agreeably, and then she gave my sister and me one Toffee candy apiece. Later that night, my mother placed a plate of water with Hour Grass on the dead man's chest. It was a local custom -a belief that Hour grass, an herb when used with water in this manner, will prohibit the belly of the dead from rising.

The following day, hundreds of relatives, friends, and well-wishers converged at the Ashton Cemetery to pay their last respects at his burial. My grandfather, Charles Stephen Stewart was laid to rest at 5:07 P.M.

Immediately after the burial, my brother Urias and I slowly walked up to the main road; there we met our great aunt, Liz (Elizabeth Simmons). Aunty Liz was crying hysterically and yelling, "Me whan, me whan." She meant that all of her brothers and sisters had died, and she was the only one still alive. With so many people crying around us, and without a teardrop coming from our eyes, we felt out of place. Instantly, I held Urias' head closely to mine and whispered in his ear quietly, "I think we supposed to cry too." He looked at me as though he was pondering but never responded.

After Dada's funeral, we calmly walked through the darkness of the night to our home, which was situated a quarter-mile away from the cemetery. As soon as we entered the little house, a feeling of sadness inundated us. We sat on the wooden floor for several hours. There we reminisce silently about the entire activities at the funeral. Sadly, our callow minds did not help us from warding off the fear of zombies that we thought might enter our house through the windows and jalousies. On that night, my three siblings and I slept together on our parent's bed.

On a Friday evening, several weeks later at school, I was sitting in class, very close to one of my classmates; his name was Godfrey (Wheels) DeRoache. I was the smallest and youngest student in that class. Amazingly, Wheels was three years my senior. While the class was in full session, he said to me under his breath, "*Ley ah-we go pick tambren* (tamarind)" (Let us go and pick tamarind). As a new student, I thought that it was permissible for us to leave the class to go wherever we wanted to. The idea of picking tamarind was like music to my ears, so I was up for it. And in excitement, I whispered, "Yes!" to Wheels. Very quickly he rolled his book firmly into a cylinder-shaped object and placed it snugly into his back pocket. Immediately, I took my books and put them into my brown school bag. Suddenly, the chalk fell from the teacher (Sincere), and as she bent to pick it up, Wheels, without shoes on his feet, quickly darted out of the building. Instantly I became suspicious and remained seated in the class. "Boy, I was nervous!" Observing that I was still in class, Wheels peeped through the window in an effort to persuade me to follow him out of the class. But, Sincere, with her keen eyes caught sight of the little delinquent and immediately demanded that he return to the classroom. He did. On that evening, Wheels' punishment was four straps on his back from the headmaster. Sitting nervously with Pee dripping in my white underpants, I can say emphatically that I had learned a valuable lesson that afternoon. What an experience! But was that the end of such a harrowing occurrence? No! Several days later, Wheels refused to sit close, or talk to me, instead, he acted more friendly to the other chaps in the class, and on one occasion he initiated a fight against me in the schoolyard. Fortunately, it was Sincere's keen eyes again, but this time, she came to my rescue. Life at Small School was quite adventurous I must say, for I can speak about an event that happened on every day of the week.

Keep reading, folks, because "Dis is weh ah we like, and, we na-e go no whey till we finish." (This is what we like, and we are not going anywhere until we are finished reading).

On a Monday afternoon at school, while sitting in class, I was struck hard on the back of my head with a book. Unbelievably, it was an exercise book that was rolled into a cylindrical shape. The culprit was Urlin Quashie, one of my classmates who was sitting on a wooden bench behind me. His nickname was *Bow-Peep*. Everyone at the school had a nickname, but I did not acquire mine as yet; it came several years later. Bow-Peep mischievously hit me while I was reading my textbook, *The West Indian Reader*. In a rage, I turned around and swung at him. He responded in like manner, and immediately a fight ensued. Instantly, the voices of the students escalated into pandemonium as the fight progressed. The raucous-like behavior of the class caught the attention of the entire school; it was, after all, *Small School*. Sharon Lewis, a new teacher of our class on that day, was standing at the window unconcerned when the incident happened. Immediately, she rushed to the class, snatched a wooden ruler from a desk nearby and without asking a single question, she began to hit us several times. I received the lashes on my hand and shoulder. Disgruntled that I should not be treated in that manner since I did not provoke the incident, I shrugged my shoulders. My action enraged the juvenile teacher who hit me again on my lower arm. I wasn't having it, and so every time she hit me, I shrugged my shoulder again at her. She finally gave up. Donna, another teenage teacher from a nearby class, saw what had happened, came across to my class and took the ruler from Sharon. Donna had hoped to teach me a lesson that afternoon. She hit me much harder on the same spot. But every time she hit me, I shrugged my shoulders at her. This went on for several minutes. But because of my unwavering tenacity, the enraged juvenile abandoned her task and stared me in the eyes.

Then Sharon said to me in a commanding voice: "Go by the headmaster." In awe, I glanced at her, for the sharpness of her voice, I thought, did not match the pleasant looking girl that I had been looking at throughout the whole ordeal. Then Donna immediately pushed me in the direction of the headmaster. The headmaster was a short, dark-skinned man from St. Vincent. His name was Mr. Brown, and he was a faculty of the school for no more than one month, I recalled. His desk was situated on the far right-hand corner of my class. Mr. Brown, I remembered, was standing with a strap in his hands as he impatiently awaited my arrival. Everyone in the school looked on intensely at me. As I got closer to him, he placed his left hand on my right shoulder, turned me slightly to his left, and delivered four stern straps on my back.

At once, the entire school became abnormally silent. Still, in a state of distraught, the headmaster ordered the abused back to his class. Accede I did to his stringent demand. Lightheaded and in pain, I slowly walked back to my seat. Instantly, I felt nauseated and was overwhelmed by a throbbing headache. For a few minutes, while sitting on the wooden bench, I felt a bit comfortable, but that was short-lived for I became frail and later slumped over into my lap. I remained in that position for a while and heard some of my classmates whispered: "Teach-arr, Jovez sleeping, Jovez Skurt sleeping." But neither of the teachers paid attention to me then, or even tried to find out about my condition. I stood in my crouched position for a long time.

When school was over that day, I rose calmly from my stupor. But by then, almost everyone was gone. Embarrassed, I gingerly walked out of the building, but before I got to the final step, I vomited profusely. Still bothered with a throbbing headache, I sat beside the excrement for a while hoping to feel better, but I never did. After a few minutes, I slowly rose again and started my journey home to Campbell. On my way home, my mother saw me at a distant, I was walking slowly without my school bag. Mom knew instantly that something was tragically wrong. I had forgotten my school bag on the floor next to my seat. Mom walked down the track to meet me. Immediately, she held me and placed her hand on my neck, then on my forehead and said to me, "Boy, you sick, you have a fever. What happened?" Horrified and worried, my mom was saying so much and asking me so many questions, all at once. But with my already perplexed state of mind, coupled with the deluge of questions, I became even more confused. She took me into her arms and carried me home. Later, while explaining the ordeal to her, she looked at my swollen right hand in disgust and tried hopelessly as tears dripped from her eyes. I saw clearly the pain in her eyes and felt morose. Meanwhile, my sister Lyris stood nearby and looked at me caringly without uttering a word; her eyes said everything. Clearly, the feeling that inundated me at that moment was more painful than the beaten, which I had received at the school. "I wonder if I should give this child ah Cafenol (Pain Killer) for the headache?" Mom asked herself loudly while staring at me in a despondent state of mind. She was referring to me as a child, conveying how delicate I looked in her arms. "I am feeling sick she said." Then suddenly she took a glass of Andrew Liver Salts (Antacid) and drank it. The last thing I remembered that evening: I was being coerced to drink a bitter cup of Bush Tea, and the waxy feeling of Soft candle being rubbed on my forehead and neck. I imagine that sleep had the better of me that evening. Several months later, I realized that I had been fed the Seed-Under-Leaf herb, a plant that is known for its great medicinal value.

The following day, still sick and traumatized, I was unable to attend school. My father visited the school early that day to speak to the headmaster and to get my book bag that was left on the floor of my classroom. He was told that the incident happened only because I was hitting the teachers. What a lie! Of the two teenaged girls (teachers), one was unable to make eye contact with me for several decades later. I can only imagine how penitent she might have felt several years later into her adult life.

Even today, some 49 years later, I still wished that I were the father of that precocious little boy that was severely beaten and traumatized at the hands of a headmaster and two children in the form of teachers. To be beaten at the hands of two young girls who were handed the responsibilities of adults? Obviously, they knew not the skills of teaching, and neither were they formally taught the art of teaching. They did nothing more than what they had observed and inherited in their immediate environment. In essence, they didn't do anything wrong but ONLY followed the dictates of their culture that is guided by nature and nurture.

At Campbell, things were happening quickly; we immediately became the owners of livestock. First, we had a dog, and then goats, sheep, pigs, fowl, and a cow too. To my amazement, a few years later we would become the owners of the most goats in Union Island. We gave most of the goats our names. These names were Lyris, Ezrard, Urias, **Sheila**, and so forth, and these animals responded to our call. Within a year, we were raising most of these animals on one of the huge pastures of Ashton named Ms. Irene's Pasture. We were fond of the outdoors; we could go almost anywhere, and that meant freedom to us. My brother Urias and I woke up early each morning to look after our goats at that huge pasture. There we would meet with other chaps who also had their animals tied nearby.

But taking care of animals at Ms. Irene's Pasture was not without challenges; my brother Urias and I had more than we could have handled from the youngsters who also had animals at the same Pasture. Almost every day we fought with one of the boys. We just could not walk peacefully to Ms. Irene's pasture without someone picking a fight with us. And some of the older chaps would encourage the younger boys to fight us just for fun or excitement. They did not like to hear us speak with a Trinidadian accent. If we were to say the following words below, they would try to correct us immediately by saying the italicized:

- Board - *- Boad*
- Bird cage *- Bud cave*
- Tiptoe *- Tippy toe*
- Door *- Dow*
- Corn *- Carn*
- Dirt *- Dutty*

They were adamant that I was saying those words incorrectly and were bent on making me pay. The fights were happening so often; I thought that they were enjoying every ounce of it, even to the extent of receiving pain themselves. Rightfully so, that senseless act of fighting had a negative impact on my quiet temperament. It permanently transformed me from my totally quiet demeanor and brought out my rebellious instinct. As a result, I can say loudly today, that even though I still possess a relatively calm demeanor, I stand as an unflinching proponent against injustices.

Another day at school while standing in the schoolyard with my classmates, an old man was walking slowly by when my classmates began to heckle him. Ole-man Shuvvy... Ole-man Shuvvy... Ole-man Shuvvy.... The old man stood up, looked at us and flung a stone into the crowd. The stone hit me on my shinbone, and immediately, the skin came off, then my foot began to bleed. Horrified by the blood oozing from the fresh wound, I stepped into the school to draw the teacher's attention to my injured foot. Several of my classmates followed me, but before I could utter a word to the two teachers that were standing next to the door, my classmates in anger, shouted, "Is Shuvvy, Is Shuvvy way hit him, teach-ar, is Shuvvy, Shuvvy pelt ah stone and hit him an he foot. If was me, I widda hit him back." The old man Shuvvy, was the father of Augustus King Mitchell (mentioned later). The teachers looked at my foot in a nonchalant manner, and said to me, "Go by the pipe and wash it off." My classmates followed me to the pipe. But at the pipe, there was no water. We returned to our class instantly and sat down for a while, yet, my situation was not addressed. It appeared that the teachers had forgotten me entirely.

Baffled, but waiting patiently for the school to over in hopes of getting some forms of solace from my mother, I sat on the bench until the final bell rang to end the day. That evening, I walked swiftly on my journey home at Campbell. Hastily, I told my mother what had happened, and showed her my injured foot with the dried blood. "What is this?" she asked. She heads to the kitchen then came back with a small container of salted water and a piece of cloth. She sat me down, raised my leg, then drenched the cloth with the salted water and placed it on my injury. The cloth with the salted water remained on my foot for approximately 10 minutes before she took it off. That was the end of the ordeal. Collectively, that was justice and clinical service, the Union Island way. That's just the way life was in Union Island. But deep within me, I could not ingest that way of life, for I had that innate sense that there was a better way.

Nevertheless, the reason why I had loved Union Island was because of the many fruits that were available there. They just weren't accessible in Trinidad, and I never had such level of freedom and wealth of privileges before. In Union Island, I enjoyed the liberty of freely picking quavers, sugar apples, mangoes, cherries, plums, oranges, coconuts, and tamarind. That was incredible, and sometimes I would sneak into my neighbor's garden (Adrian Simmons) and help myself with a watermelon or two. But I had to make sure that my mother was nowhere around. I got to admit that Campbell meant home to me –in every aspect of the word. I don't think that there are words to explain how delighted I was as a little boy. Could you imagine that I actually dug potatoes and peanuts (groundnuts) too? And amazingly, I was allowed to keep all of the peanuts that I dug. Yes, they were all mine!

I had the privilege to visit the beaches every day if I wanted to. And I took advantage of that too. I made use of the delicious seaside grapes. I walked the reefs to get conch, whelk and even catch small fishes. I dug crabs, and removed *Long Back (crustacean)* from the rocks and ate them raw. And when the rainy season came around, I fished for sharks that come in the lagoon every year. I learned the art of fishing from older chaps in the neighborhood, such as Henry John and Emerson Ambrose. I caught lots of sharks at Campbell Bay.

But amidst all of these excitements about the various fruits, I had two disappointing moments during those early years at Campbell. And even today, 49 years later, they are still salient in my memory, and I sometimes wonder why. Firstly, my brother Urias and I were sitting under our guava tree when he said to me, "Felix, I am going to get some Common Cherry by a Common Cherry tree." I had never known of these fruits before, and happy I was on hearing the word *Cherry*, I decided to accompany him to get some cherries myself. I was so excited that I could not wait to get to that tree to eat some of those freshly ripe fruits. We hastened our journey to the tree. On reaching that huge tree, I was amazed to see so many ripe cherries hanging off one cherry tree; I thought that no one else had seen the tree before; so I was bent on having my fill and then keeping it a secret from the other youngsters at Campbell. I grabbed a bunch and placed a couple into my mouth and began to chew, but almost immediately my mouth was a sticky mess. And to make matters worse, they had an unpleasant taste too, they tasted nothing like cherries, and so I spat them out in disgust. I looked at my brother and saw him struggling with one of the little fruit in his mouth while another was stuck on his chin, and the skin of the fruit was fastened to his right elbow. I was upset. After all, he said they were cherries, I though and who really needs instructions on how to eat cherries? He knew instantly that I wanted to go back home. Yet, he still had the nerve to persuade me to eat a few more. He was crazy, I thought, for all that I wanted to do at that point was to get that unpleasant taste out of my mouth. We left the site almost immediately, and from that day until now, I have never placed one of those so-called cherries into my mouth.

Secondly, my entire family was in the garden, west of our little house. It was early in the rainy season, and we were cutting the shrubs and small trees to prepare the garden for an early corn and peas crops. I was just about to cut down a very green plant that was nearby, when my mother shouted, "Don't cut that tree, it is an English Grape tree." Excited to save the plant from the wrath of my little cutlass, I dropped the tool immediately, secured the small plant, and molded it nicely. Hoping that this plant will deliver

Picture of a Banana Quit perching on an English Grape tree

some nicely grown English Grape in the near future, I watered the plant every morning. Religiously! And the plant did flourish and grew very tall. But over the years, I observed that the plant never brings forth grapes. All it did was blossomed, and whenever I took a leaf off the plant, some milky white sap oozes out profusely.

Dumbfounded by my unreasonable expectation, I never asked my mother any questions about the plant. For over the years, I had seen many English Grape trees, and all of them were devoid of grapes. I later came to the realization that the name *English* was greatly revered in the Caribbean for several centuries.

Now, back to the beautiful pasture of Ms. Irene where we have learned many valuable and interesting lessons. Every Saturday, we would spend a tremendous amount of time taking care of our animals. During one of those long stays in this remote area, we had our first lesson on matters relating to the bathroom. I can tell you emphatically that when it was time to "go," we had to go. There were no two ways about that. It simply meant that we had to find a secluded area in the bush quickly because there were literally no latrines available there. I could also remember the times when we had no toilet tissue available, but we had to "go" nonetheless. And as young chaps, we just had to improvise and use whatever was available to us. That could imply using the leaves of plants that were available in the vicinity, or even other measures that were incredibly intriguing. Today, it is easy to reminisce about my formative years and be flippant about it too, for those days rendered some fascinating experiences indeed.

Many youngsters who reared livestock at those remote areas of the island will remember vividly and can relate downright to what I am referring to. Those days…. Yes! Then as soon as we returned home from the pasture of Ms. Irene, we would be greeted with a glass of Aloe Vera juice mixed with milk, Orange juice or Seawater. Our mother gave us one of those bitter drinks once per month. God, how I hated it! And although many years have passed since we had those golden days at Ms. Irene Pasture, I still disdain the smell of the Aloes juice today. Also, during the rainy season when we ate a lot of sugar apples and other sweet fruits, mom never wasted a minute to give us her favorite laxative Broclax. Broclax was chocolate-flavored and tasty; it sends us to the bathroom quickly. With Broclax, we had to be very mindful, for there were times when we think that we were passing gas, but quickly found out that the crutches of our pants were dripping wet.

One Saturday afternoon while at the pasture of Ms. Irene, my dad took us (Urias and me) farther into the dense vegetation to an area named Colon Campbell; there we found remnants of a cotton plant from what is believed to be an old cotton plantation that once belonged to his grandfather, John Henry Stewart. It was quite surprising to see the cotton plant for the first time. We were excited to lay our hands on the raw cotton and feel the texture. We placed a few of the partially opened cotton pods into our pockets, and off we went to look after our cow. That same afternoon, we gathered some dried wood to be used as fuel for cooking, but we did not have any rope to tie the collection. Dad stripped the bark of a Black Sage tree to make a piece of rope. He tied the bundle of dried wood, placed it with a *Karta* on Urias' head, and then we left for home. Then when we get home, we had our chores too. Each Saturday, we had to scrub our white Wachekongs (sneakers) with corn chaffs, then, apply whitening on them to prepare for school the coming week.

Back in Clifton, Ma and Grandma were doing fine, but Ma never ventured far from home; the most she did was walk slowly around the house with a wooden walking stick. We continued our visits to Clifton every month, mainly on Fridays, and we usually took Tiger Malts for her; it was her favorite beverage. We must have visited her, at least, nine times, and she always had something intriguing to say to us. She was a very humble woman who exhibited great affection toward us.

One afternoon when we were about to say farewell to her,

she questioned us with her gentle voice, "Way all you going? Ashtin?" (She meant Ashton). My mom nodded affirmatively, and off we went to the district of Campbell. Sadly, it was the last time that we had seen her alive. I must admit that during this short period of visits, I had grown to love my great granny very much.

On a cool afternoon of January 22, 1969, exactly one year and five days after our arrival from Trinidad, this sprightly nonagenarian died peacefully at her home. She was only 96 years old. Her body was laid to rest on the following day at the Clifton Cemetery. She was gone. On the day of her burial, I saw my mother cried openly for the very first time. I later learned that my mom had been living with my great granny throughout her childhood and adolescent years, and they maintained a very close relationship until her death.

My great-grandmother is gone, but she left with me some valuable information, the details of which I will share in a later chapter of my life. I must admit that I remained baffled for many years. As I grew older, I asked myself several times, why did this old lady give to me such historical information that is more fitting for the mind of an adult? I questioned myself over and over again. I believed that her clairvoyance, have enabled her to recognize something unusual about me. But from a different perspective, I was not alone in that little house when she was relating some valuable historical points to me. Instead, I was in the company of my three siblings, and the keen listening ears of my mother. And although I was the center of focus, most of what she was telling me was only a reminder to my mom. My mother, in turn, had been privy to all this information since her early childhood days in that little district named Point Look Out. As mentioned before, she had been living in that house throughout her entire childhood life.

Well, life at Campbell was very intriguing. During the 1970's at Basin Beach, I encountered many incredible things that were very puzzling, and I was unable to decipher what was happening. I remained puzzled for many years; my callow mind did not permit me the wherewithal to comprehend what some of these incidents meant. I remained mum and never shared with my peers what I had seen and heard. Later those memories did set off an unquenchable desire in me to write something that I could share with other Unionites such as myself and maybe the world.

When I was 18 years old, the rest of my family had already

returned to Trinidad, and I was bored to death while living alone in

* The common-cherry tree with some freshly ripped cherries. Visit the URL @ unionislandhistory.website *

the little house at Campbell. It was time for me to reunite with them, so on the calm afternoon of May 8th, 1981; I left E.T. Joshua's Airport at Arnos Vale, St. Vincent, for Trinidad. I looked out of the airplane just in time to take one last glimpse at the little wooden house until it disappeared before my eyes. After three hours, I was back in the district of Laventille, Trinidad, once again, having left it some 13 years earlier. A week later, my mom and I visited the Piccadilly Government School to see some of my former teachers. They were Ms. Harewood, Mrs. Farrell, and Mrs. Waite. Mrs. Farrell, my favorite teacher, had died only one month before we visited the school. Later that day, I took my mother to a house where we had lived when I was only four years old, and then to the house that we had owned before leaving Trinidad for Union Island in the year 1968. She was startled at my phenomenal memory, an attribute that I inherited from her.

I was 19 years old now and wanted to write a book on Union Island's history, about things that were said to me, and also that which I had witnessed. Many facets of the island's history were unknown to us, and there was a lot to be learned, I thought. I observed that our history studies at school were totally wrapped up in the affairs of Europe. Nothing of Africa or St. Vincent & the Grenadines was ever mentioned in our history books. We lauded the British Empire. Names such as Queen Elizabeth, King Ferdinand, John Hawkins, Walter Raleigh, Admiral Penn, General Venables, Francis Drake, and Henry Morgan were revered. Many of them were knighted "Sir" regardless of their notorieties. We were taught to respect and admire them nonetheless. Many of my schoolmates I am sure, can still remember some of the nursery rhymes listed below. They were included in our textbook:

- *Percy the chick had a fall.*
- *Twisty and Twirly riding a bike to school.*
- *Pussycat, pussycat where have you been?*
  I have been to London to visit the queen.
- *There was a naughty boy, and a naughty boy was he.*
  He ran away to Scotland, the people there to see.

So, there I was, bent on writing a historic book, and I had hastily accumulated 45 pages in a notebook, which I kept with me at all times. Unfortunately, my writing came to a gridlock a few months later. I didn't have the wherewithal to write a resourceful book that would do Union Island or myself any good. My youthfulness and lack of experience were just added disadvantages. Coupled with that, I wrote almost the way I speak (Union dialect). At that time, my level of writing was way below the standard usage of grammar and mechanics that was required to write a resourceful book. My ignorance, I attribute to my depressed experience during my formative years at Small School. My dream of writing a book came to an end when I lost every piece of information that I'd accumulated.

The years were going by and time seemed to be passing swiftly with no notable events. Then suddenly, I lost my grandmother Telina, the woman who had taken me from the harbor of Clifton to my great-grandmother at Point Lookout. She succumbed to a devastating stroke at her Point Lookout home. She fell in front of her doorstep and lay semi-conscious for several hours. She was later taken to the Nurse Clouden Health Center at Clifton, where she was diagnosed and treated for hypertension. Unfortunately, she never regained consciousness and died a few days later. Her death was one of the most gruesome accidents that have ever happened on the island. Intracerebral hemorrhage was the culprit. On April 27th, 1993, my grandmother Caroline (Telina)

Roache was laid to rest beside her mother, *Isabella Roache*, at the Clifton Cemetery. She was only 82 years old.

That was an incredibly sad moment for my siblings and me, amid other challenges that I need not mention here; instead, I will reference them in another book or maybe my autobiography in years to come.

Today, I have made a concerted effort to start anew with my literary work by touching on every aspect of the lives of our people (Unionites). I hope that by doing so, I can document their authentic lifestyles in a manner that gives reverence to them, the ancestors. Acknowledge and exhibit who they were and the impact that they continue to have on us, the descendants.

In remembrance of my great-grandmother, I erected a water- well on Thursday, October 30th, 2013. This incomplete well, which is known as Well *Isabella*, is located where her house was situated at Point-Look-Out. I could not think of anything else that represented life, longevity, and fulfillment of the life she had. It is in that setting that I was fed my first historical lesson. That location is where she evoked a penchant in me for the island's history; my mind's eye has been keenly opened since. Inadvertently, she changed my little world instantly and decisively. For many years after she died, I felt empty and alone. In many instances, it seemed as though my peers and I had little in common. I later saw myself as an anomaly.

Here I am today, almost 50 years later, and it's unbelievable how excited I am. I have so much to say that everything wants to seek an exit all at once, but I will take my time to touch on everything that my memory allows. These thoughts have saturated my mind for many years -almost my entire life. I will give my candid take on quite a few things that have slipped through the cracks, and perhaps offer a realistic peep into the not-too-distant future. Sound a bit clairvoyant? Well, there are lots to talk about, so let's start with a slow, deliberate walk.

INTRODUCTION

Now, all you can see in Union Island is bush, because, dey nah-e wok the land. Nowadays, if you want ah roast-corn, way you getting it? Eh?

Union *Island's History –Servitude, Metayage, And Civilization (UIHSMC)* is an expansion of its predecessor, UITN. Like UITN, this book also takes a comprehensive look at the lives and heritage of a people called "Unionites." By delving much deeper into the island's history, you are inclined to uncover a plethora of unprecedented, but important information. And so, it is the author's hope that the contents of this enlarged manuscript that you are now holding firmly in your hands will be etched permanently into your hearts and minds. Once and for all, you will be satiated with the details of the island's history, heritage, and culture; a history that you will know like never before.

Now, for those that once called Union Island home, this unique culture that is described here with honesty and candor will be relived by turning these crowded pages. Again, those that are not native to this region, too, will automatically embrace the opportunity to learn and appreciate a new culture from this practically unknown landmass. Whether you belong to the Caribbean or not, this book's contents are intended to whet your appetites. Your reactions, I expect, will be contingent on how much you can identify with, and relate to the culture. A word of caution! Some of the information here is unknown even to the few who once referred to Union Island as "Little England" during the mid-1970s. For others, the contents of this text can be baffling, but necessary to preserve the history for the countless generations unborn.

This book speaks profoundly about evolution, something that no one can escape in his or her entire lifetime. However, for the purpose of simplicity, let us use the word *change.* Yet, how many of us are happy and contented with the changes? "Change is the scariest word in the English language," author Dr. Susan Forward writes in her book, *Emotional Blackmail*. "No one likes it," she continues, "almost everyone is terrified of it, and most people will become exquisitely creative to avoid it."

Unfortunately, many baby-boomers had failed miserably to accept things that differ from the way they were when they were growing up. Some changes are unavoidable and have significantly affected the social, economic, and academic growth of Union Island in a positive light. However, there is a need for watchdogs to sieve out other changes that may be regressive and counterproductive. Nevertheless, positive changes can engender constructive growth.

For many years, the diaspora of Unionites that lives in the Americas, Europe and other parts of the globe, have watched from a distance the subtle transformations that have taken place from time to time. Although many of them abroad have taken the opportunity to make better their lives in their settings, there is still a feeling of homesickness among them. That homesickness or nostalgia denotes a burning desire to return home someday, and of course that word "Someday" means "permanently." Amid the myriad disadvantages in Union Island, some have returned home permanently, and have released themselves from the gilded cages of the various countries abroad where they have been tethered for many years. Many others are still hopeful that they too will be able to return someday and recapture some of the joys of their formative years. Well! Such a dream is hopeless, for they must be candidly informed, or reminded passionately that times have changed, and change it has, considerably.

The following are the shared sentiments of many folks in the local dialect –Union Island's lingo. They have articulated from their perspectives the change of time in the island and the current mindsets that correlate with those changes. Invariably, the yearning for the good old days still resurfaces in their hearts and minds. I suspect that many other Unionites may share some of these sentiments that are expressed below. These are the views of five Unionites –Baby boomers of course:

Look, I is ah big man eh, and ah know that time changing all the time. But it really hard to see the way things going on these days. Ah mean, when last you see them children nowadays play games like Shick-Shout, Hopscotch, Moral, Green Bush, and marbles? This generation yah don't know nothing. You could tell them anything bout both-head when yo pitching marbles? What about *Fenn-that, go back to stars, yo bringzing*, Ah go suck them *dry*, or *Yo getting bone-ox*? And when we was lil boys we use to set traps to ketch Grun-dove and Pigeon. What is really going on today, boy? Deh talking technology, advancement, modern time and ah whole set ah thing. But this technology-thing bringing more separation than anything else e-nor. Look at them cellphone way them children have in da Azs (ears). When them children standup close to you, and you calling them, you think dey does hear you? Eh...? Them children nah-e study you, and deh acting like they ain't dey dis side. Me ain't saying time can change and all that you know. Nooo! That not what me saying, you understand? What me is saying is: If you want technology, tek technology, is aright. Tek cellphone, tek computer. But for me? Help my Gad, give me long ago. I go settle wid that.

JP-

"Growing up on Union Island was an experience that resulted in my conviction that I had the best childhood ever. Most of the customs and traditions are no more. Three things that I wished were still practiced in our culture are these:

Big Drum Dancing

The rhythm of the drums, the sensual movement of the women, and the demonstration of masculine control by the men are some interesting things to behold. The Douglas family had expertise in this area. It was a pleasure to watch them dance.

Sporting Events

Participants compete in traditional races such as Egg and Spoon, Sack/bag race, One-leg race, Thread and Needle, Rounders, Tug-a-war, and Maypole dancing. These games were fun to watch, and the entire family participated.

Moonlight Picnics

In the open pastures of Ashton, whether a church group, a community group, or just a few good friends spending time together, moonlight never ended without fun, games, and food at some hillside on Union Island. Everyone contributed to the event, and one could hear singing and laughing from miles away. It was the sound of youthfulness and clean fun. Tactlessly, those days are gone!"

VS -

I can remember very well during the late 1960s and into the 1970s when young men used to frequent the local beaches of Ashton to race some finely made sailing boats. Saturdays and Sundays were the days that they came out in numbers. Henry John and Ezzard Stewart had two of the finest sailing boats in Ashton. They were made from the local Pumpkin Wood tree, a lightweight wood that is easily moldable. I can tell you that these small yachts were splendidly made, and they sailed very well.

Like the real thing, they had a spar, bowsprit, jib, mainsail, keel, and an adjustable rudder –the whole nine yards. And while this was a sport to be enjoyed, they had to be exceedingly careful not to take their eyes away from these small crafts while racing or otherwise they might easily lose their sailboats. These small crafts were so fast that they could quickly sail away beyond their reaches in a short time. Sailboats racing is something that is practiced no more in Union Island, not even the small Coconut boats that were flanked with a huge grape leaf and a tin rudder is available today. At least everyone could make those, even the girls. I would like to see those days resurface.

KR-

You know what? I wish Union Island was still the same way it was when I was growing up. Those days was better days…. People used to care more about each other –they had more unity, love, and togetherness! Today, em, you can see a lot of advancements, but with all of them new advancements, we have a lot of problems too. I don't like it you know. Drugs for one is too prevalent among the young people. Nobody wants to work, and they don't want to plant the land neither. Look nah! When I was growing up, everybody planted corn & peas, from Bottom Campbell in Ashton, all the way to Point Look Out, Clifton. Now, all you can see in Union Island is bush, because dey nah e wok the land. Nowadays, if you want ah roast-corn, way you getting it, Eh? "Stchups" (sucks her teeth). People too selfish now. Give me ah break…. You could put today with long ago? Yo crazy? I for one, rather the olden days.

JC -

Yo tink it easy? Aye! When Union was Union, you tink them lil boys couda pass ah big man like Claude Ambrose straight an ain't say good marning? Eh? Yo making joke! One cutass he widda put on them, eh; and da dare not go home and tell deh parents, else deh get the rest ah it. Today, right yah in Crass Road, Felix, Ms. Rosa is meh witness. Dah foce-ripe boy fo Wilma, and the one whey deh say is Kedrick son, cussing mother-ass right in front ah me –ah big man like me! Felix, I cudda be da father. But the ting way hurt me is, I know when Harris baun. Is jest dearder-day he baun. And is me whey went an call Nurse Clouden when Wilma was in childborth. Now, that boy have no respect whatsoever; all he doing is cussing 4-letters all over the place. I don't want to wish that boy bad yo know. But help my Gad Felix, I done say aready, Harris have nottin good to come out. Mark my words.

DW –

Interesting uh? That was indeed a mouthful to chew, much more to swallow. However, this dialect, as raw as it is constructed, it will pose no problem to the average Caribbean man; and for those whose navel strings were buried in the heart of Union Island, it is as simple as a cake walk. But if you, the reader, in any way, form or fashion, have felt challenged, or encounter any difficulty in understanding the Jargon, then you must stop now. Turn to "*Vernacular, Twangs, & idioms*," on page 134; don't just breeze past those exciting phrases, idioms, and intriguing sentences but immerse yourself deeply into the taste and flavor of yesterday's vernacular. Then, when you have drunk in enough and have your full of this serving, please return immediately to page 28.

*Amazing, wasn't it? Yes, that was the language of yesteryear. A taste of that dialect can be got at <u>only</u> a few localities on the island, but you must be mindful that this unique Potpourri of the Africans and English languages is quickly making its permanent departure. Alas, the dialect today is typical to that of a Vincentian.

So... is the culture of Union Island changing? The response here will be a resounding YES! Thus, far, it has changed significantly. Unionites are experiencing the loss of their culture as it steadily dwindling its way into permanent oblivion. Moreover, the questions that perplex most are these: Should they be blamed for such concern? Should they be blamed for looking back constantly as Lot's wife did in biblical history? Well, older folks have also agreed that important folktales such as Bra. Ananci and the redoubtable fibs and fiction of the La Diablesse stories are also making their way into oblivion. These essential folktales, which are of African origin, were once recited and listened to during their formative years. Today, they are tenuously held, only, in the palms of the Baby Boomers and a handful of the Traditionalists, and the Silent Generation. Unfortunately, these venerable folktales will expire with them unless there is some redoubtable force of nature that is resilient to the downward spiral of Union Island's culture.

The story about Bra Anansi Spider is a folktale from the tradition of the Ashanti people of Ghana, Africa. Bra Anansi (imaginary figure) was very cunning, as always; he played tricks on other animals to get them to do what he wanted. The La Diablesse story is yet another folktale that places fear in the heart and minds of listeners. La Diablesse is nocturnal and is perceived to be a female with an elegant appearance and sensual appeal. She possesses the power of flight and can disappear instantaneously. She lures her victims (men) away from their homes into dark wooded areas. At some point, the victim becomes lost and stumbles to find his way back home. The feet of the La Diablesse sometimes change into a hoof like that of a cow. One memorable story about an incident with the La Diablesse in Union Island was when a local fisherman with a rowboat was hired to transport some strangers to Frigate Rock; they paid the fishermen two shillings and five pence, but before the boat arrived at the little island, they suddenly leaped off the boat like birds, ran into the small island, and then shouted, "Look in yo hands, goat shit, goat shit."

The fisherman, in anxiety, opened his folded palm only to be confronted with the sheep's litter. The Soucouyant, like La

An aerial view of Clifton Harbor, the commercial capital

Diablesse is another sinister character that possesses the power of flight. This character also rules the dark of night like the vampire bat in its quest for fresh blood.

Inevitably, the above folktales and much more will expire within another decade or so unless this current heedless spiral comes to an abrupt end. Some Unionites may say, "Well old ideas have been supplanted by new ideas." Such statement, of course, signifies the eventual state of acceptance of this lost. The truth is, extinction is gradually making its presence felt while many helplessly and hopelessly looked on. "Long time, long ago, or back when," are already some of the choice words that have become an active part of their vocabularies whenever some of the customs of *Union Island* is mentioned. In hesitancy, many will tacitly agree.

The long and hopefully enjoyable presentation of the education and cultural reminders that are etched within the binding of this book (UIHSMC) will begin immediately in the chapters that follow. Like its predecessor, this book possesses some essential information and references for many and may serve as an instrument of strength or fortitude. Yet, from a morbid yet realistic point of view, one can only surmise that the cultural end is wrapped up in the brevity of time. In the meantime, Unionites must salvage and savor as fine jewelry or aged wine, what is left of that rich culture. Regrettably, it appears that those footprints in

The beautiful Clifton Harbor, Capital of Union Island

the sand of time is fading quickly into utter oblivion....

Nevertheless, sit back, relax and enjoy this meager, yet significant reminder of Union Island's past in Union Island's History – Servitude, Metayage, & Civilization. Be eager to share what you have learned in this book.

Section 1 ◆ ◆ ◆ □*Chapter One*

WHERE IS UNION ISLAND?

Even after 250+ years since a forceful divorce from the motherland, the remnants of the African culture are still evident throughout Union Island.

Unknown, even to some islanders in the Caribbean, and to a larger extent, the outside world, this little Caribbean Paradise - Union Island, is located some 180 miles north of Trinidad, 40 miles south-southeast of St. Vincent and 36 north-northwest of Grenada. Nevertheless, it is safely situated in the Grenadines -exactly in the heart of the Caribbean. The spoken language is English. And although Islam may have been the principal religion of the Africans that were stolen from the motherland, Christianity is now the sole religion in this region of the globe. The currency used is the EC$ (Easter Caribbean Dollar). With the advent of the personal computer, sites such as Google Earth have given justice to many shores by providing ubiquitous access to just about every place known. To access this member of the archipelago on Google Earth, and to have a panoramic view of her neighboring sister islands, one can search 12 degrees, 35', 48.96" North and 61 degrees, 25', 49.43" West. There, a splendorous view awaits you. Please view the Map of the Grenadines at the preliminary page (**iv**) of this book to locate and discover the little paradise.

Located in Clifton, the capital and Eastern corridor of the island, the Union Island Airport of 2,467 ft. is now assessable to visitors from every segment of the globe. International airlines can fly first to the neighboring islands of Trinidad & Tobago, Barbados, Grenada, St. Lucia, Dominica, and St. Vincent. From these islands, smaller crafts (nineteen-seats) can touch down on the unfamiliar Union Island Airport in less than one hour. The Argyle International Airport of St. Vincent, which was officially opened on February 14th, 2017 (Valentine Day) is yet another hub that is aiding greatly to the accessibility of this island.

Another access route is the traditional sea/waterway. Foreign yachts are frequent in the Caribbean islands, but the Grenadines islands, which are honeycombed with myriads of shallow reefs and marine lives, provide an enormous attraction to foreign snorkelers. The sheltered bays of Clifton Harbor, Frigate Rock, and Chatham Bay are mooring grounds for the multiple foreign sea crafts that make Union Island their place of getaway each year. Another beautiful scenery in the region is the Salt Whistle Bay of Mayreau, a neighboring cay of Union Island.

Now, you may wonder about the source of the island's name or its origin. Surely, it came from Admiral Samuel O. Spann, a wealthy entrepreneur whose history you are about to read. Samuel co-owned several ships during the 1760s-1780s that conducted (triangular) slave trade in West Africa and the so-called New World. Among them were the Alexander, *Vengeance*, *Tiger*, Bacchus, Burke, and the ubiquitous *Union Island*. During such time, his ship, **Union Island** and the Alexander, were frequent on this little landmass. Many slaves (ancestors) arrived on the shores of this small cay via these ships. The Union Island, however, must have been one of his favorites, being the principal ship to engage in the Trans-Atlantic Slave Trade during the earlier years. Hence, it is safe to deduce that he named this island after that particular ship.

Union Island is one of the larger islands of the Southern Grenadines, which is located between Grenada and St. Vincent. But where do the names Grenada & Grenadines came from, and why? Obviously, these names are similar. And long before the amalgamation of the islands, St. Vincent & the Grenadines, the Grenadines for centuries was <u>permanently etched to Grenada</u>. Although there is not much to be desired from the origin of the name Grenada & the Grenadines, it is safe to deduce that these names are also of French origin. They derived from the word Grenade 'Pomegranate,' the fruit. Nevertheless, the Grenadines is a chain of 32 tiny islands that is situated between these two major islands of the Windward Islands in the West Indies. St. Vincent is located towards the north, while its sister, Grenada is located in the south. After the turn of the 20th century, St. Vincent has governed most of these small islands. Proximity might be the deciding factor here. Petit Martinique and Carriacou, two other small Islands of the South are governed by Grenada. Today, the name St. Vincent & the Grenadines is widely known throughout the Caribbean rather than the original but archaic, Grenada & the

Grenadines. Unfortunately for Union Island, during the 1890s and the early 20th century, the sentiments of the residents were sometimes mixed as to which of these islands (St. Vincent or Grenada) should assume ownership. We will take a detailed look at this situation in another chapter.

Grenada often referred to as "The Island of Spice," became known worldwide during the 1980s when it's prime minister, Maurice Bishop was assassinated. Later, it was led to believe that the American Armed Forces interceded to rescue the island from local rebels; the Caribbean community thinks otherwise.

The second largest and next to the most southerly of the Grenadines Islands of St. Vincent, Union Island was deemed the artistic center and cultural mecca of the Grenadines for many years. The reason is that the Africans, which were brought from the motherland, upheld their culture. And from every facet of their lives on this little island, it remained visibly dominant. Today, it is safe to conclude that the remnants of this culture are still evident throughout this small landmass even after 2-½ centuries of unintentional divorcé from Africa, the motherland.

To any visitor who has visited St. Vincent but has not yet laid foot on the birthplace of the luminary, Captain Hugh Nathaniel Mulzac, you must be reminded that you have not yet honored your right to exploration and discovery. Who? Hugh Mulzac? Yes! Captain Hugh Mulzac is a household name that everyone will become familiar with after reading this book.

Though it is known regionally that the redoubtable TV personality **Oprah Winfrey** once sailed on a convoy of yachts to the island of Mustique, she, too, is not absolved from the responsibility of laying her feet on the precious soil of Union Island. It is reputed that she may have been in the waters of Palm Island and Petit St. Vincent –a stone's throw away from Union Island. Her visit to the white sandy shores and reef-filled waters of the Grenadines may be good news in that her return is imminent. Imminent is the key word here for in this 21st century; this little island needs to be known, the world over.

Amazingly, the Union Island that few have grown to love over the years is virtually unknown to the world; even today. The world, as many may look at it, is only as wide and enormous as their minds are programmed and conditioned to see it. So, in fact, many may not see the world exactly as it is in most cases but only as their paradigms allow. Keep in mind that for 99 percent of the world out there, no such place is called Union Island. Though it was referred to as the "Little Tahiti of the West Indies" several decades ago, to date, very little is known of this minuscule landmass even in this 21st century.

If anyone were to walk the well-trodden streets of Manhattan in New York, from 42nd Street Times Square to Malcolm X Boulevard, 125 Street, with a large map bearing the words "Union Island," and if ten or more people were to identify with that island, then it can be said, a monumental task has been accomplished. But there are considerable doubts that this will ever happen. So, the task of writing this book encompasses the responsibility of conveying to the larger world the presence of the Grenadines of St. Vincent as a significant entity. But for now, Union Island is the primal focus.

Union Island now possesses a small but racially integrated community, and this may be a plus to engender growth from several aspects of the business environment. Therefore, it is imperative that information on Union Island be disseminated to the outside world. Union Island's History –Servitude, Metayage And Civilization hints about the African influences, mores, folkways, conventions, and local customs that are still pervasive in this unfamiliar territory. Union Island's History –Servitude, Metayage And Civilization (UIHSMC) attempts to document the complete history of the island; also, to make relevant in the hearts and minds of the readers, the details of that long crucial period that existed during the late 1750s, all the way to year the 1909. This was an incredible experience for the ancestors of the current generations of Union Island.

EUROPEANS AND SLAVERY

With the convenient use of the shack at the back of the plantations by the slave masters, integration has become akin to slavery.

Spanning the shores of Point Lookout, the beautiful beaches of Basin, Campbell, Richmond, Big-Sand, Belmont, Bloody Bay, Rapid, and of course, the exclusivity of Chatham Beach in the Western side of the island, will all give an insurmountable feeling of blithe. There is energy, a combined collective force working in concert here. There is synergy, a union, and so the name Union Island is quite appropriate to meet all of its intangibles.

The beaches, the reefs and rocky terrain are nothing short of breathing grounds for tourists who came in droves, eager to enjoy the unadulterated beauty that God and nature have created. They immediately become cognizant of the sheer liberty that exists in this beautiful southern part of the Grenadines Islands. Experience will later teach that such levels of joyous nonchalance can only be exhibited in these tropical virgin territories such as Union Island and a host of neighboring cays. Although not big on nightlife, the accommodating staffs at Anchorage Hotel, Bouginvilla Hotel, Kings Landing Hotel, Clifton Beach Hotel, Big-Sand Hotel, Islander's Inn Hotel, Palm Island Resort & Spa, and Lambi's Guest House are unquestionably second to none when it comes to hospitality. Mustique Island, a wonderful neighboring resort island, is also a little gem that is known around the entire globe. Yes! This is exactly where Union Island is situated. Like Union Island, these 31 other neighboring islands are gracefully flanked by the ubiquitous trade winds of the Atlantic Ocean.

It seems almost unbelievable that Union Island has been inhabited since 5400 BC. And according to Scientists: The Earth was formed about 4.5 million years ago. Whatever truth there is to be extracted from the above statement, it is unrealistic to believe that the world is only 2000 years old as I was led to believe during my formative years at the Christian churches. It is equally unrealistic to give credit to what history has taught us about

35

Christopher Columbus. His presence in the Caribbean or so-called New World in the year 1492 may have given rise to a newfound knowledge in Europe, and Europe only. It is not by accident that the 'The Burning Spear, a Jamaican reggae artist, and The Shadow, Tobago's calypsonian, referred to Christopher Columbus as a "Damn blasted liar," indicating that the islands of the Caribbean were already inhabited long before his so-called discoveries. Mutabaruka, another singer/poet from Jamaica, referred to Christopher Columbus, as "Christopher-Come-Bust-Us." Such label is in accord with the murderous taints that are attached to his name. Like the Frenchmen, Antoine Rigaud and Juan Augier (mentioned later), he too was a mass murderer of the Amerindians of the Caribbean.

It is clear that Christopher Columbus had visited the Caribbean approximately 6892 years after this little rock had already been inhabited. But what was it called by the first inhabitants? This is a very poignant question; the answer to this, however, may be far fetched. Why? The history of this tribe of people (Caribs) in union Island has not been properly documented. On January 22nd, 1498, Christopher Columbus (Spanish) landed on St. Vincent, but no information is available to substantiate that he actually laid foot on this little rock that is now called Union Island. Neither did he set foot on Grenada, the most southerly of the chain of these neighboring islands. During the presence of the Spanish convoy in the region, they observed Grenada & the Grenadines as a group of tiny insignificant islands closely aligned like a flock of birds. They later referred to them as Los Pajoros –the Spanish word for "The Birds." Aligning the sandy beaches of some of these miniature landmasses were the Amerindian teepees.

Christopher Columbus' presence in the New World from 1492 onwards, has opened up a new atmosphere for the Europeans to acquire the lands that have been inhabited by the Indians and other races. England, Spain, and France –the three big wigs, were eager to lay claim to these islands at any cost, even at the expense of the annihilation of the natives. So, by way of trickery, strong-arm, legerdemain, then war against these natives, they eventually took all of their lands. Inevitably, wars broke out between these major nations as lands changed ownerships from time to time. As a result, numerous agreements were drafted and signed to settle the long-standing land disputes among themselves. One of these agreements was The Treaty of Paris in 1763, which give rise to the Islands of St. Vincent & the Grenadines and

Grenada to be governed by Great Britain. This new ownership perpetually changed the landscape and atmosphere of the French dominance in the region. As a result, the native language of Union Island, though embedded with the African influence, was destine to be Anglicized, Permanently.

When he (Christopher Columbus) arrived in the region, the Amerindian tribes of South America were on Union Island and other Islands of the Grenadines as well. Archeological studies have confirmed their presence during 5400 BC up until the 1760s. These Amerindians were the Carib tribe whose origin lies in the Southern West Indies, and the Northern Coast of South America. Today, in Union Island, there isn't a meager trail of the documented history of the descendants of this once noble tribe since the French inhabited the island in the late 1750s. It is paramount that the Amerindians disappearance be questioned and thoroughly researched in hopes of amending the island's history and her-story.

The numerous artifacts that were found on the soil of Union Island provide further proof of the existence of this tribe up until the 1760s. During the 1970s and beyond, many of these artifacts were unearthed from where they were hidden, including beneath the many Manchineel trees that are found on every beach on the island. Foreign archeologists have visited and studied this pristine territory as well as the lives and customs of the Amerindians. They finally made good of the spoils, which they unearthed without consent from local authorities. They have removed all of the ancient cutlery, potsherds, vessels, bowls, and cylinders. It is believed that some of these artifacts have been sold at exorbitant prices at foreign museums in the Americas, while others remained as exhibits at various museums as well. Currently, there are no museums available on Union Island that reflect the presence of this once noble tribe, their lives, or the rich tangible legacy which they unwittingly left behind. What a Dishonor!

The Manchineel plant mentioned above is considered to be one of the most poisonous tree species in the world. The Spanish called the fruits of the Manchineel tree "Little apples of death." The milk or sap of this plant is a potent skin irritant. Even standing under this plant during a heated day was widely discouraged because doing so can cause severe skin blisters. Eating the fruit is fatal. The Amerindians (Caribs) used the milky sap of this plant to poison their arrows during hunting and also against their enemies. The poisonous leaves of this plant were sometimes used to poison the water of their enemies. The numerous Manchineel trees that were present at Chatham Bay, coupled with the unearthed artifacts at that site, have substantiated the presence of this noble tribe.

Now, it must be remembered that it was the appearance of the French in the neighboring island of Grenada during the 1650s that led to a bloody battle with the Amerindians (Carib). In the 1650s, a French expedition from the Caribbean island of Martinique landed on Grenada and established a so-called friendly rapport with the natives. Hostility became inevitable as the French exhibited their desire to control the entire island. War broke out almost immediately between the two factions when the Amerindians demonstrated an unwillingness to submit to these settlers.

Called fierce and warlike by the European invaders, these Amerindians did put up some stern resistance in a succession of battles to protect their women and lands but were eventually defeated and slaughtered. Rather than surrender to their soon-to-be successors, the remaining tribe members chose the hills of North Grenada, (Sauteurs) where they committed suicide by leaping off a cliff. The French later named the spot "Le Morne de Sauteurs," or "Leapers' Hill." The question must now be asked: Did the Amerindians of Union Island just give up the land of their forefathers to these foreign settlers/invaders, or did they put up fierce resistance, which would have been true to their nature? The detail of what happened is indeed some food for thought. Sadly, these communal people were never seen again on this island after the French settled during the late 1750s. Left, as a permanent marker on Union island's most northerly coastline, is the name, Bloody Bay. The name Bloody Bay, if nothing else, signifies that blood was shed at that site. Regrettably, the history and her-story of the indigenous people of Union Island were not properly documented, or made available for history books. Was it an attempt to hide such a barbarous act against humanity by refusing to record it into the history books? By way of research, here are some brief and tasteless extracts that represented the demise of the Indians in Union Island: "By the year 1763, the Indians of Union Island were gone," "The Grenadines became part of a long and bloody story in which Union Island witnessed," "In the Grenadines and Grenada, the French people were the Caribs main enemy, eventually causing the total destruction of the latter." In the Turks and Caicos Islands, the same can be said of the indigenous natives –the Lucian Indians. Again, here are two extracts: "The Lucayan Indians were gone from the Turks & Caicos

Islands within only a few decades of the first European contact." "Shortly after Columbus arrived in 1492, the Lucayan civilization disappeared, and the islands remained sparsely populated for about 30 years." The above information is all that can be had in regards to the details of what transpired during the European intervention on those soils. Yet, the victors were the only ones to write the seemingly sparse history of Union Island and the region.

One thing for sure was evident among these conquistadors is that human lives meant nothing to them. These settlers also knew that land ownership was the basis of power, so their intentions were to do anything that they deemed necessary, and at any cost in order to obtain land, wealth and power.

ANTOINE RIGAUD & JUAN AUGIER

In the late 1750s, Antoine Rigaud, and Jean Augier, two French merchants from the islands of Martinique and Guadeloupe set foot on Union Island, a densely forested mountainous isle that was inhabited by Amerindians. Simultaneously, Monsieur De L'isle, another prominent Frenchman laid claim to Tobago Cays, Frigate Island, and Palm Island (the latter was formerly called Prune). Frigate Island is a tiny Island that is situated approximately ¾ mile south of the Ashton Harbor. Monsieur De L'isle was also an inhabitant of the islands of Mayreau and Carriacou.

With complete disregard for the indigenous inhabitants (Amerindians) of the island, Antoine Rigaud and Jean Augier decided to settle on Union Island. But in order for these Frenchmen to conduct trade or business relationship, to have total control of the land for the introduction of the cotton plant, and for the use of Africans as chattel for the first time on Union Island, they had to make a pact with the original natives, or propagate war against them. War meant the total annihilation of these Amerindians and ownership of the island. The Frenchmen choose the later; it placed them in complete control. So, these French marauders were actually the first Europeans to own Union Island.

Because there is little to be had about the annihilation of this tribe from Union Island, many citizens are eager, more so, than before to find out the details of this undocumented war between the French and the Amerindians at Bloody Bay -the northernmost bay of Union Island. For the activities that took place at this bay may be synonymous with those of the renowned Le Morne De Sauteurs (Leapers Hill) disaster of Grenada during the 1650s. During that war, the French totally massacred the native Indians of that neighboring island. It was a total disaster. The annihilation of the Indians on Union Island at the hands of these two French merchants during the 1750's marked the first and only war that was fought on the soil of Union Island. Even the mammoth territorial tension that existed between Great Britain and France during and after the Treaty of Paris never escalated into a war on the soil of Union Island.

After annihilating the Amerindians of Union Island, these Frenchmen were now in total possession of the island, or so they thought. But the conclusion of the Seven-Year War that resulted in the Treaty of Paris would prove differently. Meanwhile, Monsieur De L'isle, the other Frenchman, who has settled on some of the smaller islands of the Grenadines, also grew a small quantity of cotton. But his specialty in the region was making White Lime for use in Building Construction. In the Grenadines, Mr. De L'isle striped the shallow surrounding reefs of the multiple corals and burned them in limekilns to obtain the finished product. One of his limekilns was located at Richmond Bay, Union Island. Because of the proximity of his limekiln to the Richmond water pond, residents referred to the water pond as Limekiln water pond, and later Lenkin, as oppose to the correct name, Lincoln Pond.

You have observed that the subject Amerindians was mentioned here on several occasions, and briefly discussed. To get a thorough insight of these people –the first to walk the soil of Union Island and the various islands in the region, it is worth taking a little time to review their origin, their life, and legacy. Turn now to the subject, "The First Inhabitants" on page 71; carefully read the short article, then resume your reading on this page. A deluge of resourceful information awaits you.

*With the tone already set for the production of cotton, Jean and Antoine brought 350 Africans from West Africa, and the Marie Galante cotton plant to Union Island. It was the crop that they intended to use to make a fortune at the expense of the free African labor. They also brought Tamarind (Tamarindus Indica), Mangoes (Mangifera Indica), sugar apples (Anona Squamosa), Hog plums (Spondias Mombin) and many other plants and livestock to the island. The latter was a major food source for the African slaves. The Calabash tree (*Crescentia cujete*) was native to Union

40

Island, and so was the Cedar plant, which also was in abundant on the island. The latter was later used for building ships and vessels and can still be found in the dense bushes of Colon Campbell, Ashton. The Calabash tree was extremely important to the slaves. It was the source of all their utensils. The calabash tree produces large spherical-shaped fruits, as huge as 20 inches in diameter. The rigid shell of this huge fruit is useful for making bowls, cups, and other water and food containers when hollowed out.

The slaves, on their arrival in Union Island, were confined to two locations -areas that was not suited for farming. Antoine Rigaud and Juan Augier, in turn, used all of the arable lands in Union Island for the cultivation of cotton. At Clifton, 20 percent of the slaves were placed at the slopes and footings of Clifton Hill, and also where the current Clifton Cemetery is situated. They thought that these areas were suitable for the slaves because they were notably stony and was considered unfit for the cultivation of cotton. That area was later called *Bottom Town*, and the shabby huts of the slave were referred to as the Niger Houses. At Ashton, the other 80 percent of the slaves were confined to the Southern footing of Mt. Parnassus, (Big Hill) north of the Ashton Harbor. That location possesses a very steep gradient. And like Clifton, this place was not suited for the cultivation of the lucrative cotton crop. This area possessed numerous tattered huts that were constructed to house this large number of slaves. As years went by, the slave population of Ashton Village grew, and new huts were expanded both east and northerly, but remained at the footing of the precarious hill above.

Called *Frigate* during the 18th, 19th, and early 20th centuries, this location through its metamorphosis was later called Pauper-land, then Ashton Village. One can observe that the population of Ashton still remained dense in that current vicinity (footings of Mt. Parnassus, page 78), even until today. The numerous conch shells that lined the Ashton Harbor are a clear indication that the Africans have inhabited this area some 260 plus years. The conch that is native to the local reefs was an important food source for the slaves.

Frederick A Fender, an expert American canoeist who sailed alone in the Caribbean with his Yakaboo during the late 19th century; on one of his trip from Grenada and Carriacou, he visited Union Island and observed that the African community was clustered at Frigate (Ashton Harbor) –the foot of Mt. Parnassus.

This is what he wrote: *I could make out the houses of a village, climbing above the shores of the bay…. A thousand natives, living in small huts clustered close together, in exactly the way their ancestors lived two hundred years ago. One change only from the early days -that of clothing, the men wear trousers and shirts, and the women wear skirts. Remove their civilized rags and you have them as they were in Africa.*

These white huts were the homes of the slaves –referred to as Nigga-houses by the slave masters. The huts were painted white with limestone, a product that was made by burning coral with the multiple Manchineel trees that bordered the beaches. In 1902, each home had to supply 300 lbs. of cotton to Mr. E. Richards.

From the onset of slavery in Union Island, during the latter years of the 1750s, the slaves were subjected to absolute squalor and abject poverty. This condition should not have been a surprise to the reader, based on the manner in which these Frenchmen took control of the island. They drove out, murdered and violently relieved the Amerindians of their birthplace –a homeland that they had inhabited for centuries. Hence, the slaves were not absolved from any harsh measure of treatment that was exhibited from these slave masters. Unfortunately, the African presence as slaves on Union Island from the mid 18th century through the ostensible Metayage (sharecropping) system of 1863 to 1909 represented a period of severe hardship, misuse, abuse, neglect, murder and death. It ultimately became a legacy of disenfranchisement, from Antoine Rigaud, Jean Augier, Admiral Samuel Spann, Charles Mulzac, Richard Mulzac and the extremist, Mr. E. Richards –all of the players of slavery in Union Island. The institution of slavery and its compatriot, the ostensible Metayage or Sharecropping System lasted for approximately 150 years in Union Island.

The picture on page 42 is rare scenery of Clifton Hill. This early 20th century photo depicts a white house at the top of the hill and many thatch huts with grass roofs that aligned the slopes of the hill. The residence of this big house was Mr. Rupert Otway, a representative of the British Gov't. Mr. Otway superseded Mr. E. Richards, the last owner, and landlord of Union Island. Antoine Rigaud, Jean Augier, Samuel Spann, Charles Mulzac, Richard Mulzac and Mr. E. Richards, at some point of their tenure as landlords, they all lived in the white house at the top of Clifton Hill –the hill that overlooks the Clifton Harbor (See also the picture on page 109). This ancient landmark (called Gov't House in recent years) has since been nonsensically razed in the year 2015.

Union Island, being a semi-arid landmass, which receives an annual rainfall of only 40.25 inches, produces abundantly only during the rainy months of May through November. Because of such low annual rainfall, there was always a dearth of water and food supplies, two prized necessities of life. Evidently, these deficits were core ingredients for life's difficulties of the slaves on a foreign land. Because the island was unable to provide enough food and ground provisions to feed the hundreds of slaves, instead, food

Thatch huts in Ashton Village (Frigate) at Union Island where the blacks have lived since the days of slavery. This location was later referred to as **Pauper Land.**

was imported weekly from St. Vincent, the mainland. The scarcity of water, though, posed a major problem; it prompted Antoine Rigaud, the slave master, to construct two major water ponds, namely: Basin at Campbell, and Lincoln at Richmond. These water catchments were used solely to water the slaves and animals. The slaves shared the turbid water from the ponds with the animals. The slave masters, on the other hand, used well-built cisterns, and other forms of water catchments to convey clean drinking water for themselves. They used water goblets and big jugs that were made of porous clay that facilitates evaporation, thus enabling the landlords to drink cooler water.

The constant demand for water among the slaves becomes insatiable, for there was an absence of cisterns and reservoirs to convey clean drinking water. The ancestors (slaves), with no alternative, were forced to share the turbid water of the ponds with the multiple livestock on the island.

With all of the above said, the slaves on the plantations of Union Island faced multiple health issues. Unsanitary living conditions, improper nutrition because of a scarcity of nutritious food, clean drinking water, and overwork; all of the above made them susceptible to various diseases. As a result, the death rates among the slaves were significantly high because of morbidity. The principal causative agent was the filthy unsanitary water, which comprises animal excretions that lead to multiple illnesses, namely: diarrhea, typhoid, cholera, tuberculosis, hepatitis, influenza, and STDs. These landlords were not concerned about the slaves' well-being; instead, their primal focus was the economic success –the cotton production and the enormous financial rewards that this plant can generate, but to the exclusion of higher ideals – the health and maintenance of the human machines in the fields. Apart from the ever-present health issues that the slaves endured, the institution in itself was one that was intensely barbaric, bloody and brutal.

Samuel V. Morse, a commanding engineer, made a timely visit to Union Island on July 22, 1778, and found that the lack of water was a major problem. Appalled by the scarcity of water on the land to supply both livestock and the slaves, he witnessed the deplorable health condition of the slaves, and the squalor that they endured daily. He found that the Europeans, on the other hand, used rainwater, which they conserved in earthen jars and well-built cisterns. This is what he had to say:

"There are no rivers in any of the Grenadines but springs in most of them, which by sinking wells supply the Negroes and stock most of the year. The water, in general, is not good, frequently brackish and disagrees with the Negroes at first, but when they are accustomed to it, does not prove unwholesome. The white inhabitants principally depend upon rainwater, which they preserve in cisterns or earthen jars."

The landlords during such time, i.e., Jean Augier, Antoine Rigaud, Samuel Spann and later Charles Mulzac, did very little to mitigate the horrible living condition that the slaves were subjected to. And so, the squalor, poor hygiene, and sicknesses escalated into infant mortality and shortened lifespan. In many cases, mothers preferred child murder rather than having their sick children live the lives to which they were subjected. Leprosy and Yaws became prevalent among the Africans and spread rather quickly because of the clusters of living quarters. The Africans that were inflicted with Yaws were placed at Palm Island (Prune), a small neighboring island; those that were infected with Leprosy were isolated at Frigate Island without aid.

All year round on the larger islands, unlike Union Island, slave masters often tried to cure their ill slaves long before they were sent to doctors. A slave that got sick meant a loss of working time, and for death, an even greater loss. Given the cost of slaves and their importance to plantation economies, slave masters organized slave hospitals to treat serious health problems. So, in the hope of saving money, they relied on the basic healthcare skills that they knew. And so, the wives of the slave masters were also heavily involved in the healthcare needs of the slaves. It was only when their healthcare treatments did not help to improve the slave's condition, they would ask the doctor to come to the plantations. Such was the case with Dr. H. N. Nichols (below); Dr. Nichols was brought in to treat the ailing slaves, but many years too late.

On Tuesday, June 11th, 1891, an American doctor by the name of H. N. Nichols visited Union island. Dr. Nichols was a specialist in Yaws, (a highly infectious disease that affects the skin and bones, but is incredibly easy to treat). This condition is similar to the unsightly disease leprosy that is written in a subsequent chapter about some ailing residents that were placed at Frigate Island. On arrival, Dr. Nichols was astounded and felt compassion for the people whom he observed were destitute and totally neglected by the Government of St. Vincent, who only adds to their woes. He said that these residents were not benefiting from the state in any way, shape or form, because they were not given anything. "Not even the roads were upkeep," he said; hence, he was astounded that these good people did not drive them off on their arrival. He also learned firsthand, that there were no concerns by the state for the wellbeing of residents who died indiscriminately when ill. Sicknesses and death occurred because doctors were not available to address their needs and concerns. "When the tax collector comes around, many residents took to sea with their little crafts to escape that burden, he said; those that could not leave the confines of this improvised rock had to pay by the skin of their teeth. They paid from the money that they barely earned through inter-island trade to Barbados and Carriacou he further stated." Below is a concise transcript of what the good old doctor, H. N. Nichols had to say:

"They get nothing from the Government. People are ill and die on the island, and no doctor can be got. There is no protection for life or property; no road kept up by the Government, and it was really a wonder when we arrived that the good people of Union did not assemble to drive us off. We gave the people nothing, we added neither to their comfort nor their happiness, and we took away the money they had barely earned by carrying their produce in their crank boats to Barbados and Carriacou."

With the above information, and the years passed, it will be prudent for one to imagine that the horrible water condition that pestered the Grenadines for centuries, should have been a thing of the past. Unfortunately, that is far from the case.

Don Carlos Verbeke, a Benedictine priest, was also appalled by the condition that he observed when he visited Union Island in 1928. He described the grave shortage of water on these islands by indicating that there was scarcely anything to drink. He went on to say that the people had to scoop water from mud-filled ponds and that the island was devoid of grass to feed livestock. Nevertheless, he was overwhelmed by the people's desire and will to overcome such impoverished state. The ponds that Verbeke was referring to were Lincoln (Lenkin) Pond, Basin (Basket) pond, and several other wells of Ashton, (pages 97, 98 and 240). Below, you will read the words of the Benedictine priest:

"Those islands at the time of my visit were literally burnt,

there being not a blade of green grass left. I have seen the sheep and cattle dying along the roadside. I have witnessed the people cutting the last leaf off banana trees to give to them. The people have no water to drink. I have seen them gathering water from ponds, mud in the strictest sense of the word. How they manage to live, to tide over this appalling misery is a mystery to me."

In recent research from the Encyclopedia of Caribbean Religions UNIVERSITY OF ILLINOIS PRESS *Urbana, Chicago, and Springfield,* this is what was extracted from an article which was written during the 1970s: *"Thus in the Grenadines, tiny Union Island, with only one school, a paucity of medial and sanitation facilities, and no systematic water supply or electricity, can boast of having an airstrip, built by the Vincentian Government to transport tourist...."*

Amazingly, this level of water shortage, miserable conditions, and squalor continued even into the late 20th century. Today, it is almost 260 years since this morbid condition was brought upon the African Diaspora of Union Island. And while living conditions have been removed from miserable and squalor to seemingly promising or hopeful, water condition has become a permanent problem in Union Island & the Grenadines, especially during the dry months of November through April.

ADMIRAL SAMUEL OLIVER SPANN

On February 10th 1763, the Treaty of Paris was signed between the British, French and Spanish. Great Britain legally became the owner of many islands in the so-called New World. Among these islands were St. Vincent and Grenada & the Grenadines. Britain needed all its new colonies to be occupied under a British rule, for there was still a legitimate form of tension in the region from the French. Some of these islands were partially occupied by her archrival, France, during this seven-years' war. Admiral O. Spann, a wealthy officer that belonged to the Society of Merchant Venturers in England (Warden). Samuel was hugely influential in the city of Bristol. He was allowed by the British Monarchy to occupy and own Union Island immediately after the Treaty of Paris. On his arrival with his brother John and two other merchants, John Hamilton, and David Smith, he met two Frenchmen, Antoine Rigaud, and Jean Augier. They had huge cotton plantations in the western part of the island, with a workforce of 270 slaves. Samuel and his crew were heavily involved in the triangular slave trade and general maritime trade under the banner of S & J Spann and Company (Samuel and John, his brother). Like the Frenchmen, Samuel and his brother John also bought hundreds of slaves from Cameroon, Angola, Ghana, Guinea, Liberia, Togo, Sierra Leone, Nigeria and other ports in Africa with his ship the Union Island. On arrival, S & J Span & Company immediately became owners of a large plantation in Union Island; brought 165 slaves, occupied 1830 acres of land, and had an annual yield of 53,000 pounds of cotton. There was another brother (Spann), whose first name is Sam. Sam had been on the island for some time but left Union Island to pursue business in Trinidad, one of the larger islands of the Caribbean.

Admiral Samuel Spann had a fleet of ships in the region; many he co-owned with some of his compatriots from England.

The Alexander was a 300 tons' ship that was involved in the slave trade. The shipmaster was John Preston. In 1801, this ship traded in Cameroon-Angola. They brought slaves straight to Union Island rather than stopping in Barbados, as was the custom.

The **Tiger** was another large cargo ship of 250 tons. This ship was owned by Admiral Samuel Spann, John Clarke, Levi Ames, John Clissold and Thomas & Robert Lucas. Specialized in the transportation of large quantities of Coffee, sugar, indigo, and cotton, she was hijacked by a squadron that was commanded by the Comte d'Estaing and sent to Cadiz, Spain.

The noted **Union Island** was a 200 tons' ship that was owned by Admiral Samuel Spann and his compatriot David Hamilton. This fine cargo ship which was engaged in the Triangular Slave Trade –From Europe to Africa, followed by the Caribbean, and then back to Europe, was manned by Master Joseph Rawle. During the Franco-English skirmish (1764 -1782) in the region, it is reported that this namesake-ship, which has brought many African slaves to Union Island, and the region, was abducted by a French privateer and sent to Cape Francois, France, in the year 1780.

The Vengeance: A 120 tons' vessel was the smallest of the slave ships. Captain Watkins manned this two masts vessel, which was owned by Samuel Spann and James Bonbous. Bound for New York in 1781, the Vengeance with Captain Watkins and crew was seized by an American privateer, Disdained, and sent to Boston.

Admiral Samuel Spann also owned two other ships that were frequent in the region. These ships were the **Bacchus** and the **Burke**. Masters Charles Thomson and James Clarke manned the Bacchus, a 300 tons' ship, during the years 1782-1783. In the year 1781, Captain James Clarke with a small crew manned the Burke.

After he named the island Union, Samuel Spann presented the two small villages of Union Island their names. These names were Ashton and Clifton; these names originated from two suburbs of Great Britain. Clifton, the capital of Union Island, is located in the east, while Ashton, the larger of the two, is located in the west of the island. During the 18th, 19th and mid-20th Centuries, Clifton, the capital, was widely referred to as Calsay, while the inhabited Ashton Harbor that is located in the western part of the island, was called Frigate. The proximity of Ashton harbor to the little neighboring island, Frigate Island (rock), may have influenced its name. The name Calsay, on the other hand, has been derived from the name Calabushice, a name of French origin. Calabushice was a rather awkward name for black folks to pronounce because of their African tongue. The name Calabushice was mentioned once by an English Engineer named Morse. Morse visited Union Island and made a report to the British colonial administrator Lord Mac Cartney on July 22nd, 1778. This word may have been misspelled for it seems to have no etymological root.

It must be understood, clearly, that Mr. Spann, this wealthy British entrepreneur did not come to Union Island as an excursionist, or a tourist, and neither was he a philanthropist to the Africans. Instead, he came to occupy the island, engage fully in the cotton cultivation, slavery of the Africans, and the Trans-Atlantic Slave Trade; he did all of the above effectively. On his arrival, the existing French merchants, Antoine Rigaud, and Jean Auger didn't vacate the land or announced their immediate retirements from the cotton industry. Neither did Monsieur De L'isle, the other French Merchant; he did not abandon his White-Lime production with the limekiln factories that was situated on the island. Instead, these French merchants co-existed with Mr. Spann and embraced both the fortunes and challenges of the lucrative cotton industry.

With an existing tension in the region, (still existing after the Treaty of Paris) a French Admiral by the name of Earl D'Estaing joined with some American privateers and attacked Grenada on July 2nd, 1770. In only one day later, July 3rd, Grenada surrendered to the collation. Technically, that made Union Island once again a French colony. Fortuitously, the two Frenchmen now had a viable reason to remain longer on the island. As mentioned before, as early as the 1780s, Admiral Samuel Spann lost some of his ships, (Vengeance, Tiger, and Union Island) to French privateers (pages 48 & 49). His alleged involvement in piracy did not do him any good either, for it may have been a contributing factor to his loss.

In 1778, the population of Union Island had increased, but not significantly. There were more French occupants on the island than English because Antoine Rigaud and Jean Augier had occupied the island for several years before the British, and with them, were other associates that also had vested interests on the island. As a result, the population now comprised of sixteen Europeans (ten French and six English). Of the six English that existed on the island, two other Englishmen were among the quartet of Samuel, John, Hamilton, and Smith. The workforce now exceeded 400 slaves that cultivated a bountiful cotton crop each year. The collective annual yield from a substantial harvest on this little island was rewarding. The island's annual income was now two hundred and fifty thousand (£250,000) British pounds per year. This income was indubitably satisfying for these new investors; they used every method possible to get the work from their subjects. As mentioned above, the British and French coexisted on the little island for almost three decades.

To settle the protracted tension in the region, another truce was signed in the year, 1783 by England, America, and France. This truce was called the Treaty of Versailles, and it was the final territorial truce in the region among these nations. With this treaty, Grenada & the Grenadines were given back to England. At this time, England had a visibly stronger grasp on these islands. And with her imposing dominance, it substantiated the fact that two forces cannot occupy the same space at the same time. The French Merchant Antoine Rigaud, realizing that he had no sturdy leg to stand on left Union Island immediately. Augier, on the other hand, remained on the island for a number of years but eventually left.

Finally, with stability in the region, a military defense system was put into place on Union Island. The island was now fortified with numerous cannons that were positioned at strategic points of the isle to stave off potential enemies and invaders. Today, most of these cannons are intact and can be found at the following locations: Bloody Bay, Rafale, Fort Hill, Fort Basin, and

Clifton Hill.

In 1791, the initial phrase **"Grenada & the Grenadines"** came to a screeching halt as England divided the Grenadines into two factions. The majority of these islands were to be managed by St. Vincent in the north, while Grenada in the south was given a lesser responsibility. It is now called **St. Vincent & the Grenadines.** The islands of Petit St. Vincent, Union Island, Palm Island, Mayreau, Canouan, Mustique, Bequia, Balliceaux, Petit Nieves, Bettowia, Isle de Quadre, Les Piloris, Pigeon Island, Petite Mustique, Petit Canouan, Savan, Tobago Cays, Frigate Island, and several other cays north of Union Island are governed by St. Vincent. Carriacou, Petit Martinique, Diamante, Les Tantes, Ronde, Lie Large, Lie Callie, and all other small islands south of Petit Martinique are governed by Grenada. While the separation ended 150 years of common governmental history between Union Island and Grenada, England was adamant that this division would make the multiple islands challenge much more manageable.

Here (Above) at Gardenfield Cemetery lies the disintegrated tomb of Oliver Spann (grandson of Samuel Spann). During the latter part of the 19th Century, in the month of October, Oliver died at the ripe age of 93. He was the husband of Mariana Spann.

Mr. Spann, whose principal home was in Bristol, England, subsequently made Union Island his entrepreneurial home. He is known to have a daughter and a son whose names are Ann Bartlett (nee Spann) and Samuel Spann Jr. respectively. Two of his brothers were also in Union Island; they were John and Sam Spann. Other members of the Spann family also descended on Union Island, Carriacou, and Trinidad to enjoy the fruits of early industry and economy. They inevitably became the principal residents on the islands as the family grew in numbers. They buried their loved ones at their private burial ground in Gardenfield, Ashton, as opposed to the older cemetery that is located at the foot of Clifton Hill or the Ashton Cemetery which is located at Frigate (cemetery of the slaves). The Spann's burial ground was fenced, but among the tombs were numerous orange and plum trees. Visiting this old site, one can still see the boundary that represents this once fenced plot of land. Remains of several badly eroded tombstones are still visible. Among them are two tombstones that are partially intact. They are engraved with the names Oliver Spann, the grandson of Admiral Samuel Spann, and Lavinia Cuthbert, the first wife of Richard P. Mulzac, (mentioned later). She was the mother of Richards' first two sons, John, and Edward.

At the foot of Clifton Hill, lies the tomb of Elizabeth Scrubb; only 31, she died on Nov 23rd, 1893. Although the institution of slavery had been abolished in the year 1838, the customs and function of this institution were well alive even into the early 20th century.

Admiral Samuel Oliver Spann, the wealthy merchant of Bristol, England, who once owned Union Island, restored it as a

British colony after the Treaty of Paris, named the island, and who's genealogical footprint is still evident on the island, later died in England between the years 1795-96.

The legacy of cotton farming continued under the S & J banner for almost one hundred years. During such time, poverty and squalor inundated the island, and the slaves unavoidably wallowed in adverse and miserable conditions. With a lack of adequate water and the filthy condition that they were subjected to, poor hygiene led to sickness, infant mortality and shortened lifespan. As mentioned before, many mothers preferred child murder rather than having their sick children live the lives to which they were subjected. The deplorable water shortage, miserable condition, and squalor continued even into the early 20th century.

The first cemetery, Clifton, (at the footings of Clifton Hill) lays the tomb of Cecelia Robinson, who died on May 14, 1874. Who was this lady? Many other tombstones lie in the vicinity with epitaphs that shows the short life expectancy of the black community back then.

With the abolition of slavery in the West Indies in 1834, but Union Island in 1838, came a subtle change of tide on the plantations. Unfortunate for the lucrative cotton industry, it never returned to its former stature. Sixteen years later, in 1850, S & J Spann and Company had seen enough on Union Island to call it a day. That same year, the company sold the island to Major Collins, a resident of St. Vincent. With little to do on the island regarding generating a comfortable income, many of the Spann family went back to England in pursuit of better life. Some have migrated to the United States of America while others went to the nearby Caribbean island of Trinidad, where another faction of the Spann family resided. Currently, descendants of the Spann bloodline are prevalent throughout Union island and Trinidad. Samuel Spann and other slave masters of that day had multiple children with their female slaves; this was because of the convenient use of the shack at the back of the plantations as opposed to the use of the slave master's house. It was the status quo for these plantation owners. History teaches that William Pinchback, a slave master of Mason County, Georgia, had ten children with his slave, Eliza Stewart. George Washington and Thomas Jefferson, former presidents of the U.S.A., they too fathered children with their slaves. Hence, it is widely questioned whether integration had been tightly knit into slavery because of the sexual use of the female slaves? Evidently, many of the black families of Union Island are descendants of their slave masters. At one point, the descendants of Samuel Spann were the largest family to exist on Union Island post-slavery.

CHARLES MULZAC'S LEGACY

With so little to attain through their tedious efforts on those plantations, inevitably, the Africans developed an aversion to working the lands.

For nine decades, S & J Spann and Company has ruled Union Island with an iron fist. These British slave owners have profited immensely from the once lucrative cotton industry. But the effects of natural disasters and the Abolition Act of 1838, the Spanns had seen enough to call it a day. They knew that the industry could not return to its heyday. In 1850, S & J Spann and Company sold the island to Major Collins, a businessman from St. Vincent. Then 15 years later, (1863) a sharecropper of French origin took an interest in Union Island and later leased it from Major Collins for £150 per annum. That sharecropper was Mr. Charles Henry Malzac/Mulzac. He was born on the Caribbean island of St. Kitts. Charles' influence on this little island was profound; it later shaped, molded and fashioned the island's culture -an impact that is still evident today, approximately 155 years since he laid foot on the little Island. Charles was the grandfather of Captain Hugh Mulzac, now a household name in St. Vincent & the Grenadines.

Mr. Charles Henry Mulzac, a Kittitian, who had been in the region for several years, came to Union Island with his wife Mrs. Mulrain, the daughter of a wealthy Jewish family that lived in St. Vincent; she was also a distant relative of the Mulzacs. They had five children. They were: Richard, Mary, Charles Jr., Emma, and John. At such time, Richard, his oldest son, was only twelve years old. Unlike the Spann family, whose interest on Union Island was limited to cotton, the Mulzac family became dominant entrepreneurs throughout the island. Celebrated for their enormous skill in shipbuilding, the young men of this family manned many cargo vessels throughout the region. They were also adept at whaling and fishing, which they did extensively in the islands of the Grenadines. Consequently, the legacy of whaling is still alive in the sister island of Bequia. Shipbuilding is still practiced in Carriacou, another sister isle. With the cotton crop forcefully kept alive, Union

Island was also rife with livestock, and the Mulzacs were the sole supplier of the island's milk and meats.

It is now 155 years since Charles Mulzac laid foot on Union Island, yet many names of the early Mulzac family are still evident in the younger generations. Names such as Ada, Una, Roselyn, Charles, Hugh, Cuthbert, Richard, Henry, John, and Edward can still be found in the family as descendants take honor in bearing these names with dignity and pride.

Richard Mulzac, Charles' first son, married his sweetheart, Lavinia Cuthbert (white woman) while he was still a teenager; she was older than him. She bore him two sons, John, and Edward (twin). Unfortunately, Lavinia became extremely ill and later died on January 28th, 1878; she was only 28 years old. She was buried at the Spann's cemetery at Gardenfield, Ashton.

** The Excavated Tombstone of Lavinia Cuthbert, Richard P. Mulzac's first wife. **

In 1885, seven years after Lavinia's death, Richard, 34, wedded Ada Donowa, a black woman, and mother of one. Her parents were from Antigua, in the Leeward Islands. From this marital union, began the life and legacy of a legendary hero and a historic giant named Captain Hugh Nathanial Mulzac. Richard and Ada had seven children, namely: Hugh, Irvin, Una, Lavinia, Lamie, James, and May. Richard affectionately named one of his daughters *Lavinia*, the name of his deceased wife. Richard Mulzac later had four additional children out of wedlock from two other non-conjugal relationships with black women in Union Island. The names of these children were Theresa, Radford, August, and Thomas. Like the Spanns of the mid-18th century, the legacy of white landowners having children with their subjects is evident in the Mulzac family of the 19th century, and later the Richard families of the early 20th century.

Fully aware that the institution of slavery was no more, or at least had dwindled a bit in its physical abuse of the Africans, Hugh's grandfather, Charles Mulzac, elected to use the Metayage System in a stringent manner to keep the fading cotton industry afloat. This method had a tragic, long-lasting impact on farmers (Africans) of Union Island.

Metayage, or Sharecropping, was a system of agriculture in which a landowner allowed a tenant to work the land in return for a share of the crops that he or she had produced (e.g., 50 percent of the crop). Unfortunately, there was no significant economic change post-slavery, and sharecropping did very little to boost the local economy. As a result, Charles Mulzac demanded 66 percent as his allotment of the cotton crops. He bought from the Africans their 33 percent share of the cotton crop, but paid so little that it was utterly senseless for the sharecroppers to remain as farmers on the plantations if they wanted to survive. And even worse, most of the stringent aspects of Slavery were perpetuated during the Sharecropping period. With so little to attain from their tedious efforts on those plantations, these Africans inevitably developed an aversion to working the lands. This aversion has spiraled down through the ages and is notably evident in today's generation.

The already deplorable living conditions of black people (slaves), which existed during the tenure of the two Frenchmen, and Samuel Spann's rulership, deteriorated drastically. To add to the current hardship and living condition that these people endured, the land yielded nothing to compensate for their hard work. As a result, they refused to work hard. This rebellious attitude of blacks on the plantation escalated to its acme when Mr. E. Richards, a merchant from St. Vincent, assume ownership of Union Island during the threshold of the 20th century.

The yield of the cotton crop continued to decline considerably during the latter part of Charles Mulzac's rulership. Observing his father's health was quickly deteriorating, Richard

Mulzac, the eldest son, immediately assumed command of his father's assets and businesses. In 1893, exactly 30 years after laying foot on Union Island, Charles Mulzac, the bearded old man who had significantly impact the culture of this little island, quietly died in penury; he was laid to rest at the Frigate Cemetery in Ashton.

Now, the 66 percent allotment that Charles had claimed for sharecropping was not an asset to the steadily declining economy of that day. Furthermore, the 33 percent of the spoils that the Africans received from selling the cotton to Richard Mulzac was worth next to nothing. Poverty and hardship were strongly felt by these Africans who continued to be troubled by the uncertainty of the cotton crop -their only source of income. Without an alternative, these Africans shifted their focus heavily to cultivating other crops such as cassava, potatoes, fruits, corn and pigeon peas, which they also had to share with Charles, and later Richard.

The corn & pea crops flourished bountifully each year and quickly became the main crops of the island. But life remained a challenge for those farmers (Africans) because these two crops were only a food source; they did not generate an income. Life remained difficult, and the aversion to working the land escalated drastically. These Africans wanted to do better, but there was nowhere to turn. It prompted many young men and fathers to leave the island in search of greener pastures. Leaving wasn't an easy task, because they did not want to abandon their wives and children; to remain in Union Island meant that they would have been obligated to work the land and live in abject poverty. And by working the land, they would have been subjected to misuse and abuse by the vicious landlords. Again, leaving was not easy, for they first had to have somewhere to go. Some young men never left at all, and even for those who reluctantly left, most of them were never seen on the soil of Union Island again.

The reality is that there was nothing attainable financially on those plantations other than the food, which they were able to consume themselves. Could they abandon agriculture altogether? No! For there was nowhere else whereby these people could have turned. Regrettably, this tacit aversion to working the land had been handed down throughout the years and has placed today's generation at a deficit on the farmlands. Hence, it is not a surprise that the corn and pea crops of Union Island are eventually at its lowest.

With the state of the declining economy, the Windward Island hurricane of September 1898 further devastated the cotton industry of Union Island. Miraculously, the tenuous cotton crop was still alive on many farms, but at that time, its yield was significantly low compared to its original stature.

Having experienced all of these major challenges, Richard Mulzac, the father of thirteen children, unwittingly surrendered the land ownership back to an aged Major Collins at the turn of the 20th century. This was exactly seven years after his father's death in 1893. His capacity as a landlord on Union island represented a tenure that lasted for three consecutive decades. Richard though, remained the go-to person where cotton was concerned. He processed the raw cotton with the sole cotton gin on the island. With the help of his sons Irvin, John, and Edwards, Richard focused his attention on shipbuilding and making a living at sea. Richard and his family were some of the principal owners of vessels in the region. As in the neighboring island of Bequia, whaling was an art that was also practiced in Union Island, and the Mulzac boys were no slouch in that discipline. Whales were butchered on Frigate Island (Rock). Amazingly, the bones of many slaughtered whales were still visible on the little island up until the 1970's. John, one of the first sons of Richard, was a fierce captain at sea who captained several fishing boats in the region. He manned the Sunbeam (ship) throughout the Caribbean waters for several years. John later fell victim to the unpredictable regional waters during a hurricane in 1921. At that time, he was taking his vessel, the Evelyn Guy, into port. Since then, countless lives of local seamen have been lost at sea, a subject that will be discussed in a subsequent chapter.

In the year 1900, Richard Mulzac relinquished the lease of Union Island to Major Collins of St. Vincent. Tactlessly, but true, the Mulzac's presence in Union Island as proprietors represented 37 infamous years of entrepreneurial dictatorship.

MR. E. RICHARDS -Last Landlord

By the year 1902, Union Island had changed ownership once again. Unlike Charles Mulzac and his son Richard who had least the island, Mr. E. Richards a merchant of St. Vincent, bought the island from an aged Major Collins for £3,000. Having knowledge of the many challenges and the mammoth destruction of the cotton crop at the hand of the 1998 hurricane, Mr. E.

Richards was determined to make this crop an income earner at the expense of the peasants' labor. He applied the same method of sharecropping that he inherited from his predecessor, Richard Mulzac. In this Metayage System, 2/3 of the cotton goes directly to the landlord while the peasants' gets 1/3. He used every measure possible to contain the peasants and have them comply with his stringent demands. His rulership represented one of the worst life's experiences for the people of Union Island, post slavery. They suffered tremendously.

At Frigate, Mr. E. Richards convened all the peasants of that district under a huge Hog-plum tree in the vicinity of the Anglican Church and made his stringent demands. At Clifton, he gathered the peasants of that district at his residence at Clifton Hill, (called Yard) and made the same demand. Firstly, Mr. E. Richards decreed that each house must furnish him with at least 300 pounds of cotton per annum with the seeds already removed. He gets 2/3 of the seeds while the peasants got 1/3. He paid them very little for their produce. The fact was, Mr. E. Richards inherited a dissatisfied recalcitrant population that was living in tenements at *Frigate* and the slopes of Clifton Hill for many generations. Frigate was later referred to as Pauper-land, while the location of the peasants at Clifton Hill was called Nigga House. The population had severe health issues. Health issues that derived from share poverty and the squalid environments that they were subjected to. As mentioned before, Union Island has a semiarid climate and receives a very low rainfall each year, and as a result, there was always a scarcity of water. The two manmade ponds (Lincoln & Basin), and later, the well at Frigate, which was constructed during the time of Antoine Rigaud and Juan Augier, were used to water slaves and livestock. These ponds were the only sources of water that were made available to them. The other source of water was the cistern at Calsay (Clifton), but they were prohibited from catching water there; it was the ONLY repository of clean drinking water on the island, but was solely for the landlord' use. With no recourse, the poor people of Union Island resorted to the turbid water from the ponds to stay alive. And so, with the consumption of unsanitary water, illnesses escalated into an epidemic, and living conditions deteriorated drastically. Subsequently, Enteric fever inundated the land, yet, Mr. E. Richards, the uncompromisingly intransigent landlord, made no effort to address the plight of the ailing people. Instead, he remained true to his core existence on Union Island. His sole objective was to make his entrepreneurship in Union Island a lucrative one. He yielded not to any pieces of advice, and as a result, his dictatorial approach did backfire on him.

His demand for 300 pounds of cotton per annum from the peasants was utterly impossible because the soil had been used consistently for over 160 years but was never replenished with fertilizer. He prevented the peasants from planting other crops such as corn, peas, potatoes and cassava among the cotton. But the people were destitute and could not depend on the meager income that the cotton generated. As a result, they planted food crops among the cotton crops. Mr. E. Richards thought that the peasant's interest had diverted towards the food crops rather than the cotton crop. As a result, he brought people from St. Vincent to destroy the minor crops that they planted. Mr. Richards also prevented the peasants from rearing animal such as goats, sheep, cattle, pigs and fowl –their principal source of food. He expelled one man from the island and tried to expel other residents whom he accused of stealing his cotton. He also brought litigation against them, but because of lack of evidence, he was forced to withdraw. He prevented vessels from coming to Union Island. And so, the inhabitants could not get supplies anywhere. Instead, they had to depend on his shop for ground provisions or any other commodity. His shop was the only one allowed on the island.

The distressful condition on the plantation was way over two decades old. It was during that period of time that *Isabella Roache*, made mention of a sick black man who begged for his life to be spared. "Massa me nah dead yet, Massa, me nah dead yet." Unfortunately, his cry for help fell on obstinate ears, for he was later buried alive. "Carry um go bury um," (take him and bury him) was the last order given by the plantation owner to have his subject buried alive. But why was this happening on the plantation when slavery was abolished since 1834? The answer to this question is simple. It is because the "Massa-slave" relationship, which was the only form of relationship on Union Island, was still existent on the plantations long after the abolition of slavery. In fact, the abolition document was *only* a paper file at best that was **never** respected and honored. Clearly, its contents did not worth the paper that it was written on. The atmosphere on the island was still one of servitude. As a result, the so-called freed slaves (peasants) were still dependent on their superiors or the patriarchs of the island.

The year was now 1909, and these Peasants (Africans) who

had nothing to call their own, had seen enough abuse and victimization, and hence refused to be docile and pliable to this tyrant. But because the island had belonged to him, he yielded not to any advice, but continued to make life a hell for the Africans. On the brink of rebellion, they forcefully presented a petition to the administrator of that day. It was on Thursday, September 30th, 1909. The petition requested that the government assume immediate ownership of the island, the establishment of a peasant proprietary, and an annexation to Grenada. Unfortunately, the latter was impossible; Grenada could not shoulder such financial responsibility, and so, Union Island remained under the ordinance of St. Vincent. The petition also states: Mr. E. Richards prevented the residents from building better homes. The peasants explained to the administrator that living condition deteriorated so horribly that it was worded in the manner below: "We *were opened to all insults and blood-curdling horrors which for decency's sake we dare not breathe in your Honor's ears.*" The truth is, the actual story of the horrors that the people of Union Island endured, (Amerindians & Africans of the 18th century, to the descendants of Africans of the early 20th century) was never properly documented. In fact, it may have been too hideous to be made available in Caribbean history books.

Two opinions are better than one, right? Not always! For in Carriacou -the neighboring island, the magistrate of that day was asked for his perspective about the petition from the people of Union Island. In his letter on October 19th October, to the Administrator, this is what he had to say in his euphemism of the grave conditions that the sharecroppers explained above:

"It is rather overstating the case to describe Mr. Richards as a tyrant. He is merely endeavoring to carry out as a landlord the absolute owner of the island estate, a system of management that might have been appropriate some 50 years ago, but is now unsuited to the present conditions of the island, and its people. Mr. Richards, since becoming owner of the island, has in no way broken the law of landlord and tenant, but his strict enforcement of it presses hard on a people who for generations have been accustomed to a very light and easy yoke."

It is evident that the horrific climate of Massa-Slave relationship existed even during the dawn of the early 20th century. And so, it clearly substantiated the fact that the story of *Isabella Roache*, who described the horror of a slave on a Union Island

Plantation, is factual. This slave, she said who refused to work, was subsequently buried alive under a huge Hog plum tree at Bajan Corner on Clifton Road. That location was considered haunted from such time until the late 1980's. She also referred to another slave who had the roof of his house yanked off. This man's watch-house was located in Clifton, where Ms. Eldine Clouden now resides. The current location is adjacent to one of Mr. E. Richards's estate. Mr. E. Richards had also prevented the Sharecroppers from cultivating food crops; he wanted them to focus on cotton, and cotton only. In some case, he destroyed the food crops of the Sharecroppers to dissuade them from cultivating more in the future.

With so many complain of injustices from the residents to the administrator, the landlord, Mr. E Richards was pressured into selling Union Island to the British Government or Crown. On June 1st, 1910, the island was bought for £5,000. At that point, it was referred to as "Crown Lands." The British Crown then subdivided the land into parcels of two, three, and four acres' parcels to be sold to the residents. At £4 to £8 sterling per acre, the first sale began in 1911. Mr. E. Richards, now the former landlord purchased a significant amount of the best land on the island, so did the Mulzac family, the descendants of the Spanns, Joseph (Daddy) Alves and Allan Scrubb. They had belonged to the upper echelon of society on the island. On the other hand, the former sharecroppers or residents being under abject poverty were unable to buy their plots of land outright. Evidently, a land credit scheme was put in place; it gives residents the opportunity to make small down payments on the properties that they intended to buy, and to make subsequent payments throughout the years that follow.

But with the lands being under the authorized credit scheme, Mr. Rupert Coleridge Otway, a representative of the British Government, prohibited each resident from setting up living quarters or dwelling on these farmlands. It was believed that the presence of living quarters or shacks on these farmlands would have taken away from the meager volume of land space that was available. That would have also compromise the cultivation of the cotton crop. Instead, the lands were to be used only for the cultivation of cotton, and other short-term food crops. So, it is evident, that even after the slavery and sharecropping years had essentially met their demise, the element of servitude and patriarchal dominance was still alive in Union Island. With poverty pestering the land, regrettably, some folks were unable to purchase lands for themselves. Instead, they reluctantly remained sharecroppers, but in servitude to their former oppressor.

Many years had passed; yet, poverty in Union Island refused to go away. As a result, several parcels of lands remained unsold. And although many residents had great pride in being landowners for the first time, those that were tied to the land installment contracts could not obtain their deeds because they were unable to pay up their amortization even in the year 1930. It was only after the year 1931 that the residents began to leave the foothills of Clifton and Mt. Parnassus and Clifton Hill to build better homes. The result is evident throughout the island seventy-five years later.

For the Spanns -slave masters that ruled Union Island, traces of the their bloodline are still evident on the island. Today, the family name *Spann* has dwindled to an alarming zero on Union Island. This may be due in part to the fact that many young women (Spann) after marriage may have been compelled to assume the family names of their husbands. Nonetheless, the principal contributing factor must be attributed to the legacy of migration, a system that will be explained in detail in another chapter. In humility, the author referred to it as, The Exodus Factor. Regrettably! It has become an integral part of the life and legacy of every Unionite, and by extension, anyone who have lived in Union Island for a considerable amount of years. And for the rest of the Caribbean islands? Ditto.

Unlike the Spanns, Mulzacs, and Richards, whose bloodline was proliferous throughout the island long after their departures, tactlessly, there hasn't been the faintest sight of any Amerindian bloodline on Union Island after the 1760s. Neither are descendants of the Frenchmen, Antoine Rigaud, and Jean Augier. Nonetheless, there are some physical reminders that can be attached to the French presence in Union Island. They are: Ms. Pierre, Bordeaux, Mt. Taboi, Mt. Parnassus, Petit Bay and Chatham Bay. These are names of districts, mountains and bays on the Island. For Monsieur De L'isle, another compatriot of Antoine Rigaud and Juan Augier, traces of his bloodline can be found on the island of Carriacou.

On the following page is a sample of the first deed that was granted to landowners during the early 20th century. Sadly, 99% of these improvised peasants could not hold a deed or Crown Grant to the lands that they were indebted to. It was only after 1930 that they were able to bring their lingering amortizations to an end.

Saint Vincent.

GEORGE V. by the Grace of God of Great Britain, Ireland and of the British Dominions beyond the Seas King, Defender of the Faith Emperor of India

To all of whom these presents shall come.

Know Ye that in consideration of the sum of *three* Pound ....shilling and.........................Pence paid by *Charles Stewart* of *Union Island*.........................*to* the treasurer of our said Colony of St. Vincent we do hereby grant unto the said *Charles Stewart* and his heirs all that piece or portion of land situated on the acquired Estate of *Union Island* in the parish of *Southern Grenadines* in the said colony of St. described Vincent being one *lot* in the extent number *19* and bounded as shown and in the diagram heron and also on the plan recorded in the office of the superintendent of works or however otherwise the same may be bounded known or described. Together with all buildings and appurtenance and easements thereto belonging. To have and to hold the said piece or portion of land to the said *Charles Stewart* his heirs and assigns forever subject however to any Regulations made by the "Governor in Council" under the provision of "The Land Settlement Ordinance 1899" and the conditions therein continued. If the said *Charles Stewart* shall fail to comply with the said Regulations, the Present grant may, pursuant to the said Regulation of any time after such failure be revoked by US or the Officer Administrating the Government of our said Colony of St. Vincent and the said piece or portion of land may be dealt with pursuant to the said Regulations.

The Crown reserves to itself the fee simple out of the grant hereby made all mines, veins, beds, deposits or accumulation of Minerals and Mineral Oil already found; or which may hereafter be found under the premises aforesaid with full liberty at all times for the Crown to enter and inspect the same, for the purpose searching for, getting, winning and taking away the said Mineral and Mineral Oil, subject to such compensation for injury done to or upon the surface, or any building standing thereon as may be determined by two arbitrators of whom one shall be appointed on behalf of the Crown and the other by and on behalf of the Grantee, or such other private party (if any) interested for the time being in the said premises, or in the event of disagreement between such arbitrators, such compensation as may be determined by an umpire, who shall be appointed in writing by such arbitrators before they enter on the matter so referred to them or on any matter upon which such arbitrators may differ, and in such event the decision of the umpire thereon shall be final and binding.

In testimony, whereof we have caused these Our Letters to be made Patent and the Great Seal of Our Said Colony to be hereto affixed. Witness our trust and well beloved *James Henry Garret Esquire;* office administration and Government of Our said Colony of St. Vincent this *23rd* day of *September 1930* and in the *twenty-first* Year of Our Reign.

William P. Dolly F.S.I

Superintendent of works
Date of allotment 01:01:1931

N

ow, with the departure of Antoine Rigaud & Juan Augier, during the late 18th century, the Spanns during the 19th century, the Mulzac's and Mr. E. Richards during the turn of the 20th century, the island was left with a population that was predominantly Africans. A population that was totally useless to these merchants after slavery was challenged by the act of abolition. And although these Africans were partially loosed from the chains of physical bondage, they were left with several impediments that inevitably haunted their offspring over a period of 100 years. One major obstacle is the inability to read & write – an essential element of life (discussed in another chapter). Another major impediment is that the ancestors were rooted out of Africa, brought to a strange land, and were forbidden to practice their beliefs, morals, laws, acts and customs, that was fundamental to their livelihood. As a result, they lost their names, languages, religion, culture, folkways, mores, and norms. On arrival, to the West Indies, they were introduced to a new life –chattel slavery. They had no choice but to forcefully adapt to their slave master's way of life and customs -a way of life that they had loathed, and hence it never took root into their psyche.

Consequently, if anyone were to take a cursory glance at the institution of slavery, he/she may never understand the detriment and long-lasting impact that this wicked establishment has brought on a single race of people -the inoffensive sons and daughters of the largest continent of planet earth, Africa.

Fortuitously, some of these Africans of Union Island were prospective owners of the same land that they once worked for their superiors. They were able to reap the entire benefits of their labor. Unfortunately, the cash that they were receiving from selling the raw cotton to the Mulzacs was disheartening, for they were unable to make ends meet. The Mulzacs, on the other hand, who now had a monopoly on the cotton crop, were not willing to negotiate, or give the farmers a better price for their hard-earned produce. And so, with poverty pestering the land, many young men were forced to pursue work on new frontiers (outside of Union Island) to get money to take care of their families, and also to earn enough money to buy lands that were available for sale. Some left Union Island on boats such as the Sunbeam, Lady Osprey, Ocean

King, and Wanderer, which conducted trade in the Caribbean waters. Others ventured to Europe and America in hope of improving their standard of living. Regrettably, many were never seen or heard of in the region. As a result, their offspring are scattered throughout the globe. Therefore, in the Americas, no one should be caught by surprise if they were to discover that their landlords, next-door neighbor, or supervisors are their blood relatives; the possibility exist that their bloodlines might be traced all the way back to Union Island.

In Union Island, several other young men, who were also eager to arrest the wretched hardship, left the island and ended up on the soils of Trinidad & Tobago, Cuba, Aruba, Curacao, Venezuela, Colombia, England, U.S.A., and even at the massive construction site of the Panama Canal. Their hopes and dreams were to return to the island of their births with enough money to live easier lives. With a labor force that consisted of 90% black men from the Caribbean, the construction of the Panama Canal began in 1881 and ended in 1913. Unfortunately, there was a huge death toll at this site that resulted from the indiscriminate spread of diseases while working in such an unsanitary environment. The aforementioned Charles "Mindo" Stewart" was one of the few Unionites who had worked there for several years. He was adamant to defy the formidable Exodus Factor by returning permanently to the land of his birth –an accomplishment in itself. Sadly, most of his friends and compatriots, became tethered by the countless entices that were too addictive to avert. The late Samuel Oliver Alexander, the brother of Presaul Ambrose (mentioned earlier) is a typical example. Impecunious and gaunt, the late Oscar John and Preston "Kayber" Ramage of Ashton village quietly returned to Union Island during the 1970s. They too had left Union Island during their youth to seek employment on foreign soils. Regrettably, they returned long after they had passed their productive years. They died several years later.

With boatbuilding fully introduced to the island by the Mulzac family, some young men had the opportunity to learn the skill of shipwright. With such a remarkable skill, the gloomy future of the island seemed to be waning quickly, or so they thought. A few years later, many youngsters became owners of several small fishing boats and vessels, which they built themselves. The lumber that they used to build these crafts was obtained from the forest of Colon Campbell, Ashton. During those years, Colon Campbell was rife with cedar trees that were cultivated during the earlier years when the French and English inhabited the island. During the 1930s up until the 1970s, many Unionites had owned vessels, and they conducted interisland trade throughout the Caribbean. With this type of business venture, the economy of Union Island was in better standing than during the tumultuous years of sharecropping. The names of several vessels that were owned by Unionites are listed in another chapter.

During the first quarter of the 20th century, the Mulzac's entrepreneurial power in Union Island began to dwindle. Many of the Mulzac families had left Union Island and ventured abroad for greener pastures. Today, traces of the Mulzac family are present in the USA, but are derived primarily from the offspring of Hugh and his younger brothers James and Lamie. Concurrently, two remarkable residents of Union Island came to prominence almost immediately. They were Joseph Alves (Daddy Alves) and Allan Scrubb (Ba Allan). As vessel owners, these two gentlemen conducted marine trade in the region and were very successful entrepreneurs. Unlike the average resident who was poverty-stricken under the aforementioned sharecropping era; these businessmen, Joseph Alves & Allan Scrubb had the financial wherewithal and were able to buy more lands than most residents.

Daddy Alves, born on the neighboring island of Carriacou during the late 1870s, was an influential businessman. He also was a shopkeeper in Union Island during the 1920s through the 1940 & 50s. He was fond of Union Island and hence made the village of Ashton his home. His wife, Edith, who was born on the neighboring island of Bequia in 1885, was the teenage girlfriend of Hugh Mulzac before he left in 1907 for his endeavors at sea. Daddy Alves and his wife Edith was loved and respected by Unionites from all walks of life. This Kayak (native of Carriacou) with his thick accent, was noted for a line he coined some seventy-plus years ago: *Vincentians, from collar & tie to barefoot, none nar good.* This translates to: Vincentians from the highest echelons of society to those in the throes of poverty are considered to be untrustworthy. This saying is still recited and echoed by a few older folks in the community whenever Daddy Alves' name is mentioned. Allan Scrubb (Ba Allan), another entrepreneur in his own right, was also a fine shopkeeper at Ashton Village. He was the first black resident to build a concrete house on Union Island. Before the year 1931, no one was given authority to erect any structure outside of the footing of Mr. Parnassus and Clifton Hill. Mr. Scrubb completed this historical task at the foot of Mt. Parnassus in the year 1922.

Today, although Unionites seldom own vessels like those of their forefathers, they are proud owners of very small fishing boats that can easily comb the waters of the Grenadines. Of the legacy left from Richard Mulzac, the entrepreneurial mastermind of Union Island, boatbuilding and whaling are completely extinct. Although interisland marine trade has diminished considerably over the years, animal husbandry and fishing remained an active part of the island's culture.

The absence of these local customs can be rather devastating in that it will push the little island deeper into a state of poverty.

THE FIRST INHABITANTS

Sadly, the bountiful treasures (Artifacts) that were unearthed never made their way to any museum of St. Vincent & the Grenadines.

The history of Union Island has a Genesis. Yes, it does! And that Genesis begins with the people that first called Union Island home. But the history of the indigenous people of Union Island is one that is seldom spoken or written of. Fortunately, fragments of the history of this little island have been handed down from generations to generation. Many elders speak passionately of what they witness and were told by their parents and grandparents –slaves and sharecroppers. And so, a lack of written documentation is understood and acceptable, for the slaves and sharecroppers were unable to read and write; hence, they used the only viable asset that they had, and that was their memories.

To complete the history of this island, extensive research has been done regarding the lives of this indigenous tribe. Regrettably, very little is attained of this race of people that is believed to be the first to live in Union Island. One may ask what was the name given to this island by the first inhabitants? This we may never know, for the sparsely documented history of Union Island began only when the Europeans came. What you will read below will affirm that the Amerindians did inhabit Union Island during the 15th to 18th centuries when the European arrived in the region. This tribe of Amerindians was notably called the Caribs.

Let us now expand our horizons by taking a look at the Amerindians –this race of people who walked the soil of Union Island thousands of years before Christopher Columbus (sighting), Antoine Rigaud, Jean Augier, Samuel Spann, his colleagues, John Hamilton and David Smith; Charles Mulzac, and Mr. E. Richards. They were the first settlers of Union Island, the indigenous natives –people who were never weary of a community lifestyle.

The Amerindians are believed to have migrated from the Orinoco River area in South America to settle in the Caribbean islands. Union Island and many other islands of the Antilles have been inhabited some 5400 BC. Dominica, St. Lucia, Grenada, and St. Vincent were rife with this tribe of people. Later, during the 17th century, the Caribs of St. Vincent were integrated with Africans that escaped a sunken slave ship in the waters of Bequia Island and St. Vincent (A subject you will read about in a later chapter of this book).

In Union Island, the Carib communities were dense at Chatham Bay, Bloody Bay, and Ms. Pierre. Like many communities that toiled the lands to produce their foods, the Caribs worked this semi-arid landmass and planted many root crops such as yams, cassava, sweet potatoes, dasheen, eddoes, and also corn. Nevertheless, their principal food source derived primarily from the sea, for fishing was an integral part of their livelihood. They fed extensively on the fish and turtles that are native to the region. Manicou, iguanas, crabs, and birds were also hunted for food.

Archeologists claimed that these people were in existence in these regions some fifty-four hundred years BC. To substantiate this, the presence of numerous artifacts on Union Island is indicative of a community that once existed and flourished there for several centuries. Sadly, there is a sparse collection of the documented history of these people. The fact is, this indigenous tribe had been violently removed from the soil of Union Island in a provoked war. This transpired during the mid 18th century by two marauders, Antoine Rigaud and his colleague Jean Augier. It was these two Frenchmen from Guadeloupe and Martinique that brought slavery to the shores of Union Island after assassinating these Indians (Caribs). Such heinous crime was vaguely documented; hence, there is seldom any historical recording of the indigenous people (Caribs).

As mentioned earlier, it is common knowledge that Bloody Bay, the most northern bay of Union Island, had gotten its name from the bloodshed that occurred during a French instigated war against the Caribs. But the dearth of documented information on the history of Union Island makes it much more difficult to attain the details of what transpired at that bay during the late 1750's. Moreover, what is factual in the region during the European existence must be highlighted; for even the high territorial tension that existed between Great Britain, France, and America during and after the Treaty of Paris never escalated into a war on the soil of Union Island. There were small skirmishes among these factions, as the French were weary of the presence of these Indians in the region. The Indians too were distrustful of the pale-skinned enemy after they annihilated their brothers and sisters in Grenada during the provoked war in the 1650s (Le Morne de Sauteurs).

After the Treaty of Versailles in 1783, Admiral Samuel Spann, the owned of Union Island, saw it fit to fortify the little jewel with defensive weapons in the form of cannons.

Now, with the annihilation of the Caribs in Union Island by Antoine and Rigaud, one can only surmise that these first inhabitants should be honored by their tangible past -the artifacts that they left behind. The artifact encompasses the stone tools, bowls, smoking vessel, shards, pottery, jewelry, amulets, clay pots, arrowheads, and Ica stones. But where are these artifacts today? When were they removed from the soil of Union Island? When were they swindled? Where have they been taken?

For decades, (1970's -2000's) three adventurous visitors that later became residents on Union Island, dug up pots and many other valuable utensils throughout the island. During such time, the authority from St. Vincent & the Grenadines did not assume guardianship of what has been excavated. Sadly, the bountiful treasures that were unearthed never made their way to any local museum of St. Vincent & the Grenadines, but instead were swindled and taken away to foreign soils. The question that many Unionites have been asking themselves in recent years is this: "Are we not deserving of the island's natural heritage and artifacts?" Firstly, these Amerindians were annihilated, and then the artifacts that they unintentionally left behind were stolen. As a result, the history of the Amerindians of Union Island that dates back to 5400 BC and onward is now etched into the wilderness of nothingness.

Several residents (males), who were goaded by foreigners to unearth, these priceless treasures, only for a pittance, have attested to what they have seen and found. As mentioned above, the artifacts that were excavated at the beaches of Union Island included stone tools, bowls, smoking vessel, shards, pottery, jewelry, amulets, clay pots, arrowheads, and Ica stones. "During the 1970s, we had dug up a lot of stuff, one resident explained. In fact, there were so many artifacts that it literally filled the small shed that was used as a repository. And amazingly, a lot of these materials were still in good shape."

The late Clem Stewart, the third generation of the renowned William McDowell Stewart, (mentioned later) speaks vehemently of his encounter with a group of foreigners who were trespassing on his land at Chatham Bay. "They had with them instruments to detect objects that were buried," he said. "I chased them out," he continued, "They never asked for permission to come on my land; they came to steal all the gold." But Mr. Clem Stewart was not always present at Chatham Bay, so time and time again he encountered large areas on his property that had been dug up. The roots of huge Manchineel trees were left exposed or partially covered.

Ignorant of the presence of these foreign trespassers on his land, Mr. Clem Stewart never knew what their real intentions were. And without opposition from the local authority, these looters finally dug up and swindled everything, down to the last amulet.

It is reputed that a large number of artifacts was unearthed from the numerous shores of Union Island, and can be found at the museum on the neighboring island of Carriacou. The author has made numerous attempts to locate such items that were removed from the soil of Union Island to the sister isle, but to no avail. Nevertheless, the Caribs, the first natives of the region have left an indelible mark on Union Island. And fortunately, that memory of Union Island's History, which has finally made its way to the pages of this history book, will last for eternity.

The French that fished extensively in the region used Union Island, as some of the other islands of the Grenadines as a hub. But after 1650, when the French had attacked Grenada, the Caribs that inhabited all of the neighboring islands were aware of this deed, and became even more distrustful of the French; they were considered enemy number one. The two factions would sometimes wage war against each other at sea. Adenet and Vandangeur, two French fishermen, were inadvertently left on Union Island when the native Caribs with five canoes viciously attacked their vessel. As a result, the two French men (above) remained on the Island for seven months. Below is a detailed French story of what transpired on an eventful experience in Union Island, then to Grenada.

In May 1654, a boat from Martinique going to Grenada with the Captain Fontaine Heroux stops in Union, which is an island of 4 to 5 leagues in circumference, 10 leagues away from Grenada. Then we start fishing, taking wood and water, that which were needed. As all of us are about to enjoy life and the small necessary commodities, the savages appear in five canoes at full speed to take our boat if they can kill us. When the Captain sees them, he calls all the people who are all about and leaves the slowest ones in order to save as much as he can. Anyway, during the time taken to run, people get wounded, two of them get killed and a third one died 2 or 3 days after. The Captain seeing his weakness and the strength of his enemy who is trying to surround him and cut off his retreat, takes the open sea, the savages sending arrows and them firing back. During all these events, Sirs Vandangeur and Adenet who were hunting in the forest arrive and see their boat far away with the savages behind and curse their bad luck. They are left there without gunpowder, lead, bread, and without any commodity or assistance except that which may come as a miracle from heaven. As for the land, it is out of hope to get any for a long time and know not if they have to live or die. Another concern is that the savages who have missed the boat had come back to Union in the hope of finding someone who had not been able to board the boat in time. As soon as they landed, they start searching everywhere for someone on whom they could vent their rage and anger, but whoever God wants protected is well protected. These guys are so well hidden that no one can find them. After they leave, the savages keep in mind that the boat has left someone and the desire to catch them makes them come back often on the spot. They are searching everywhere and sometimes very close without seeing them. God is blinding them not to lose whomever he means to save. They find human footprints and ashes from a fire recently made in a cave, and this makes them sure about their feelings. They go in and back, they run, they keep searching, but that was a waste of time. Then they stop their search not knowing what to think about the prints and ashes. Our poor guys get away with their lives. Hunger makes them eat crabs, shells, and conch -only rubbish and garbage. They can say what Saint Job said about sitting on the dunghill, "That "the meats that they disliked now seemed delicious as they no longer have the right to choose." Necessity forces them to eat anything they find. When they see a passing vessel on the sea which is no farther than two leagues away, they bawl for help hoping that one would pick them up, that they have nothing to fear from them, that they are French. But perhaps they do not see them or hear them or trust them and the vessel goes for fear of a trick. This sad state of affairs continues for seven months. The Captain who has brought them thinks of coming back to Union to get them if they are still alive. But bad luck on bad luck fails under Grenada, - there is no wind. After a long way round, the Captain at last reaches Martinique where he reports the event of what has happened to Vandangeur and Adenet. One feels sorry but no one tries to help the situation, maybe as they believe that the savages have surely caught them and slaughtered them, or as they don't really like them or care about their loss, or also as no one is really interested in their story or trust to take them out of their misery. Then, finding the time long enough, and not being able to subsist, as the unpleasant is sometimes ingenious, they *make a lightwood raft and with it, reach Grenada. They land at Fond Du Grand Pauvre, and from there, they climb to the Carib huts where by luck the savages have fled out of fear of being caught by our people. Then they stay around eight days feeding on sweet potatoes and afterwards they go to Fond Des Fontaines where hearing a gun shot. They find a hunter who had been more frightened of them than they of him, but let me tell you the story: The hunter believing that they were savages, put his gun on them, so they hurry and tell him not to worry as they are lost French people and so he doesn't have to be scared. So, the hunter stops his shot and his mind gets quiet, and he notices that the savages do not in fact look as they do. Then they go closer, talk and recognize each other. They come to the Grand Fort all ugly, faceless, not recognizable, this happens around Christmas. They report their story, and their misery was enough to soften any rock. They praise the loving protection of God, to have kept them amongst so many dangers, and to bring them to such a good harbor without any bad encounter with our enemy, who will not spare them by immolating them with cruelty and fury, at the peak of their rage and at the most bloody time of their war. As well, God never left his own people....*

Today, it is well over 400 years since the European presence is felt in the territory of St. Vincent, Grenada & the Grenadines, alas, the indigenous communal natives (Caribs) that once peopled this region some 5,400 years BC is now a highly endangered tribe.

♦♦♦□*Chapter Two*

EXPLORING UNION ISLAND

The rocky terrain of this little island is much more pronounced than that of her sister islands throughout the Grenadines.

Mountainous by nature, with several peaks such as Mt. Olympus, Parnassus, Mt. Tabor, and a mountain range that extend from Mt. Parnassus in the central to Mt. Campbell in the west, Union Island is by far the most precipitous isle of all the Grenadines. This rocky terrain makes hiking a must on this little island. Volcanic in origin, this island is approximately three miles long and one mile wide (3.54 square miles) with a meager population of approximately 3.500. With an annual rainfall of 40.25 inches and an average temperature of 27.5 °C, Union Island is made up of two villages, namely: Ashton and Clifton.

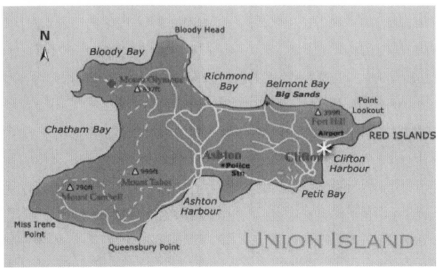

Map of Union Island

Samuel Spann gladly named these villages after his hometown of Bristol, England. Ashton, which is the larger of the two villages, consists of Ashton Village, Campbell, Valley, Bordeaux, Garden Field, Dominique, Bonnet, Richmond, Belmont, Jerome, Chatham, Rapid, Ms. Pierre (Ms. Pay), Ms. Irene, and Colon Campbell. Areas such as Campbell, Ms. Pierre, and Ms. Irene attained their names from female plantation owners who once farmed these lands with the use of slave labor during the famous cotton era. The district of Campbell was called Ms. Campbell until recent years.

Clifton, on the other hand, consists of Point Lookout, Clifton Village, Moure, Downson, Penfield, Cotton, and so on. Having such small landmass makes Union Island one of the most densely populated small islands in the region, but it does not appear to be so, because there are still numerous acres of lands that are vacant and uncultivated. Some of them are still referred to as Crownlands.

Ashton Village (Pauper land). From the mid 18th century until today, the population remained dense at the footing of Mr. Parnassus.   Photo: Herbert Thomas.

The rocky terrain of this little island is much more pronounced than that of her sister islands throughout the Grenadines. Mt. Tabor, at an altitude of one foot removed from officially called a mountain, is not the only prominent peak that grasps a visitor's attention. Mt. Olympus and her sister peak, Mt. Parnassus, (locally called Big Hill), cannot escape the gazing eyes of any first-time visitor to the island.

These two peaks are both a smidgen lower than Mt. Tabor. Mt. Parnassus, which overlooks the central village of Ashton may appear alarmingly precarious to a first-time visitor. However, its bold presence is not a deterrent to any of the residents whose parents and grandparents have lived their entire lives looking up at it. A visitor noted some thirty-five years ago that the first time she was driven to Ashton, she felt timid, as she got closer to this huge hill. "It appeared as though it was moving aggressively toward me," she said. After visiting the island time and time again, she expressed that it was like a different kettle of fish. Mt. Tabor is part of a range of highland that runs in a westerly direction that ends at the peak of dense vegetation named Mt. Campbell.

Many of these highpoints proved to be good lookout sites against enemies. Numerous cannons are still intact at key points throughout the island. These archaic weapons are rather eye-catching to tourists, who seize every opportunity to visit these locations, take pictures, and make historical documentation where necessary. Bloody Bay, which is situated on the northern coast of the island, speaks of the massive bloodshed associated with that particular region during maritime wars. It is the blood of the original settlers of Union Island, the Amerindians? Sure, it is! Did they not fight to their bitter end when the French first laid feet on the island to claim their land? To date, there is very little historical documentation available to indicate or reflect the total debacle of this tribe. Yet available or easily accessible to the people of Union Island is the history of Henry Morgan, John Hawkins, and his younger cousin Francis Drake. They were marauders and notorious British pirates that were honorably knighted "Sir" for their countless savage acts at sea. What a shame!

From an aerial view of St. Vincent and the Grenadines, one cannot escape the picturesque beauty that lies beneath. The long spans of reefs that engulf the white sandy beaches are enticing, not only to the marine biologists and anglers, but also to the average visitor. Amazingly, there are also hot springs –underwater volcanoes with continuous bubbles. The water temperature changes dramatically, becoming very warm at times. Also present is an abundance of outstanding corals in this vast expanse of reefs.

Boat-racing, snorkeling, spear fishing, waterskiing, game fishing, yachting, scuba diving in shallow water, and other aquatic sports are just a few of the enormous marine activities and attractions that exist on the island. Diving in these pristine territories offers opportunities to capture a panoramic submarine view and coexist with marine creatures in the shallow. Some of these Marine creatures are: the Frog Fish, Nurse Shark, Octopus (locally called the Sea Cat), Barracuda, Stingray, Manta Ray, Porcupine Fish, Congo Eel, Green Eel, Christmas-Tree Worm, and many other that inhabited the underwater world.

On the website, Grenadinesdive.com, are some pictures of the pristine underwater elegance in the confines of St. Vincent & the Grenadines. The famed diver, Glenroy Adams has captured and brought the elegance of the marine ecology at our fingertips.

Like the many trees, multiple land animals are residents to Union Island; among them are Goats, sheep, Pigs, and cattle that are domesticated. There are well over forty species of intriguing birds that are dispersed throughout the island. Some can be found at the seashore, in swamps, in pastures, and amid the dense vegetation inland. The **Green-Throated Carib**, locally called the Hummingbird, is the smallest species known. It can be seen extracting the juices of flowers during the ephemeral rainy season. The largest of the birds is the **Brown Pelican**. This excellent diver is seen mainly in the air and sea, and in most cases, is accompanied by its marine counterpart, the **Laughing Gull** (David) another excellent diver that follows fishermen out at sea. Wherever fish abound in the sea, these predatory birds are found in clusters. The Brown Pelican, locally called the Gramazier, is edible and is sometimes hunted for its meat.

The **Belted Kingfisher**, another native bird, has characteristics similar to those of the aforementioned birds. This bird can be seen mainly in the shallow coastal waters. The **Carib Grackle**, or blackbird, is quite an intriguing character to contend with; the detail of how this menace operates is the subject of a later chapter. Another bird that children were warned to keep their distance from is the **Grey Kingbird** (Petchary). This one is locally called the *Pickery*. It earns this name from its willingness to ward off any potential threat, even humans. During its breeding season, this bird is exceptionally aggressive toward anything that ventures near its path. It is extremely protective of its eggs or young ones. The **Zenaida dove** (mountain dove), Rameau, and Ground dove belong to the same species of the dove. The Rameau is the largest of the dove family in Union Island. Its proper name is the Scaly-

Naped pigeon, and like the rest of the doves, it is adorned with beautiful feathers. This bird, though, is blue and has bright red eyes. It can be seen only on tall trees or in the highlands. During the onset of flight, the wings of these regal birds exude a melodious sound.

** The domesticated sheep, reared for its meat**

The **Tropical Mockingbird**, similar in size to the Grey Kingbird, is locally called the Parka Change-Jay. During the late 1970s, this was one of the most proliferous birds found on Union Island. On the numerous Kashie trees (thorny trees) of Campbell, they were found hovering in huge fleets. The **Cattle Egrets** are white, lanky, long-legged birds that share the grassy pastures with cattle. Because they prey on insects and other vertebrates that are parasites to these larger animals, they can be sometimes seen standing on the back of these hosts.

The **Rufous-Vented Chachalaca** is very timid and wild and are seldom seen, except in the dense vegetation of Queensbury, Colon Campbell, and other densely forested areas. This brown bird that resembles the domestic fowl also has some notable characteristics similar to those of the turkey. It is locally called the Cocorico and is the national bird of Trinidad & Tobago.

The **Osprey** is a huge predator that almost all other birds on the island fear. The locals call it the Chicken Hawk. Whenever a domestic fowl is frantically seeking cover, there is a probability that a hovering Osprey is nearby. Other birds of the island include the Smooth-billed Ani (Jumbee Bird), the Black-faced Grass Quit, Banana Quit (page 17), Green Heron, Caribbean Martin, Bare-eyed Thrush, magnificent Frigate (scissors), and a host of other eye-catching feathered creatures.

Two species of snakes are native to Union Island: The **Tree Boa** (Corallus Grenadensis) locally called the Congo Snake, and the **Grass Snake** (Mastigodryas Bruesi), called Black snake by the locals. The colorful Congo snake is the larger of the two species and looks very much like a python. This nocturnal reptile is incredibly lazy and can be found wrapped up like the shape of a ball, sleeping on the branches of a low tree. In pursuit of its prey, this animal moves slowly but gingerly, aided by its gift of camouflage. The Congo snake grows to an average length of four feet. The Blacksnake, on the other hand, is shorter and much slenderer. Although called black, the actual color of this adult snake is dark brown, but its underside is bright white. This agile creature grows to a length of approximately 32 inches. Unlike its larger counterpart that sleeps openly on trees, the Black snake's home is mainly in the holes or burrows of large trees. Both reptiles are nonvenomous and are very timid by nature. They can be seen in the dense bushes and highlands rather than in the lower coastal region. To date, there has never been an incident of snakebite on the island. They both feed on lizards, snails, and other small vertebrates.

The opossum, called Manicou by the natives, is an animal that was hunted for its meat during the earlier years, dating back to the Amerindians. It was once considered a menace to farmers with large flocks of domestic chicken (fowl). Over the years, the lifestyle of the natives has changed so drastically that today there is seldom any chickens raised at home for meat and eggs. The hunting of this dog-like animal has long been a thing of the past. Other than humans, it has no known predators, and as a result, its population is expected to increase bountifully.

Like the armadillo, the tastiest of all wild meats, the opossum was once considered a delicacy in Union Island. But unlike this swift creature that is hunted in broad daylight, the opossum was hunted during the midnight and the early hours of the morning. The Flambeau or Massantow were the only sources of light for hunters through the entire course of this nocturnal mission.

Manicou are prevalent during the rainy season when the Manicou apple trees are laden with ripened fruits. But Manicou apples are not the only food that makes up their diet, for they would not resist the temptation to feast on the local fowl that sleep on trees during the night. This seldom happens, but whenever it does, a cornucopia of noise erupts from the rest of the birds, which are forced to leave the comfort of their resting place to the ground beneath.

Dogs have always been man's help, man's best friend, and so, these animals have been an integral part of hunting. On a good night of hunting, three young men, each with his dog, would descend on every Manicou apple tree in the vicinity. The hairy Manicou, on seeing the lights and hearing the sounds of their vicious predators, become intensely nervous and immediately seek cover in the highest branches of the trees or on the ground. Those that seek refuge on the ground are at the mercy of the carnivorous jaws that await them. A climber can also shake to the ground those that make the higher branches their sanctuary; they eventually become victims too. The almost lifeless catch is then taken into a holding bag, preferably the caucus bag. The hunters visit a few more trees, or even revisit the same tree, causing the catch to grow in number.

At the end of the hunt, the catch is taken to one of the hunters' homes, where a fire is lit, and the fur is cleanly burned off the skin. The animals are then cut open and gutted. Special parts of the animals are cut off and given to each dog for his hard work. These parts are areas of the endocrine system, such as the groin, testicles, glands, feet, and other parts that are said to stimulate the dog's aggression during hunting. The huge catch is divided equally among the hunters, who then disperse and head to their respective homes, where the bulk of meat is then cut to pieces, washed, and seasoned. One of the condiments used is local thyme, which is called Spanish Thyme or Big Thyme.

The Spanish Thyme or Big Thyme has its great medicinal value that will be explained in a later chapter. Fresh sea salt, which is harvested from a local salt pond, is also used. The abundant fresh wild meat is cooked and devoured within a few days. During those olden days, refrigerators were only a dream deferred.

The iguana is another animal that abounds in the rocky terrain of this mountainous cay. An adult iguana is much larger than the opossum, its counterpart. This reptile can be seen lurking on the brink of rocks during the early evening hours, or even on rocks overhanging the sea. In the words of Dr. Amos N. Wilson, "Power is a chameleon; it takes on the texture of its environment." These multicolored reptiles are exceptionally adaptable everywhere. Like the opossum, the meat of this reptilian wonder is also edible; everyone tends to associate its taste with that of chicken. The skin of the opossum is burnt in a light fire before it is gutted, clean and season. By tradition, the meat of this animal is seldom eaten by the natives.

Hotels, Restaurant, Bars

ANCHORAGE YACHT CLUB

Anchorage Yacht Club at the vanguard of Clifton Harbor, Union Island.

Making your way across the Caribbean blue waters of the Grenadines takes you into a whole new realm. You have arrived at The Anchorage Yacht Club on Union Island, a casual and comfortable hotel along the white beaches of the crystal clear turquoise waters of Clifton lagoon, far away from the mass tourism. The exotic romance continues with the resort's accommodation – all the rooms are waterfront, some on the first floor with a panoramic view over the marina from a spacious balcony; the rest is directly on the white sand of the beach.

If you are staying at the Anchorage Yacht Club, how convenient to come out of your room and have lunch or dinner next to the famous shark pool! The Anchorage restaurant serves pizzas, meat, lobster and delicious fresh fish. It also has a bar, free Wi-Fi and a beautiful view over the lagoon. The Anchorage Bar is a nice place to relax after a kite or surf session. Sit next to the shark pool and enjoy the view while enjoying an excellent colorful cocktail.

Union Island has a wide choice of restaurants, whether you look for a fast lunch or a romantic lobster dinner. The nightlife on Union isn't huge, but it has a special Caribbean vibe. What better way to end your day than with rum and coke or beer listening to reggae tunes and looking at the sunset...

CAPTAIN GOURMET

Run by a French couple; Captain Gourmet is the place to be every morning to enjoy the best breakfast or brunch in the Grenadines. You will find a different kind of coffees, French croissants, and baguettes, or you can also choose the amazing breakfast with eggs, bacon, tomatoes, spring rolls, etc. In the meantime, you can use the free Wi-Fi and see what's going on around the world.

BOUGAINVILLA RESTAURANT

Next to the Anchorage you will find the lovely Bougainvilla hotel, bar, and restaurant. The restaurant has a lot of choices; my personal favorite is the fresh sashimi with the secret sauce. The surroundings with the huge, beautiful aquarium and the view of the lagoon make it a romantic place to have lunch or dinner. Bougainvilla has a friendly staff and tasty drinks. You can enjoy a drink at the bar while your lunch is getting ready.

UNION ISLAND AIRPORT

During the late 1970s up until the 1980s, Union Island Airport was one of the busiest airports in the Caribbean.

Union Island Airport was constructed in the year 1974. Its construction marked the birth of the long-awaited airstrip at Point Lookout, Clifton. Mr. Andre Beaufrand, the entrepreneurial mastermind who constructed this once private airport, was of French origin. This 2,467-ft. long airbase now replaces a coral reef, a mangrove marshland, and a very tiny island known as Red Island. For centuries, Unionites have called this very tiny island (Red Island) by the name *Mancheuse Seen at* (Gettyimages.com) Boats in Harbor off Union Island Creative # 585999330. The mangrove marshland mentioned above was once the breathing ground for a wide variety of crabs. These crabs were hunted for

An aerial view of Union Island Airport. Palm Island (Prune) is seen in the distant rear.

local dishes and to a lesser extent, marketing to the island of Trinidad. Natives frequently visited the large coral reef and shallow water that spanned throughout the easterly part of Point Lookout

Beach to hunt numerous whelks, crustaceans, and delicious conch delicacies in the region.

During the late 1970s up until the 1980s, Union Island Airport was one of the busiest airports in the Caribbean. Although, at that time the airport was half its current size, it was home to numerous airplanes that landed almost every twenty minutes. Union Island, during those two decades, has experienced its most prosperous and economic years to date. Today, even though there are many touchdowns from various countries, the airport is far from what it used to be some three decades ago. In short, there has been a drastic reduction in the air traffic over the years.

Among the multiple aircraft that can be seen in this remote part of the globe are The St. Vincent & the Grenadines Airways (SVG Airways) that conduct regular daily flights between St. Vincent and the Grenadines islands –Bequia, Canouan, and Union Island. LIAT is another airline that takes passengers from Barbados to St. Vincent & the Grenadines, Trinidad, and Grenada via the regional islands.

There was once a tiny landing base that was situated on Palm Island (neighboring cay) many years before the Union Island Airport was built. This little airport was a boon to the Palm Island Resort and facilitates tourism in the region befittingly. Palm Island, which was formally called Prune, is one of the hidden treasures of the Grenadines. The Palm Island Resort, which is situated a stone throw away from the tourist-filled Clifton Harbor, Union Island, is second to none.

In 1995, almost 20 years after its construction, the Union Island airstrip was expanded approximately twice its length. The expansion was done so as to accommodate larger aircraft. The terminal was relocated, and a host of modern facilities was set in place. Then in May of 2009, a major restoration project was conducted. This process was scheduled in two phases. The first phase entailed asphalt resurfacing of the runway, taxiway, an apron (an area for almost 250, 000 sq. feet), pavement marking, and minor landscaping of the area.

In the second phase, rocks were placed towards the western end of the landing strip to increase the protection of the newly renovated infrastructure. Although the CCA Limited swiftly executed this process, the airport still had to be rendered out of commission, but only for a short period.

* **Aerial view of Union Island's Airstrip. Located at Point-look-out, Clifton.** *

Today, with the availability of several landing bases in these seemingly remote vicinities of the western world (Bequia, Canouan, Mustique and Union Island), the Grenadines islands are easily accessible to the entire globe; it requires only the simple click of a mouse.

FRIGATE ISLAND (ROCK)

"Give meh son this bake for meh please," she uttered in the dialect of that day.

Frigate Island is a tiny, uninhabited island that is situated approximately ¾ mile off the southern coast of Union Island. The name Frigate Rock will be used for the remainder of this book when referring to this little landmass; it is the only term that is used by Unionites whenever they refer to this little cay.

During the late 1750's, the Frenchman, Monsieur De L'isle, ruled this little island while his counterparts Antoine Rigaud and Jean Augier settled on Union Island. Mr. De L'isle used the shallow surrounding reefs to obtain coral, a vital commodity for the manufacture of limestone, a legacy that remained in the Grenadines until the 1970's. Although Union Island is a separate landmass from the neighboring sister, Frigate Rock, these two islands were always regarded as one. Perhaps the two cays were connected to each other centuries ago. Not too long ago, residents used to walk the shallow reef that separated Union Island from this nearby four acres' landmass. Walking was much easier during low tide than when the water level was higher. This reef was called "Grass" and was home to many crustaceans. The conch and sea urchin, both native to this reef, were hunted and eaten as delicacies. The presence of "Grass" may be a clear reminder that this presumably single landmass had been eroded centuries ago.

As Hugh Mulzac mentioned in A Star to Steer By: someone could walk out into the sea for a mile or more in water no deeper than their waist. On one particular instant, Hugh eagerly took his father's rowboat from Ashton Harbor to row his way to Frigate Rock but almost face disaster. He had witness his father's crew of fishermen hauled up a huge whale on the rock, and he wanted to see the huge creature. That evening, he got a beating of his life. Frigate Rock was a butchering site for whales caught in the region.

And so, the span of water that exists between Union Island

and Frigate Rock is exceedingly shallow and has experienced land erosion over many years. One can observe a sudden 90-degree drop from the southern part of Union Island that is closest to Frigate Rock in the vicinity of the late Meldon John's house -a former resident of Campbell Village. This area is arguably 40 feet or more above sea level and has shown evidence of water erosion in the past, and erosion is still evident today. In that area, lots of boulders can be found on the sea floor.

The Ashton Cemetery that lies along the coastline and opposite of Frigate Rock has also fallen victim to the advancing sea. This severe erosion over a prolonged period has resulted in many human bones or fossils that became visible along the shoreline as the encroaching sea dug its way into the nearby Ashton Cemetery. In the mid-1970s, a construction project was conducted at that site to prevent further erosion. The use of wire baskets filled with boulders has been laid along the shoreline. As a result, there was no evidence of further erosion.

Frigate Island from a northwesterly view. A partial view of Petit Martinique is seen at the rear.   – Photo Josiah Stewart

Frigate Rock is currently uninhabited. Approximately 30 percent of this small island is flat and is suitable for a tourist resort. For many decades, tourists have used the sheltered water of this island as a docking port for their yachts and the calm waters for skiing. Just like Fort Charlotte on the mainland of St. Vincent, Frigate Rock had been used to house the African, who were afflicted with yaws and leprosy during the late 19th century. They were separated from the rest of society but were cared for only by relatives, and were encouraged to bathe regularly in the sea. Bathing in the sea was widely encouraged because the high saline content was believed to bring salutary results to these ailments.

During those earlier years, the disease leprosy, which causes deformities of the face and extremities, was somewhat prevalent in these geographical areas but is almost nonexistent today. It is believed that this leprosy, or Hansen's disease, is spread via respiratory droplets. Studies have shown that it can be transmitted to humans via armadillos that harbor the Mycobacterium Leprae, the causative agent. The Armadillo is an animal with very sharp claws that digs for its food. It also carries a very strong armor that protects it from predators. In Trinidad and Tobago, the meat of this animal is considered the tastiest of wild meats. A few years ago, this animal was introduced to St. Vincent by way of Grenada. It is said that these animals are multiplying very rapidly in the Greggs and Richland Park areas of the mainland (St. Vincent) and are in the initial stage of becoming an agricultural menace. Nevertheless, armadillos are nowhere to be found in Union Island. Leprosy is seldom seen in the Caribbean nowadays.

Yaws, on the other hand, is a very contagious disease that affects the skin, and can penetrate the muscle all the way to the bones. This disease, which is also known as Frambesia, is of tropical origin. It was prevalent in Africa, South America, East Asia, and the Caribbean. Fortunately, this disease, which also causes deformities of the face and skin, can be easily treated with a single dose of antibiotics.

It is prudent to surmise that Dr. H. Nichols' (American doctor) presence on Union Island on Tuesday, June 11, 1891, was not by accident, but to treat those who were affected by these contagious ailments. During his visit, he was appalled by the deplorable conditions that afflicted the Africans on the plantations. He later expressed the distastefulness of his observation.

Obed, the son of Ann Edwards (Ma Dee), an old woman from Clifton Village, was afflicted with leprosy, an unforgiving disorder, and hence became a resident of Frigate Rock. There was little that Ma Dee could have done for her beloved son regarding the condition of his health. Nevertheless, she was satisfied that she had the opportunity to send food, clothes, and anything edible for him. She knew ahead of time that a fishing boat was heading in the direction of Frigate Rock the following morning. That night she prepared a roasted *coconut-bake*, and early the following morning when the boat was leaving, she handed a package containing the bake to one of the crew. *"Give meh son this bake for meh please,"* she uttered in the dialect of that day. Delighted that she was able to do something worthwhile for her son, she knew very well that he, too, would appreciate such gesture of his mother's affection.

She immediately ran off from the beach where the boat had just left for its destination, and up she went to the highland where the Catholic Church is situated (a popular landmark). There she stood as the boat made its way through the reefs and shallow areas into deeper waters. Ma Dee was alert and watchful, as the little craft got closer to Frigate Rock. Unable to contain her excitement, she began to wave at the fishermen as though they would be able to see her from such distant. Her excitement quickly turned to gloom, and finally into anger, as she watched the boat slowly sailed by the little island.

Instantly, she began to bawl loudly, expressing her hurt and dissatisfaction. In only a few minutes, her inconsolable sobbing caught the attention of the entire Clifton community –a community so small that everyone literally knew each other fairly well. By midday, everyone was quite aware of the heinous act committed - that of neglecting to deliver the mother's gifts to her son. Such a crime, of course, was not tolerated in the close-knit community, where cohesiveness was always the order of the day.

On returning from their fishing trip, these sailors did not have any reason to visit Frigate Rock, for they had already devoured the contents of the package (*coconut bake*) on their long day at sea. That afternoon, residents expressed their displeasure by physically beating members of the crew to make an example out of them, and to assuage the pain of the aggrieved mother.

The little island of Frigate Rock was also used as a lookout point for the local fishermen of Union Island. They climbed to the pinnacle of the island, where they could have a panoramic view of the fishes' movements from the deeper water to the shallow. When fish is present in the vicinity, they appear very dark in the lighter blue waters. These smaller fishes, being chased by the larger predatory fishes, swim into the shallow lagoon-like area for shelter. It was at the pinnacle of Frigate Rock that a local fisherman named David John, aka Gayman, would bellow at the top of his lungs, "Fish-oooooooh," alerting other fishermen on Union Island that there were fish to be caught. The waiting fishermen, with their seins on board, would hastily roar their roar boats to the location of the fish. Meticulously watching the movement of the fish while in a ready position, the fishermen would seize the first opportunity and cast their huge nets in hope of engulfing their prize.

If the fish were caught about a hundred yards from the shoreline, the fishermen would haul the catch ashore. Because news got around very quickly, numerous young men would rush to the site of the catch to lend a helping hand to pull the prize ashore. On completion of this process, everyone was guaranteed to leave with a small portion of the catch. This communal venture makes his evening's effort worthwhile.

Today, the young fishermen of Union Island seldom practice this fine art of fishing (sein casting). Instead, spearfishing is much more prevalent throughout the Grenadines.

In the early 1990s, the government of St. Vincent & the Grenadines made a gallant attempt to construct a 300-boat marina at Frigate Rock and Ashton Harbor. This was indeed a practical endeavor to generate income in the region and to create employment and economic stability on Union Island. While the project was in full swing, it did make vehicular transportation viable to and from the two neighboring cays. It is reputed that the French company that procured this major project went into receivership, and the project came to a crashing halt. Although this major undertaking was designed to generate a newfound income in the region, it did affect the ecology in the nearby mangrove region of Union Island quite negatively. The constructions of numerous pillars in the shallow water have prevented the free movement of water in the area. Consequently, the water of the eastern region of Ashton Harbor is somewhat stagnated and murky. Conch, lobsters, corals, and all sorts of marine lives have been destroyed. A venerated Grunt-fishing ground was utterly destroyed during the construction of this major marine project. This fishing ground was located midway to Frigate Rock from the northern side of Ashton harbor, lining up with Sail Rock at its easterly lower point; only the seasoned fisherman of today will remember profoundly the site where these Grunts were once fished.

The seawater at the most easterly end of Aston Harbor and Top Yonder Bay has become stagnated since the project began," said one resident. "The saline content at that area has been severely compromised," he added. The narrow water passageway between Union Island and Frigate Rock is no more in existence. Small crafts can no longer use this shortcut in and out of Ashton harbor; instead, they have to circumnavigate the entire cay of Frigate Rock to and from their requisite destinations. The shoreline at the Ashton Cemetery shows no further threat of erosion; rather, it has a renewed beach from the copious deposits of sand. The downside of this is that the influx of sand in that region has smothered and destroyed the coral reef and sea grass, resulting in further ecological damage to the fish, lobsters, and conch population.

At the turn of the 20th century, Frigate Rock and the famed Toy Yonder Bay were shipbuilding sites for the respected Mulzac and Mulrain families. They were adept at this craft, and it is out of this legacy that Union Island produced some of the best shipwrights in the region. Vibrant young men such as Eastman Stewart, Gurry Stewart, Solomon Stewart, Incoman Stewart, Paul Wilson Percival Thomas (Brother Tom), Sonny Wilson, and Tanil Sandy were proud products of the Mulzac's shipwright of Union Island. A young Hugh Mulzac, still in his teens, before he ventured out at sea in 1907, had learned the art of shipbuilding also. Even the deceased Centenarian, August King Mitchell, did his share of shipbuilding during his formative years. These men built and launched their boats at Top Yonder Bay.

Frigate Rock was also a huge getaway site on most weekends and the home of some huge whelks too. Residents frequented the sandy coastal lowlands of this little cay to have their regular picnics. Elaborate cooking for those local events was done at home ahead of time. Pelau was often the dish of choice on these occasions. Pelau is a very delicious dish made primarily on weekends and especially when family and friends get together on special occasions –to "lime," as is said in local parlances of the Caribbean. The main components of this dish are rice, green pigeon peas, and chicken/beef or any meat of choice. Sadly, much of these communal activities have declined over the years. Frigate Rock's receptive arms remain just a few minutes away from the Ashton Harbor –an area that was once called Frigate because of its proximity to Frigate Rock. To visit this beautiful Isle, a rowboat might be the ideal, or the vehicle of choice to gain access.

WATER CONSERVATION & USAGE

Lincoln Pond (Lenkin) was by far the best and most preferred pond on Union Island even into the mid 20th century.

Semiarid, with a very low rainfall of 40.25 inches per annum, the absence of rivers, coupled with the November to April dry season has caused the natives of Union Island to use water very sparingly. More than 2-½ centuries ago, numerous seasonal ponds and wells were dug to conserve large quantities of water. These wells, sometimes called waterholes, were located at the following locations: (a) at the Anglican Church, (b) next to Gospel Hall Church (c) at the sand hole next to the United Friendly Society, (d) Chatham Well, at Chatham Bay, and (e) Campbell well, at Bottom Campbell. The latter is less than eighty years old. Two major ponds were dug during the late 1750s for the purpose of watering the slaves and animals during that time. Unfortunately, there have never been wells at Clifton, even until recently. During the early to the middle part of the 20th century, many residents at Clifton had their private ponds that they also referred to as waterholes. Most of these ponds were located at their homes. The owners of some of these ponds were *Isabella Roache*, Ms. Victoria Hypolite, May-May Hutchinson, John Snagg, and Ce Mammy; others had ponds located at Belmont and one at Top Hill, Clifton.

Some of the more significant ponds of Union Island were Pappy-Son waterhole (situated at Colon Campbell), John Stewart (Papa) waterhole, Downson Pond, Rapid (Rapeet) Pond, Mulrain waterhole, and the two huge ponds were Lincoln and Basin (Basket) Ponds; they are located at Richmond and Ms. Irene, Ashton respectively.

The sites of the water wells and ponds were the locations where clothes were laundered. Natives took their huge bundles of laundry, along with wooden tubs, washboards (jerking boards), blue soap, and corncobs, to do extensive washing by hand. Washing by hand was the only means whereby the natives could have gotten their clothes clean. The cob of the corn was locally called "corn stick," and it was used widely as a scrubbing brush. In this case, the cob was utilized for scrubbing clothes, especially jeans—or dungarees as they were called then. Most people preferred to use the ponds and wells on Thursdays and Fridays for this purpose. On-site, their clothes were washed and sometimes partially dried to reduce the weight before they took them home. At the homes, the clothes were hung on lines with wooden clothespins, where they would thoroughly dry later. Lincoln Pond was by far the best and most preferred pond on Union Island, even though Basket Pond (Basin) may have been the largest. Lincoln Pond had a spring, and hence, when most ponds were dried up during the severe dry seasons, water was still available at Lincoln Pond. For that reason, most washers could be found there on both days of the week. The water there was very clean and drinkable; it did not have a taint of saline content.

(Above): A 19th-century picture of a typical water well of Union Island. This well was dug during the mid 18th century to supply the slaves at (Frigate) Ashton Village. It is located in the same vicinity of the Anglican Church, which was built a century later. This well is still used today for washing clothes and feeding livestock.

It is well over seventy years since proper water reservoirs were built in Union Island. The challenge of water shortage had to be addressed, and the reservoirs immediately aided the residents, who had to contend with the dearth of supply they experienced annually. There are two of these facilities. The larger is situated in Ashton Village, a few hundred meters above the Adventist Church. This reservoir provides water for the nearby Ashton community.

The chief recipients are those without huge concrete cisterns to conserve their catches of water during the evanescent rainy season. The other is located in the east of the island. This Clifton reservoir obviously is not as big as the aforementioned Ashton repository, but it serves the Clifton residents. Some dry seasons can be severe. The scarcity of wells, coupled with the abandonment and extinction of water holes, has given Clifton residents no alternative but to depend on transported water from St. Vincent. This water is then taken by trucks and sold to residents who made requests. In the eastern end of Clifton Harbor, a desalination plant is situated. This plant provides an adequate and efficient amount of water for those commercial enterprises, hotels, and guesthouses that are tethered to the beaches. This makes the water shortage a non-issue to tourists and visitors, even in the heart of the dry season.

This is a 2001 photo of the same water well that is seen above. With over 250 years of service to the residence of Ashton village (Frigate), this refurbished well takes on a completely different appearance.

The water situation is still a major challenge to residents, but is not exclusive to Union Island, for the rest of the Grenadine Islands encounter the same plight of water shortage annually. They had hope that the governmental authorities in St. Vincent would have addressed this condition a long time ago.

In the eyes of many residents, Union Island has never been treated fairly by the state of St. Vincent. As a result, Unionites openly expressed their desire to be governed by the neighboring island of Grenada at the turn of the 20th century. Unfortunately, Grenada declined such a responsibility base on the financial burden that accompanies this task. Moreover, it is interesting to note that such level of neglect by the state of St. Vincent is not recent, but one that dates back to the advent of the British in 1763.

Samuel V. Morse, a commanding engineer who visited Union Island on July 22, 1778, found the lack of water rather daunting. Appalled by the scarcity of water on the land to supply both livestock and the slaves. Samuel Morse also observed the deplorable health condition of the slaves and the squalor that they endured daily. The Europeans, on the other hand, used rainwater, which they conserved in earthen jars and well-built cisterns.

Don Carlos Verbeke, a Benedictine priest, was also appalled by the condition that he observed in 1928. He described the grave shortage of water on these islands by indicating that there was scarcely anything to drink. He went on to say that the people had to scoop water from mud-filled ponds and that the island was devoid of grass to feed livestock. Nevertheless, he was overwhelmed by the people's desire and will to overcome such impoverished state. The ponds that Verbeke was referring to were Lincoln (Lenkin) Pond of Richmond in the North, and Basin (Basket) pond which is situated at Miss Irene Pasture in the South of the island.

But it was 38 years prior to Don Carlos Verbeke's presence on the island, i.e., on Tuesday, June 11th, 1891; an American doctor by the name of H. N. Nichols visited the island. He was a specialist in Yaws, (a highly infectious disease that affects the skin and bones but is extremely easy to treat). This disease is similar to aforementioned leprosy (Hansen disease) written earlier about some ailing residents that were placed at Frigate Island. On arrival, Dr. Nichols was astounded and felt compassion for the people whom he observed were very poor and totally neglected by the Government of St. Vincent, who only adds to their woes. He said that these residents were not benefiting from the state in any way, shape or form because they were not given anything. Not even the roads were upkeep; hence he was astounded that these good people did not drive them off on their arrival. He also learned that there were no concerns by the state for the wellbeing of the people who died indiscriminately when ill. This is primarily because doctors were not available to address their needs and concerns. He further indicated that when the tax collector comes around, many residents took to sea with their little crafts to escape that burden. Those that could not leave the confines of this improvised rock had to pay by the skin of their teeth. They paid from the money they barely earned through inter-island trade to Barbados and Carriacou.

In a recent research from the Encyclopedia of Caribbean Religions UNIVERSITY OF ILLINOIS PRESS *Urbana, Chicago, and Springfield,* this is what was extracted from an article that was written during the 1970s: *"Thus in the Grenadines, tiny Union Island, with only one school, a paucity of medical and sanitation facilities, and no systematic water supply or electricity, yet, can boast of having an airstrip, built by the Vincentian Government to transport tourist...."*

This form of disenfranchisement and neglect of basic needs, necessities, and services had been perpetuated on the people of Union Island for several decades. So, on the brink of rebellion on Thursday, September 30th, 1909, Union Island observed a change for the first time. As a result, the island was subdivided a year later, and the Africans ostensibly became landowners. But marginalization and neglect from the government returned for several decades, even unto the 1970's. What made matters worse was that the population of Union during such time was not in support of the incumbent Labor Party. And Union Island not being a constituent of this political party added only fuel to an already escalating flame; as a result, the wrath of the Cato Administration was upon them. With a striving tourist industry, Union Island could have single-handedly shouldered all of its financial responsibilities and more, yet the island was still immersed in poverty. It was the expectation of the residents that a fraction of the island's income would be spent on the development of its infrastructure. Unfortunately, that was not on the current agenda of the iniquitous government. In fact, it had never been.

The people of Union Island was now discontented and resentful by being marginalized, used terms such as *The Weather Green* and *Time hard like Guava Crop; these phrases they used* to describe their woeful economic hardship or that day. Their frustration grew to an alarming height until one Friday morning, December 7th, 1979 a contingent of young men that called themselves Union Island Freedom Fighters (UIFF) under the leadership of Lenox Bomba Charles (page 256) staged a rebellion against the iniquitous state. They used paint to stencil the streets of Ashton with captions that read: UIFF, *Free Union Island, and Union Island is for Unionites.* These messages, which expressed the strong sentimental disgust among the people, remained on the streets for several years later.

The quest of Lenox and the prevailing sentiments of the islanders were for Union Island to be entirely separated from the tentacles of the St. Vincent's autocracy, and instantly usher in a new government by the people of Union Island. But the rebellion that had been envisioned to engender a favorable outcome was short-lived. The Royal Police Force of St. Vincent & the Grenadines was quickly deployed to the shores of Union Island.

The revolt that started early that morning with the sound of dynamites and gunshots at a pivotal location came to a screeching halt later that day. There was but one casualty unrelated. A curfew was immediately imposed on the entire state to restore *So-called law and order* on Union Island. Understandably, the prime minister of that day, (Sir Milton Cato) still frightened by the existing hostile atmosphere on the neighboring island of Grenada (Grenadian Revolution) immediately invited the help of the Barbadian troops from the Tom Adams' administration out of Barbados. Approximately seven days later, they were on the soil of Union Island. Being presented with a vacation-like atmosphere and nothing to do in the way of restoring harmony on an already peaceful island, the trigger-happy armed force became restive. They remained on Union Island for approximately one month before returning to Barbados. Fortunately, there were no additional casualties.

EDUCATION AND HOMES

One of the first board houses built in Union Island was at Ashton; the owner was the late Mrs. Courtney Wilson, a native of Barbados.

Union Island does possess some of the most beautiful homes throughout St. Vincent and the Grenadines. Yes, indeed! And this is not by accident, for the people of Union Island love beautiful homes and will go an extra mile to make this possible. If you are on Union Island right now as you turn the pages of this book, chances are, you may have already acknowledged this. Still, take a few minutes to look around just one more time, but now, use all your keen senses as you view some of those beautiful new homes. Now, you too have arrived at a mutual conclusion.

Yet, some older folks cannot forget the wattle & daub or thatch houses that they once lived in during the early 20th centuries (page 42 & 43). "During those olden days, those small houses were very beautiful and well kept. "Even though they were small, the older folks took great pride in up-keeping them," said the late Ethneil Mitchell. "And they were painted white every year, with limestone at Christmas time." She added in excitement.

During the mid 18th century up until 1940-50, the village of Frigate and Calsay were rife with hundreds of thatch houses. But a construction revolution began soon after 1931 when many residents were able to pay off the lingering land amortization that had plagued them for well over 20 years. They, in turn, were privileged to build better homes outside of the vicinity of Mt. Parnassus and Clifton Hill (townships). Board houses were built almost everywhere, as thatch house became sparse and later nonexistent. Then in the 1960's onward, marked the end of the construction of wooden houses, as brick homes became vogue on the island.

One of the first wooden houses that were built in Union Island was at Ashton Village (Frigate); the owner of this Bungalow was the late Mrs. Courtney Wilson of Barbados, West Indies. Built during the first quarter of the 20th century at the foot of Mt. Parnassus, this house was located at the corner of the famed Crossroad (Green Corner). Everyone amicably called Mrs. Courtney *"Ce Courtney,"* a form of respect that was bestowed on folks during their senior years. This structurally intact board house braved all the hurricanes of her time. Even the noted Hurricane Janet of 1955, did inflict any physical harm to her. This beautiful landmark was later razed during the turn of the 21st century. The second board house was also built at the foot of Mt. Parnassus in Ashton Village, opposite the first government primary School (Small School). Mr. John Louis Archer, a noted schoolteacher of the Anglican Church School, was the owner of this beautiful structure. Every senior citizen above the age of ninety speaks well of Mr. Archer's excellent teaching capabilities and acumen during his stint in Union Island. Mr. Archer too was of Barbadian descent.

A 2010 photo of the refurbished St. Matthias Anglican Church. Erected in the year 1875.

The government's wall house of Clifton, (page 109) was the first concrete house built on Union Island. Immediately following that was the first concrete house of Ashton that was constructed in 1922. This house too was built at the foot of Mr. Parnassus. The owners were the late Mr. Allan and Ce Alice Scrubb of Cross-Road. Ba Allan, as he was called, was a much-respected gentleman in the community and had a shop that was located at Crossroad. He was the grandfather of Mr. Cecil Scrubb, who now resides in America, and Mrs. Icena Wilson, an octogenarian who is currently living at that residence.

It should be noted, that only a handful of residents were able to construct wooden and concrete homes before the year 1931. These residents were the likes of Louis Archer, Allan Scrubb, Joseph Alves, and of course, the Mulzacs. They, however, were members of the upper echelon of society in Union Island. Their homes were built in the vicinity of the Anglican Church and other locations, east of Frigate or pauper land, but close to the main road. It meant status to anyone who could have built a home in that vicinity, whether they held ownership of the land or not.

It is intriguing now to take a few backward steps to glimpse what is now referred to as history. The shortage or lack of many facilities on Union Island during her earlier years did not appear to be a significant impediment to the ancestors who had not known any better. Airports, electricity, telephones, vehicular transportation and a host of other integral necessities were nonexistent, as were a proper health-care center, pipe-borne water, and adequate roads. One can only imagine what those ancestors may have undergone in severe instances, particularly health-wise. But by and large, they survived with what they had during that time. Post-slavery, the demand for education had been a sore evil, for want of a better word. This condition was not circumscribed only to the residents of Union Island, but also in all of the colonies that were subjected to slavery. This institution had successfully done its job, and it was time for recovery. Improvement, however, was on the way, but painfully slow.

The first real institution of transformation on Union Island was the Anglican Church School, which was built during the same time as the Anglican Church. This school was situated on the same plot of land where the current Rectory is now located. It was a pay-school, and only the folks who were monetarily efficient were able to send their children to that institution. The Anglican Church, which was erected in 1875, stands approximately one hundred yards opposite that site.

At the Anglican Church School, the first teacher was Mr. James Donowa, the father of Ada (Hugh's mother). Mr. Donowa was a highly respectable man who came with his family from the island of Antigua. He taught the Mulzac children and other children of white parentage, for they were the only ones who could have paid for the cost of everyday schooling. On most Sundays, Mr. Donowa conducted a primary educational class for the children of each African church member. Although the primary goal of this endeavor was to teach the black children basic reading and Arithmetic skills, it did encourage other black parents to join the church. By joining the sole church on the island, their children too were able to reap the benefit of learning to read and write. Reading and writing were remotely taught to the natives. Sometimes, a class may be conducted under a tree, notably, the huge Hog Plum tree at Frigate. Unfortunately, the basic skills of reading, writing, addition, and subtraction became the acme of the African's educational development in Union Island. Tastelessly, this modest level of education that the Africans had aspired to, remained for several decades later.

Many years later, during 1911, the British Government in conjunction with Barbados, her colony, sent a young teacher from Barbados to Union Island; his name was John Louis Archer. Archer's responsibility in this virgin territory was to teach the progeny of the hundreds of Africans who had never attended school before. These Africans, long after the abolition of slavery, had been free for the first time. They were now aspiring landowners and were not the chattel of any Massas, overseers or landlords whom they had been subjugated to since their existence on Union Island. But the reality is, they were still living a life of servitude, yet, a false sense of independence. They were fastened to their former landlords -it was the only way of life that they had known. They could not instantly break loose from the imaginary umbilical cord from which they were attached. Also, the system in Union Island was such that, the Africans had to rely on these former landlords for survival.

As aspiring landowners, these Africans did acquire a subtle sense of identity and self-worth. Their children, on the other hand, who were no longer the property of the slave masters or landlords were no longer ushered onto the plantations at extremely young ages. Instead, they were a part of a family structure, but their sole obligations to their parent's land and menial work remained their responsibilities. These Africans had never seen the doorsteps of any school or educational institution; hence, they did not know the importance of reading & writing, attending school nor acquiring an education. It surely was a legacy of deliberate academic disenfranchisement that they had undergone since they arrived during the late 1750's. The Africans knew full well that the Anglican

Church school was designed *only* for the well to do. Hence, the legacy of marginalization, which they had endured over 1½ centuries, was enough to dissuade them from sending their children to such an institution.

At the arrival of Mr. John Louis Archer, the Anglican Church School was now a governmental institution that was free of charge to all comers. From the inception of his tenure, there were very poor student attendances; yet, most of the students who attended the school came from of Ashton Village (Frigate), which was in the proximity of the school.

* The home of the late Barbadian-born teacher, John Louis Archer. *

For several years, most parents at Clifton seldom send their children to this distant school. Instead, they find other menial chores for them at home and on the plantations.

Mr. Archer, the young teacher, on witnessing this low student turnout at the school, took up the responsibility to persuade and cajole the African parents to send their youngsters to the lone school at Ashton. Regrettably, his effort, for the most part, was futile, for the children of Clifton were still not attending school regularly. Mr. Thomas Ambrose (Brother Can), a descendant of Admiral Samuel Spann, made a request to the Government of St. Vincent. He advised that the upper floor of the Cotton House at Clifton should be utilized to conduct the school. "This should encourage better attendance," he said. The Government accepted the recommendation and immediately followed through by having a school in that district. Several months later, the Cotton House was utilized and became the first school at Clifton. This school was conducted for several years under the watchful eyes of Mr. Barlor and Mr. Keen, two newly assigned teachers from St. Vincent. Although the new school was advantageous to many Clifton residents, the attendance rate was incomparable to that of the Ashton school. The reason was, the population of Clifton (Calsay) was four times smaller than that of Ashton (Frigate) coupled with the reluctance of the parents to send their children to school.

Advised by a renowned Catholic priest of Carriacou, the neighboring island, the lone Catholic Church of Clifton was built of wood in 1919. Apart from the regular worships that were held on Sundays, this wooden church was significantly used on weekends as an educational institution to reduce the high level of illiteracy on the island.

At Ashton, the Anglican Church school remained under the sole stewardship of Mr. Archer. Mr. Archer found the task of teaching several classes were challenging, but he was bent on making his job manageable. He groomed five of his best students to take care of each class while he was teaching one himself. These students became an integral part of the school and were able to conduct classes under his watchful eye. Among his helpers was an exceptional student who had a natural love for mathematics and a desire to lead. Little did he know that this student-helper would later become the most astute entrepreneur the island had ever known? That student was none other than the late Mr. Augustus King Mitchell. Amazingly, he engaged in entrepreneurial service of the people in Union Island—a responsibility that he has held for well over seventy years without reaching the acme of his significantly illustrious career.

During those early years, under Mr. Archers Stewardship, though the slate was initially used for writing, students were also taught penmanship, and with penmanship under the British system, students developed the proper methods of writing. It is no surprise then, that the older folks, even with their educational limitations had excellent handwriting. Take a minute to observe an older folk forming an "S." It is intriguing to observe the pen in motion. Mr. Archer, who was also in charge of the Anglican Church, later attained the professional help of two male teachers, namely Mr. Williams and Mr. Glasgow. After many years of service as a pedagogue to the youngsters of Union Island, Mr. Archers lost his ailing wife, Roslyn. It is reputed that she had been sick with tuberculosis for quite some time. Her sister, who was part of the same household, also died as a result of the same ailment. Mr. Archer later married a young Christian girl of the same denomination by the name of Patience (Lena). Decades later, in 1931, a well-deserved school was built to replace the deteriorating Anglican Church School. It was erected opposite of the Archer's residence at Ashton and was the first government primary school on the island. It was nicknamed "Small School" then, a name that continues even to this day.

This noteworthy Small School has left an indelible mark on the hearts and minds of every Unionite, who has sat on those long wooden benches. Those long wooden benches were once a part of the school's furniture. Older folks can still remember some of their teachers, who were the first to provide service to the school. Mr. Williams, Mr. Barlor, Mr. Keen, Mr. Charles, and of course, Mr. Archer were some of the teachers who molded and fashioned many young callow minds.

Meanwhile, at Clifton, student's attendance at the famed Cotton house had increased, but not significantly, for many parents still had not sent their young ones to school. The upper floor of this building housed only a few classrooms. In less than ten years as an educational institution, the doors of this school were closed to the service of the Clifton students. As a result, the students at Clifton once again, with no alternative, had to journey to Small School, the lone government primary school at Ashton. The Cotton House was immediately utilized as the island's revenue office, courtroom, and post office.

On a Wednesday night, December 13th, 1995, the landmark Cotton House that served as a repository for the harvested cotton, an institution of learning, a courthouse, Revenue Office, and the sole post office that handled all governmental affairs for the life of Union Island, was destroyed by arson. The tragic burning of this building rendered the island devoid of its already sparse database and a vital historical landmark.

The education system that was adopted from England had a stranglehold on all of the British Caribbean islands. In the early twentieth century, the school structure of Union Island under the watchful eyes of Mr. Archer was just about to scratch the surface.

Completing one's schooling in Union Island marked the end of his/her education lifespan unless he/she leaves the island to further his/her education. But the level of education was so deplorable, that the state of being able to read and write was considered a mammoth achievement, or a great acmatic feat.

Aware of the limitation of education on Union Island, Richard Mulzac, the astute father of Hugh Mulzac, knew it was important for his son (Hugh) to get an education outside of the island. So, at the turn of the 20th century, Hugh Mulzac became the first black student to leave Union Island to enhance his schooling at the St. Vincent Grammar School.

A 2009 Picture of *Gov't House*, Clifton Hill, Union Island –the oldest structure on the island. During the 18th, 19th, and early 20th Centuries, the incline of this hill was rife with thatch houses that were referred to as Nigga Houses. (See page 42)

Twenty-six years later, in 1957, the Ashton Government Primary School at Clifton Road was built. This larger school was to accommodate a greater volume of students and provide higher-grades. It served both communities for numerous years. Several years later, the Clifton Government Primary School of Clifton was also constructed. It enabled students from the district of Clifton to attend a learning institution that was actually in their community.

Then in early 1971, the construction of the Union Island Junior Secondary School was completed. Its doors were opened to the first batch of excited students in September of that year. One year later (i.e., September 1972), another two classes entered; they were Forms 1A & B. A month later, on October 24, the ribbon was cut by the late Princess Margaret to officially open that school. She was the younger sister of Queen Elizabeth II of England. Like Tommy Hilfiger and Mick Jagger, she owned property on the neighboring cay of Mustique Island.

Before the turn of the 21st century, two new schools came into being at Union Island. They are the Stephanie Brown Primary, and the Mary Hutchinson Primary Schools of Clifton and Ashton, respectively. These two schools bear the names of two female political representatives of the Government of St. Vincent & the Grenadines. In the year 2010, another secondary school was constructed at Campbell Village, Ashton. This new school supplants the first secondary school that was built in the year 1971.

But amid all the refinements that now contribute to the educational transformation in Union Island, the schools of long ago had their flaws. Today, a young female student can be an expectant mother and remain comfortable in the classroom with her classmates. In the past, that would have been considered an egregious crime. If a teenage woman were to be found in such situation, she will have to kiss her school days' goodbye, even if she exhibited the wherewithal necessary for a productive academic future, she would have still been expelled nonetheless.

This action had put an end to many young careers in a system void of alternatives. Because of the indignity that was attached to this seemingly indecent act, any young woman who realized that she was pregnant will wittingly abandon the classrooms rather than facing the embarrassment of expulsion.

Earlier, in STIMULUS, mention was made of teachers that taught at Small School during the first quarter of the 20th century. The educational system during such time was bad. A travesty, to be frank! Any students who attended the school and never made an effort to further their education were sure to encounter numerous academic challenges —challenges that will inevitably impact them throughout their entire lives.

For the author, he had devoted most of his adult life to catch up on education. This is because of his early childhood years at Small School were weak; yet, he was considered to be an "A" student. Imagine? His teachers were only 15 years old. They were just out of 6th Grade and attained what was called a *School Leaving Certificate.* That diploma enabled them to teach the students in lower grades. After several years of teaching, they will eventually graduate to teach the students in higher grades.

Because of this early childhood deficit, many things that he (the author) had learned, he later discovered were misleading. Living in America and assimilating to the language, culture, and lifestyle was extremely difficult. For someone to excel and widen his/her scope abroad he/she must devote himself/herself to some form of vigorous learning –and that may entail learning the English language all over again.

This again, is not exclusive to Union Island, for many Caribbean folks themselves cannot effectively assimilate into the American or Canadian way of life because of their many deficits as well. It can be extremely embarrassing, for it engenders many constraints in their social lives. Their regular itinerary of such victims commences at home where they leave early each morning to their place of employment. Then from their jobs, they travel back to their homes at the end of the day. Now, they may attend local functions, churches, and funerals, etc., but infrequently; in reality, they are literally confined to a boxed-life in North America Nevertheless. This is another subject that we will dispense with for the time being, for it might be more fitting for another time. Now, back to the Schools of Union Island.

During the olden days, no one wanted his or her children to take the wrong path in life, so they did not spare the rod (applicable corporal punishment). Not only the parents of that child but also by any parent in that community that practiced this method of discipline. This form of discipline was further extended to every teacher of that day, and the leather belt was often the authority of choice. The male student was much more likely to feel the belt on his behind, or the palm of his hand as opposed to females, who were viewed as delicate and undeserving of this kind of chastisement. However, a few could not escape, especially if they exhibited any masculine characteristics. A student's shirt out of his/her pants, tardiness, cutting school (playing hooky), and insubordination were issues that warranted the use of the strap.

Again, those were the days of yesterday; today, the customs are quite different, fortunately. I meant, unfortunately.

Union Island Junior Secondary School came into being in 1972 and was a timely venture that has since given rise to a much higher level of learning. It also provided employment for the yearly-graduating students who were fresh out of the schools from St. Vincent and needed some form of employment. Returning students from St. Vincent, such as Audlyn, Christine, Dillon, Umlyn, Renrick, Edison, Nadine, and the late Denzil Stewart were able to attain employment as first- time teachers. Mickey Hutchinson, who completed his studies in Trinidad & Tobago, was another vibrant young teacher. They all did an exemplary job in rendering their services to the little island. But then came the inevitable, like a pull of gravity and unfortunately, they, like many others, have succumbed to the forceful enticement of The Exodus Factor. Thus, the United States of America, Canada, and elsewhere has since become their respective homes.

Below is the concise biography of one of Union Island's first fatality of the redoubtable Exodus Factor -a man whose life was compounded with multiple challenges, and agony. This man is the honorable Captain Hugh Nathaniel Mulzac.

◆◆◆☐*Chapter Three*

CAPTAIN HUGH NATHANIEL MULZAC

"No matter how well one prepares oneself for life, the future is always in others hands! There is no frustration greater than that of being completely powerless in the face of injustice."

Captain Hugh Nathaniel Mulzac   *Hugh in his latter years*

℞he Honorable Captain Hugh Nathaniel Mulzac was born on March 26th, 1886, at Ashton Village, Union Island. Like his father and two older brothers (John and Edward), young Hugh had a natural disposition for sea life. As a boy on Union Island, during his first time out alone in a rowboat, he lost control during a heavy current and had to be rescued by his father's friends. Hugh indicated in his autobiography, (*A Star to Steer By*) that he got the beating of a lifetime from his father. On that afternoon, the young man had seen from a distance that his father's company had hauled up a whale on Frigate Rock. He was eager to visit the site to get a close look at the massive marine mammal. Unfortunately, a strong current between the two islands was too much for the Hugh to overcome. He yelled for help as his small craft was drifting quickly into deeper waters; he was later rescued by another boat.

On Tuesday, March 12th, 1907, Hugh left the shores of Union Island to improve his fortune, then to return to Union Island to marry Edith, his girlfriend. In 1910, his journey home was tragically derailed; he lost all of his savings, an engagement ring for Edith, and other valuables at a hotel in Kingstown, Jamaica when an intruder ransacked his room. Tuesday, March 12th, 1907, was the last time that he had seen his father, many close members of his family, and his childhood friends. In 1921, his older brother John was lost at sea. On February 14, 1930, his father Richard P. Mulzac (Dad Sonny) died and was buried at the Ashton Cemetery by Hugh's younger brother Irvin Mulzac. Richard was 79 years old.

Hugh's remarkable marine life of courage and fortitude began immediately after his tenure at a high school in St. Vincent; he was still a teenager. After a brief sailing experience on the Sunbeam, a 90-ton schooner that was owned by his father, Hugh bid the region farewell. The Sunbeam, which was manned by Hugh's older brother John, was engaged in inter-island trade. On Monday, March 18th, 1907, he left the harbor of Bridgetown, Barbados, on a ship named the Aeolus (A Star to Steer by). A tall blonde Norwegian named Leif Granderson was the captain. They sailed first to North Carolina, America, then to Europe. After several voyages with the Aeolus, he bid Captain Granderson farewell to pursue better marine opportunities. He served on several British schooners as an efficient seaman, but later returned to America, a land of many prospects.

Hugh became a resident of America and resided in the state of Maryland. In 1916, he married a pretty woman by the name of Sadie Harris. On February 18th, of that same year, Sadie gave birth to a beautiful little girl; they named her Elaine. Regrettably, his marriage ended in a divorce a few years later because Sadie was much more attached to her girlfriend than to him. Huge nevertheless, was undeterred by such occurrence. Determined to make life better in the United States of America, the young man set out on an educational journey at Swansea Nautical College in the UK. He thought if he obtained a shipmaster's license it would be a mean for upward mobility, a condition for employment, a route to higher pay and a source of recognition. He was right! In

1918, two important things happened in Hugh's renewed life. On December 9th, 1918, he became a US citizen, and then two weeks later the enthusiastic youngster sat for his shipmaster's license and passed it with flying colors. This license qualified him to command a ship, but he was never given the opportunity to do so because racism was still the order of the day. Two years later, on Monday, September 30th, 1920, Hugh married Miriam (Marie) Avis, a native of Linstead, Jamaica. This girl was 18 years his junior; they would have four children, namely: Joyce, Una, Claire and Hugh Jr.

That same year, (1920) Hugh met the vibrant Marcus Mosiah Garvey, president general of the Universal Negro Improvement Association, and also president of the Black Star Line. Overwhelmed by the desire of race pride and the opportunity to sail again as an officer of the Black Star Line, Hugh immediately joined the Universal Negro Improvement Association and purchased five shares of stock. With Hugh's experience at sea, and having a shipmaster's license, Marcus Garvey immediately awarded Hugh the position of Chief Officer of the Yarmouth. The Yarmouth was a fine vessel that was built in Scotland in the year, 1885. But at the time it was purchased for a hefty $165.000, it had long lived out its better days, and was not worth a penny over $25.000 (A Star to Steer By). "To add insult to injury, Hugh lamented, though she was always referred to as the S.S. Frederick Douglas in Black Star publicity, the Yarmouth she was and the Yarmouth she was to remain till the day she was sold for scrap." Because of multiple disagreements with Marcus Garvey's administration, Hugh resigned his position in 1921. Alas, the Universal Negro Improvement Association and the Black Star Line, without adequate administrative and business acumen, collapsed soon thereafter.

In late 1921, a highly motivated Hugh Mulzac founded the Mulzac's Nautical Academy at 442 St. Nicholas Avenue, New York. This school was designed to teach navigation, engineering, and wireless to young aspirants. In only a few weeks, the school amassed a multiplicity of black students from all walks of life. These ambitious students were aflame with the spirit of the Marcus Garvey movement and were making noticeable progress. After the fifth month of promise, a dark cloud fell over the entire project; the Black Star Line, headed by the Marcus Garvey Movement was declared bankrupt. Consequently, the Academy doors were closed for lack of business. In the hope of keeping the school alive, Hugh Mulzac reached out to every student of the academy and insisted upon his attendance at a special meeting. Despondently, the students turned up at the meeting. This is what one student had to say on behalf of the entire class: "Captain Mulzac," he said, "we can't afford to waste time learning to be officers when there's no future in it for us. The *Black Star Line* has failed. Even if we get our third mate's tickets, where will we get jobs? No white company will hire us. We think it's better to learn something we can make a living at after we graduate."

In December of 1941, when America entered World War II, it was a good reason for Germany to station many of its submarines off the East Coast of the United States. With the subs located at such strategic points, they disproportionately sunk numerous American supply ships that were heading for Europe. In 1942, an average of 33 allied ships was sunk per week, and the death toll was ascending steadily. America had no place to turn. She was in dire need of seamen, and undesirable that included the disenfranchised black man that made up the population of the United States of America. The black man can now be used conveniently, she thought, and she did just that.

And so, it was not because of his qualification why he attained such position, for obviously, it is more to it than meets the eyes. The principal reason nevertheless, is because of the heavy losses of both ships and men why Hugh Mulzac, a Unionite, had been considered to captain a ship in the U.S. Merchant Marine. Yet, the U.S. Maritime Commission wanted him to captain a vessel with a segregated, all-black crew because he was a black man. The unwavering black Unionite from the village of Ashton Union Island blatantly refused the offer. This is the content of his verbal retort: "Under no circumstances will I command a Jim Crow vessel," he told the Maritime Commission. Caught without an alternative, the commission eventually acquiesced to his retort and demands. Subsequently, he was given a ship to captain with 18 different nationalities. In his autobiography two decades later, (A Star to Steer By) this is what the captain had to say: "If there was ever a moment when the real meaning of democracy could and had to be demonstrated to the peoples of the world, the moment was now! And what was America's answer in this hour of need? A Jim Crow ship! Named for a Negro, christened by a Negro, captained by a Negro, and no doubt, manned by Negroes!"

On Friday, October 23rd, 1942, during World War II, Hugh Nathaniel Mulzac became the first black naval officer to command a ship in the United States Merchant Marine. The name of the ship was the SS Booker T. Washington. This proposed assignment was met with great disapproval by the white establishment; this manner of discontentment continued throughout Hugh's tenure as a captain in the United States Merchant Marine (Picture and caption on Page 118 & 124). Also on page 119 is a letter to Pete Jarman, a member of the U.S House of Representatives from Alabama's 6th district; this letter which was drafted in 1940, depicts the racially hostile atmosphere that existed in America –the land of the so-called free. Moreover, such activities were just a smidgeon of the turbulent years that Hugh Nathaniel Mulzac had faced throughout his years in America. Although he had been a qualified officer for some twenty-four years earlier, yet he was diabolically denied such an opportunity. Fortunately, his perseverance and propensity for such an enormous task had never waned. At a pivotal point in his challenging life, he indicated that thirty-five years of rebuffs had undoubtedly prepared him for multitudes of disappointments.

The SS Booker T Washington in 1942 – A Liberty Ship, which was manned by the late **Captain Hugh Nathaniel Mulzac** (A Unionite) during World War II.

With a crew of eighteen nationalities under his captaincy, Hugh manned the SS Booker T. Washington through the seas of Europe and the Pacific. There he made twenty-two round-trips over a period of five years and had a troop of approximately 18,000. In his book, *A Star to Steer By*, he deemed it as one of the happiest days of his life when he walked on the Booker T. Washington's bridge. He stated, "There really are no words to express how I felt that evening when the final 'I' was dotted, and the final 'T' crossed, and I was master of my own vessel. Everything I ever was, stood for, fought for, dreamed of, came into focus that day. The concrete evidence of the achievement gives one's strivings legitimacy, proves that the ambitions were valid, the struggle worthwhile. Being prevented for those twenty-four years from doing the work for which I was trained had robbed life of its most essential meaning. Now, at last, I could use my training and capabilities fully. It was like being born anew." He went on further to say: "Sailing with such men made the years from 1942 to 1948 the happiest years of my life. It does not come to many men, much less many members of the colored races, to realize fully their true function. It is difficult enough, indeed, to discover what our function is, let alone achieve it."

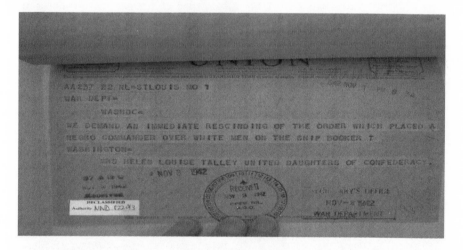

The above is a 1942 copy of a racially oriented document. Turn now to page 124 to attain a clearer view.

Hugh later indicated in no uncertain terms, *"No matter how well one prepares oneself for life, the future is always in others hands!"* Indeed, the future was in another authority's hand. And so, the challenges of life continued for the captain as tragedy struck his home in 1946 –Marie, his bride of twenty-six years, died abruptly after a long struggle with diabetes. Twelve years later, (1958) his first wife, Sadie Harris died in the city of Baltimore.

On December 16th, 1949, at 35 West 125 Street, Captain Hugh Mulzac held a gala grand opening of the Mulzac Travel Agency, featuring Sunbeam Tours to resorts North and South. Sunbeam Tours were designed for Caribbean people and thousands of more blacks that were looking for places to vacation without humiliating racial intolerance and segregation. Luminaries such as Sarah Vaughn, Billy Eckshine, Lionel Hampton, Errol Garner and Hal Jackson welcomed the gala, and it was a success. Because of multiple challenges and lack of business acumen in that industry, the Captain was forced to close the door to this promising endeavor in 1950.

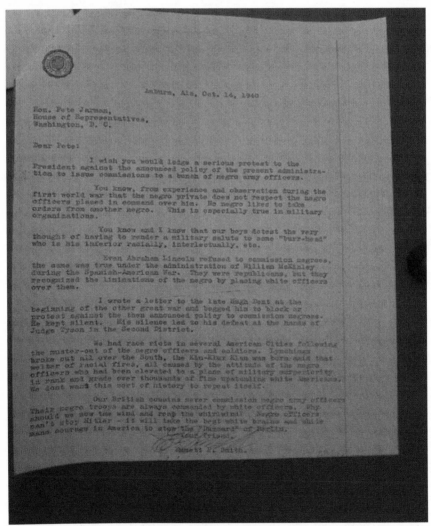

This letter, which was drafted in 1940, depicts the racially hostile atmosphere that overtly existed in America during the time of World War II. *(Turn now to page 265 for a clear view of the contents of this letter).*

Eager to find something worthwhile to occupy his time, the captain aligned himself with Vito Marcantonio, and Sidney Hillman, two high-ranking members of the American Labor Party (ALP). He was later nominated as the party's candidate for Queens Borough President. In 1950 he made his political bid but lost the election, having gotten 15,500 votes. One year later, the Unionite (born in Union Island) was again blacklisted. This time, not for being black, but because of his alignment with the (ALP), which was considered a communist party. Because of political affiliation, many shipping companies blacklisted him. As a result, he was unable to find work. The Government too, made life more difficult for him by revoking his seaman license. But Hugh by then was accustomed to the numerous methods of marginalization that were done to black folks in America. Almost a decade later, (1960) a Federal judge reinstated Mr. Mulzac's seaman's license; he again found work as a seaman, but it was his last years at sea in America.

Today, the name Hugh Mulzac is a household name in St. Vincent & the Grenadines. His achievement as the first black man to captain a ship in the U.S.A. Merchant Marine is a symbol of pride and strength to the people. He is an inspiration to every Vincentian at home and abroad. The bitter truth is that the Honorable Captain Hugh Nathaniel Mulzac's life was a testimony of hard work, struggle, and disenfranchisement from the day he left the Caribbean Sea for a better life north of the equator. His entire life at sea was very challenging and daunting for lack of a better word.

Being the son of the leading entrepreneur on Union Island, young Hugh Mulzac had a privileged upbringing. His Grandfather Charles and father Richard were Caucasians, descendants from Scotland; hence, young Hugh was considered "near white" by most residents in the Caribbean- a negative impact of slavery, which enabled the descendants of slaves to look at the high melanin content of their skins as a negative characteristic. Hugh's numerous encounters of racial prejudice have been particularly daunting compared to the good life he left behind on Union Island. Undeterred, the young chap persevered.

Another young man, Hugh's contemporary, was Henry "Bine" Stewart, the great uncle of the author. He also left Union Island during the years 1906-1907. This young lad, who had been a sailor for several years, found life much easier in America, where he worked very hard and sent his money back home to his father, John. Like Captain Hugh Mulzac, Bine was not absolved from the wrath of racism. For although slavery had been abolished in 1834, there was no change in the abusive and discriminatory attitude of white folks towards the Africans. Several years after he obtained a job in America, he succumbed to an untimely death provoked by racism. This strong black stallion was brutally hanged in the city of New Orleans, Louisiana. Unfortunately, the dead remains of Mr. Bine were never returned to his family in Union Island for proper burial.

The young Hugh Mulzac's exodus from Union Island during his early years 20th century established a migratory trend that has since become a legacy - one that may never meet its demise among today's generations. Nevertheless, Hugh's life at sea was typical of the numerous fathers of Union Island, who left their wives back at home to sail on the National Bulk Liners in order to make ends meet. These fathers will return home once every year, but only for a short period of time. Then off again to their lives at sea, leaving their wives pregnant one more time.

In the year 1961, Hugh youngest brother Lamie fell from the mask of a ship and died later. On a cold winter night, January 18th, 1963, tragedy struck home once again. This time, it was Ada Donowa/Mulzac, the Captain's mother. She died at a ripe age of 94. Later that year, Hugh lost another brother, James, who died suddenly; that same year, the captain published his autobiography (A Star to Steer By). In 1965, two years later, the Captain Hugh Mulzac, returned to the land of his birth, Union Island –an island that he had not seen since his departure on a Tuesday morning, March 12th, 1907. Regrettably, most of Hugh's contemporaries were nowhere to be found. Edith Mulrain, his teenage sweetheart, had already been deceased. Hugh in a state of emptiness also expressed that the government of St. Vincent had done futile little in the way of the development of the island. He later visited St. Vincent, and stayed at the once prestigious Paynter Guest House, at Kingstown Park, an outskirt of the capital Kingstown. He quickly found solace in his new environment and later purchased a two-bedroom house from a local businessperson named Ira Young – current owner of the local business, Value Electrical. He paid a hefty sum for the little dwelling and hired a maid to take care of all his menial and domestic chores at home.

During Hugh's sojourn in St. Vincent, he was adamant that the locals referred to him only as *Captain Hugh Mulzac* –an accomplishment he valued considerably as a veteran of the U.S. Merchant Marine. During his stay in St. Vincent, he conducted a navigation school at the Peace Memorial Hall, and the Grammar

School –pivotal locations at Richmond Hill, Kingstown. These sites were made available to him by the then government which he used free of charge to teach several up–and–coming seamen. As his social responsibility and gift to the people of St. Vincent & the Grenadines, Captain Hugh, in turn, rendered all of his services free of charge. Having been a painter for several years back at home in New York, the Captain also gives lectures in painting and saw it fit to donate some of his paintings to the local public library at Kingstown. One of his students was Mr. Wilfred Stewart of Ashton, Union Island, now a resident of Canada.

In December of 1969, at the ripe age of 83, the captain was now an old man and had seen enough in St. Vincent & Grenadines to call it a day. He wanted to return to the place that he truly knows as home. He expressed his desire to hand over his property to Glenford Stewart, his grandnephew, but the young man immediately declined his offer. The captain later willed the little house to the woman who rendered four years of service to him as a maid. Bidding the region farewell just one last time, he left St. Vincent in December of 1969 and returned to his home in Queens, New York. Indeed, it was the last time he was seen in the region – a place he once knows as home. Tried, he did, but regrettably, he too could not refute the awesome pull of The Exodus Factor (mentioned later), which was inevitably kept alive once again.

On Sunday, January 31st, 1971, two months short of his 85th birthday, the Honorable Captain Hugh Nathaniel Mulzac died

The burial site of Captain Hugh Nathaniel Mulzac in Queen, New York. A grave that is situated thousands of miles from the little village of Ashton, Union Island where he was born. Photo by Kwame Stewart.

and was buried at Plainlawn Cemetery, Hicksville, New York. Tactlessly, at the time of his death, he was not recognized for the enormous contribution that he had made as a serviceman to the armed force of United States of America. Thus, he was laid to rest as an ordinary citizen (picture of his burial site below unveils the simplicity of his tombstone). Surviving him at such time were his children: Mrs. Elaine Hackley, Mrs. Joyce Chamberlayne, Claire Mulzac, Hugh Mulzac Jr., and the revolutionary Una Mulzac, owner of the famed Liberation Bookstore at 421 Lennox Avenue, Harlem, New York. Her bookstore was opened in 1967 and closed in 2007.

Much has been written about the late Captain Hugh N. Mulzac, but there is another lesser-known Mulzac of Vincentian origin whose own son earned a prominent place in American History. Possessing just an 8th-grade education, James "Jim" Mulzac (page 126) was the younger brother who benefitted off the proverbial coattails of his better-educated and elder brother. "Jim" was a man of meager means who worked as a steward or cook on steamships. Eventually immigrating to Baltimore, Maryland with his wife, Mary Ramage, they became American citizens. To aid his struggling parents and their family from the financial hardships of America, John I. Mulzac, their eldest son, joined the Army Air Corps. Against tremendous odds in an era of racial segregation, John became a pilot with the vaunted Tuskegee Airmen. Being only one of just 919 men who in 1941 formed the first American Black Military Pilots and crewmen to serve during WW II. It was the success of the Tuskegee Airman in Europe that paved the way for the integration of the Unites States Armed Forces.

The captain Hugh Mulzac's achievement abroad has earned him much respect from the natives of St. Vincent & the Grenadines, and by extension, the world at large. With the Formation of National Security in St. Vincent & the Grenadines in the year 1986, two coast guard vessels were donated to the St. Vincent Government. These ships were given the names: 'Hugh Mulzac and the Mc Intosh respectively.' The American Government donated the Hugh Mulzac, while the Mc Intosh, on the other hand, was donated by Great Britain. To further honor the Captain for his historical contribution in the global black community, the Captain Hugh Mulzac Square was erected at Clifton Harbor, Union Island in the year 2004 -the Island of his birth.

When the young Hugh Mulzac, at 19, left Union Island in 1907, he thought that his stay abroad would have been for a few years, and a few years only. The young man was far from being accurate. Like many others today, he too was totally unaware of the formidable might of The Exodus Factor. But as he indicated in his autobiography: "No matter how well one prepares oneself for life, the future is always in others hands!" Indeed! Captain Hugh also mention before in no uncertain term: "Even when planned activities are conducted with the best intentions and skills, they don't always turn out as expected." This is an uncontrollable condition that most Unionites (males) become aware of, especially during their unproductive latter years. Regrettably!

The conclusion of the life experience of this icon takes us below to another intriguing subject that needs not be overlooked. The impact of this lone phenomenon surely will determine the future of Union Island -an Island that was home to thousands of migrants during the earlier years of their lives.

AA237 22 NL**ST LOUIS MO 1
WAR DEPT **
        WASHDC **

WE DEMAND AN IMMEDIATE RECINDING OF THE ORDER WHICH PLACED A NEGRO COMMANDER OVER WHITE MEN ON THE SHIP BOOKER T WASHINGTON

        MRS HELEN LOUISE TALLEY UNITED DAUGHTERS OF CONFEDERACY

The above Caption is copied from a racially oriented document on page 118.

THE EXODUS FACTOR

"The temptations in America are enormous, no one really gets into that ideal state of mind to leave permanently. And before you know it, you are already old and feeble."   *- Kwame Stewart.*

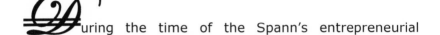uring the time of the Spann's entrepreneurial presence in Union Island (1760's -1850), the Spanns did fairly well with the lucrative cotton industry but left soon after the industry took a nosedive upon encountering financial impediments. Financial difficulties meant the abolition of slavery, the effects of the great 1831 hurricane, the aridness of the land -which resulted from the low annual rainfalls, and the infertility of the land, which stemmed from its overuse without maintenance. The abolition of Slavery, which was the major blow to the industry disallowed the slave masters some of the rights that they had over their chattel. The two French merchants, Antoine Rigaud, and Jean Augier left the island several decades before the Spanns, for the Treaty of Paris of February 10th, 1763 and the subsequent Treaty of Versailles 20 years later, negatively affected them.

In 1863 when Charles Mulzac leased Union Island from Major Collins of St. Vincent, he brought with him his wife and five young children. It appeared that he came to the region to settle. Yes, he did! He governed the island for almost four decades, and with his method of governance, his eldest son Richard, the father of thirteen, later became the entrepreneurial mastermind on the island. They amassed hundreds of livestock and supplied milk and meat for the entire island. They were excellent fishermen, whalers, and boat builders, and also conducted interisland marine trade throughout the Caribbean. They monopolized the cotton industry; hence, they were the only ones that made a profit from it. In essence, the Mulzac family was financially sound; yet, the children of this savvy entrepreneur left the confines of this Caribbean Paradise and were seldom seen again. Mr. E. Richards, a callous businessman later supplants the Mulzacs on Union Island; he was a nuisance. His method of rulership was nothing short of disaster to the black people of Union Island. Unable to generate commerce on the island, he disappeared immediately when the island was taken out of his hands. Some of his children and grandchildren, who subsequently became estate owners with lands bequeathed to them, later left Union Island to pursue life on greener pastures.

Let us take a look at the Mulzac family during the turn of the 20th century, and the time when they left Ashton village to pursue a life outside of Union Island.

A rear picture of Hugh and his brothers, (l-r) Hugh, James & Lamie (born Unionites) They all left Union Island more than 100 years ago to make better of their lives on foreign soil. Unavoidably, they became some of the earliest fatalities of the Exodus Factor.   Photo-   Henry Mulzac.

On Tuesday, March 12th, 1907, the island's prodigy, Hugh Mulzac, just about to turn twenty, left Union Island to pursue his navigational career and life at sea. Later that year, he ended up in America. During such time, he maintained his burning desire to return to Union Island to reunite with his family, and a young lady named Edith Mulrain. Edith was the love of his life. In 1910, his dream to return to Union Island almost came to reality when he left America on a ship to the Caribbean with a large amount of cash, which he had saved for three years. He had even bought an engagement ring for the young lady. Unfortunately, his journey home was significantly derailed in Jamaica when someone at his hotel stole his clothes, the engagement ring, and every penny that he had saved during his years away from Union Island. As a result, he was forced back into the tentacles of America, where he had to start life all over again. That derailment later took him another 50 years before he visited the island of his birth.

In 1912, Hugh's younger brother James, who was only 18 years old, migrated to America to join him. Then in the years 1914, Lavinia, his sister, at age 24, also left Union Island to accompany them, then followed by another brother Lamie, and his mother, Ada. They all lived together at Hugh's residence in Maryland. What remains difficult to understand is that although these youngsters had come from a well-to-do family, and had a good life, after they left, they never returned to Union island to call it home again. Many other Unionites likewise left and never returned. So, the logical question that must be asked is, what is that influence or gravitational force that has such an impact on many Unionites whenever they venture abroad? "Do they became enamored and later tethered by the sudden niceties of their new environments? Or do they choose migration as a means of escaping the bleakness of life in Union Island?" Four of Hugh's sibling, Edward, Irvin, and Una later migrated to America. May, his last sister was the only one that remained in Union Island throughout her entire life. In her latter years, she was fondly called Mother May.

There isn't any detailed information regarding the whereabouts of Charles Mulzac's other three children: Mary, John, and Emma, except that John (Johnnie) once ran his father's rum shop. Therefore, the current generations of the Mulzac's family that reside in Union Island and bore the surname "Mulzac" are primarily the descendants of Richard. Edward, the son of Richard Mulzac, was the father of the late Leonard Mulzac (Dogma), a life-long resident of Union Island. There may also be descendants of Irvin Mulzac, the younger brother of Hugh. (Tombstones of the Mulzac can be seen at the first Clifton Cemetery). While still living in Union Island, Irvin buried his dad Richard at the Ashton Cemetery on Friday, February 14th, 1930.

As mentioned above, Captain Hugh Mulzac was in is latter years, (1960's) when he had returned to St. Vincent with the intention to settle. Why did he make up his mind at such a late stage of his life? Was it a blunder? This is a critical question to consider. Well, during Hugh's sojourn in St. Vincent, he gave multiple lectures and classes in the art of painting. He also exhibited to local yachtsmen the vast knowledge and experience he had attained at sea while in Europe and North America. Regrettably, his stay in the region was short-lived, for he returned to America soon thereafter.

Among Unionites living abroad, men make up the larger percentage of the ones who wish to return home permanently. Women, on the other hand, are more adaptive of their new environments and are willing to settle almost anywhere with their families. But is there a right time to return permanently to Union Island to satisfy that nostalgic yearning? If so, when? It must be understood that Hugh's nostalgic yearning to return to Union Island was inevitable, but the feeling of wellbeing that he once had as a youth in Union Island never returned when he finally visited the island of his birth in 1965.

Andy Kwame Stewart, a native of Union Island, thinks that if anyone has that burning desire to return permanently to Union, then he or she should just pack up and leave. "The temptations in America are enormous," he states. "No one really gets into that ideal state of mind to leave permanently, and before you know it, you are already old and feeble. Do not wait," he exhorted, "the time will never be just-right."

It is approximately a century now since Unionites have been migrating steadily to other countries. During the first half of the 20th century when Unionites were venturing out in droves, their primary purpose was for employment. Although employment remains an essential reason for today's migration, there is a myriad of other necessities that can only be attained via migration. And regrettably, most of these necessities can only be achieved abroad.

In general, whenever a Caribbean person ventures in the America, Canada, or England, they seldom return to their native land. Such is the case with many Unionites that have traveled abroad; the percentage of returning Unionites is insignificant compared to those who make these foreign countries their homes. Currently, there is a large concentration of Unionites in America, Canada, UK, and Trinidad & Tobago, notwithstanding the many that are scattered throughout the globe. In recent years, Unionites have been setting up homes on the island of St. Vincent. But St. Vincent is located only 40 miles north of Union Island. So again, why? Now it must be observed that in recent times, it is the younger members of the families that leave the island for greener pastures. And whenever any resident of Union Island leaves the island for that purpose, there is only a slim possibility that they will return to call Union Island home. Often they leave their parents and grandparents behind. They at some point become parents themselves; their children are born outside of Union Island for sure, which leaves the island with a low percentage of birthrate from the original Unionite population. The numbers are surely dwindling quickly; meanwhile, the island is facing a massive brain drain. Unavoidably!

Some of you are probably scratching your heads on reading into the reality of this phenomenon, but you've already made it this far, so stick with me as I attempt to bring clarity to your already curious minds.

So, what really is The Exodus Factor? Is it a custom, a legacy, an established system in Union Island in which migration has become the inevitable? Is it status quo that a better life is easily attainable abroad, where multiple opportunities abound as opposed to the limitations of the region? Indeed, there are a few salient factors or influences, however, completely explains the necessity of this ever-present trend. So yes, this significant question will be answered in many ways, long before the final page of this book is turned.

If a survey were to be conducted in every home in Union Island, commencing from the last house at Campbell, Ashton, which was owned by the late Presaul Ambrose (Presey) to the first house at Point Lookout, Clifton, many would be amazed. It would be astounding to realize that each home on that island has, at least, one member of its family that has left the island permanently. For other families, the parents are the only ones left at home. The members of the families who have left are now living abroad or on another island in the region. Just a minute here! Does this indicate that there is a dislike for this beautiful Caribbean paradise? Absolutely Not! For emigration is also evident in several other Caribbean countries. But for Union Island, many will tacitly agree that *Exodus* has become the inevitable.

On Sunday, October 27th, 2013, the author had reason to visit a funeral service that was held at the Seventh Day Adventist Church at Ashton, Union Island. There, he met with one of the local minister named Aldon Ambrose. They had a protracted discussion about the scenery, childhood days, and the changes that the island has encountered over the years. But they could not sidestep the fact that every member of the deceased family besides the father was living outside of Union Island. To commiserate with their sobbing father, and be a part of that funeral service, every sibling of that family had to return to Union Island from their homes abroad. This concern is not exclusive to that family, for it has become status quo on Union Island, Unfortunately.

Minister Ambrose mentioned that he observed this unforgiving trend several years ago when he returned to Union Island from Canada to visit his parents. "I was literally shocked, he said. As a result, I made it a concerted effort to leave Canada for a while in order to accompany and facilitate my parents who were literally living alone."

Fortunately, for the many that have migrated abroad to improve their lives, a significant number of them have made good of the opportunities available to them. In some cases, they have made sacrifices to obtain those opportunities. Many of them are now doctors, judges, lawyers, engineers, professors, clergies, bankers, accountants, schoolteachers, principals, building contractor, nurses, healthcare providers and a host of other professionals from a myriad of other disciplines. But respect must be paid to the sons and daughters who have chosen to remain as productive citizens on Union Island. For those who have been actively involved in the social, religious, economic, academic and cultural development of the island, their commitments and contributions are laudable amidst the myriads challenges that exist. And most importantly, their will and characters to avert the magnetic might of the Exodus Factor; such is courageous.

To dispense with the above, we will now take a look at a scenario of a family who has migrated to the Americas or Europe.

An average family in Union Island entails a mother, father, and their four children as oppose to a large number of children that were evident in the families of Union Island yesterday. A dearth of academic opportunities on the island would only engender migration at some time in the early lives of the children. Because that has become the inevitable, as mentioned previously, the authenticity of the original culture of Union Island is notably declining. These children who migrate to other countries for economic and academic reasons are apt to have their parents with them at some point in time. The lifestyles in those countries are different; their parents are quick to point that out after they have lived out their novelty stage. The complaint about their confinements in homes where doors are bolted with two or three locks, windows are shut tightly, and radiators are constantly going to maintain heat during the horrid winter months. Another downside to this is that people's mobility is grossly compromised by a 180-degree turn from the previous walking habit they enjoyed over the many years spent in Union Island. One can only imagine the many health issues that stem from not being able to do the things that they once enjoyed. Nevertheless, this new atmosphere and environment have become their homes, and in most cases, their final abode.

While youngsters sometimes assimilate very well into their new environments, their parents, on the other hand, struggle with their new lifestyles. They are persuaded and in some cases, coerced into dwellings that are far removed from their true definition of home in Union Island. A trip or two back home (Union Island) is quite in order for the parents, but that is about it, for they are later returned to the unfamiliar lifestyles of Europe and the Americas. The opportunity to meet, greet, and converse with neighbors on a daily basis has dissipated. Older folks have genuine respect for their peers, so neighbors in their new environments will not hesitate to extend hospitality. But the sad thing is that the neighborly customs of America, Canada, and Europe differs immensely from the customs and traditions of the Caribbean as a whole. Nostalgia becomes evident among these older folks while boredom and stress seep in quickly. These, of course, are cogent ingredients for accelerated aging.

A final request by the parents to be sent back home permanently often falls on the obstinate ears of their children. Boredom, stress, and depression continue as the end approaches. This is basically the trend of today's generations. Many are of the belief that in the next two decades, the population of the indigenous Unionites will dwindle its way into insignificance. Many have witnessed that the dead are buried on wherever turf they meet their ends; their bodies are seldom sent back home for burial at the local cemeteries. Above all, it **must** be acknowledged that The Exodus Factor is there to stay.

The picture below shows *Captain Hugh Mulzac*, a native son

of *Union Island* with his family at a 1940s dinner in his honor. In this rare picture, three earlier natives of Union Island are seen. *Ada Mulzac* (Ma De-De, Mandy), the widow of Richard P. Mulzac (Dad Sonny), her son *Hugh*, and daughter *Lavinia*, they were all residents of Ashton, Union Island during the Nineteenth and early 20th centuries. Like many natives, they too, walked the soil of Union Island. Their permanent departures have made them the forerunners of the ever-present *Exodus Factor*. To date, this is a condition that has plagued the 3.5 sq. Miles landmass for well over a century. *Ada is also the mother of the late May Mulzac (Mother May)*, a former resident *of Ashton Village, Union Island.*

Back row: Captain Hugh's four daughters: Elaine Hackley & Husband, Joyce, Claire, and Una Mulzacs. (Front row) Hugh's mother, Ada (Ma De- De), sister Lavinia, Captain Hugh Mulzac, his wife Miriam (Marie), and son Hugh Jr. (All have deceased).

Denied the opportunity to work as a citizen of America, this *Unionite* (Hugh Mulzac) in 1942 at the age of 56, became the first black man to captain a Navy ship in the U.S. Merchant Marine. During his tenure, he commands an integrated crew during World War II. His ship was the SS Booker T. Washington, yet the establishments never honor him for his mammoth contribution to the armed forces of America. To date, his gravesite remains shamefully simple and ordinary compared to many who have done lesser deeds, yet have been buried with great pride and honor. His tombstone, seen on *pages 122* speaks voluminously.

 Of all the Mulzacs that have left Union Island and migrated to the United States of America during the early 20th century, Hugh was the most recognized among them. He was a seaman, and later, a Captain in the US Merchant Marine. He also had a propensity for painting, an art he exhibited during his later years. His youngest brother, Lamie, became a carpenter, while James, another younger brother, (mentioned earlier) became a chef on a steamship. The sisters, Una and Lavina (Aunty Venee) became Seamstresses.

VERNACULAR, TWANGS & IDIOMS

"O Gad Dorothy, you-self? If yo see ah ghal fo Ce Clouden, yo go pass um straight. Ah telling yo! You nah go mek um out at-tall, at-tall. And the ting of it, ah ghal look so old and knack-up. Dorothy, I tell you, that could never be the Urmain whey we know from Battam Campbell. Never!"

Strangely, but we all must agree that everything has its origin or genesis. So is the above paragraph, which depicts a dialect that is home, ONLY on Union Island. Before we get started, let us now inquire a bit deeper into the root of this lingo. New accents are formed when people of a different country and tongue learns another language. Such is the case when Africans from the West Coast of Africa were brought to Union Island and were forced to learn the European languages. They were not successful at mastering these languages; hence, the African influence remained predominant on Union Island today even after centuries of colonization. Obviously, as with anything new, there were challenges, and in this case, challenges in pronunciation that resulted in a myriad of variances of some words. Most of these variants were mispronounced, perpetuated, and eventually acknowledged. This ultimately resulted in acceptance or recognition of the frequency of the errors, then the birth of a new language, but not a broken one, as is the public's opinion.

Before we delve into the dialogue that follows, let us again take a keen look at the italicized paragraph above, and see what we can make of yesterday's dialect –the voice of the ancestors.

Jane Ann: Minchude, Minchude...(loudly) O Gad, ah ghal go run up meh blood pressure. Minchude...! Minchude...! Ah wander way ah ghal dey so lang? Wah mek ah nah-e answer?

Tan-Tan: Well who da e barl Minchude this urly marning? Jane Ann ah you? Good marning. Oh Gad nabe, you aghen? You and ah ghal nah tired get-way? Ah know she damn well own-way, but ah long to see she. She is the only chile way favar the gran modder, Ce.

	Chamney.
Jane Ann:	Who da? I ain't ketch the voice. Oh...? marning...(responds to Tan-Tan under the breath), and mumble as she stutters) ...Ah.... too damn fast and Raaven. Ah Makko nah know me and ah ghal is whan? If you shitting and you see that woman, I tell you, you better sit down pan ah shit
Jane Ann:	O Gad, well whey Minchude cud dey so lang?
Minchude:	Tanty look meh yah, whey yo want?
Jane Ann:	Minchude, yo tek up ah clothes from off ah line aready?
Minchude:	Tanty, me ain't come yah to wok out meh Soul-case enna.
Jane Ann:	O Gad, Minchude every marning so? Eh?
Minchude:	Tanty me nah e go no way. Help my Gad Tanty, ah wayry yo see me yah.
Jane Ann:	Whey Dentan? He get up yet?
Minchude:	Yo ain calling him fo grine ah carn fo mek ah carn Pap?
Jane Ann:	Ghal, know yo place! I know when to talk to Dentan!
Minchude:	Well sid-down dey, see how ah carn go grine for make ah pap this urly marning. He mus-e think he have ah maiden in the house.
Jane Ann:	Ghal, me have a bad win in me stomach, and ah wayry talk to Dentan.
Minchude:	Well, he day-e walk up an down one-two, one-two like he dotish. He ain't going, he ain't coming. Just looking like poor-me-whan. He better go look fo wok to do.

The above, a typical conversation, was still the dialect of Union Island up until the last fifty years but has changed considerably in recent years. Below, is an accurate interpretation.

Early morning in her garden, Jane Ann, an old lady, observed that her niece, Minchude, who is spending some time with her, is nowhere to be found. She calls Minchude loudly, gets no response and wonders where can she be. She thinks that Minchude has heard her but refused to answer. She also believes that Minchude, her niece is stressing her out, and the stress will eventually cause her to have high blood pressure. She calls Minchude a couple more times.

Tan-Tan, the neighbor hears the bellowing and asks who is calling Minchude so loudly in the morning. She acknowledges Jane Ann and bids her good morning but further asked if she isn't tired of the constant bickering with the headstrong Minchude whom she hasn't seen for a long time. She indicates that Minchude resembles her grandmother. Jane Ann realizes the voice is that of Tan-Tan, her neighbor and responds "Good morning." She mumbles under the breath and stutters badly, but implied clearly, that Tan-Tan is too damn inquisitive and ravenous, and she should be mindful that Minchude is her blood relative. She also indicates that if anyone doesn't want their name and deeds to be in the public's domain, they ought not to do anything in her presence. Minchude finally shows up and says to her aunt, "Aunty, I am here." Jane Ann then asks her if she has already taken up the clothes that are hanging on the line. Minchude retorted, "Aunty, I did not come here to work as a slave." Aunty Jane Ann responds to Minchude by asking her, *why every morning she always has something negative to say to her?* Minchude replies, "I swear that I am not doing anything. I am tired." "Where is Denton? (Jane Ann's son) Is he out of bed yet?" Jane Ann asked. Minchude responds, "Are you not calling him to grind the corn to make corn porridge?" Jane Ann retorted: "Girl, have some respect for me." I know when to ask Denton to grind the corn." Minchude responded to her by saying "If you remain cavalier, the corn will never be ready to make porridge; he thinks that he has a maid in the house. Jane-Ann responds, "Girl, I am feeling sick. I have got gas in my stomach, and furthermore, I am tired of asking Denton for favors." Minchude replied, "Denton is walking slowly and aimlessly as though he is stupid and needs help. He is not making any progress in his life. He is stagnated; therefore, he needs to find himself a job."

Now, although the original dialect of Union Island has evolved over the years, its influence is still evident throughout the island. There is a modicum of residual effects of the dialect that is present among the younger generation of today. Below are a few sentences, phrases, and clauses that were used then. The italicized captions indicate what they actually mean in today's English. This transcription is meant ONLY to conjure up memories and ceaseless laughter from events of our formative years on the island. Please be reminded that in only a few years, this unique dialect with all of its colorful flavors will be nothing else but defunct. Enjoy!

0. **Leh –ah-we go**--*Let us go.*

1. **Ah ghal fo Mildred too frontish and out ah place**------------------*Mildred's daughter is too brazen and disrespectful.*

2. **Gwan, Elsa go do fo yo ---**-------------------------*Go on, Elsa will humiliate you.*

3. **Yo en hear da say Dolton hold down Meryl under the big hog plum tree by Ms. Leah? Yea-s! Urly this marnin. I tell you; that is advantage eh?** --------*Haven't you heard that Dolton raped Meryl early this morning under the hog plum tree by Ms. Leah? My goodness, he really took advantage of her.*

4. **Less e naise, yo deh in chuch** ----------------------Be q*uiet, you are in church?*

5. **Who dah pan ah mango tree?** ----------------------*Who is on the mango tree?*

6. **Well Fethan, Oh Gad, ennah way-re lie? Deh put yo so?** -----------------Oh my God Fethan, aren't you tired of telling lies? *Are you possessed?*

7. **Gertrude, whey yo dey? What yo doing outside this hour ah de nite? E-nah-e bring anether belly in this house enna** ------Gertrude where are you? Why are you outside so late? If you get *pregnant, you cannot live in this house.*

8. **Oh Gad, Melvina, wadda e?** ----------------------Oh my God Melvina, w*hat happen / what is wrong with you?*

9. **Ah ghal fo Elma downcay eh? Who she bring?** ----------------------- *Elma's daughter is careless,* isn't she? Whose attitude and traits does he possess?

10. **Who-fah chile yo have in yo hand dey?** ----------*Whose child you have there?*

11. **Ah lil ghal fo Helena too harden; ah nay-e A'rrr**----Helena's little daughter is very stubborn; she does not listen.

12. **Clesfield, why e nah put up e discose; kibber yo tongue** ------------*Clesfield,*

no one wants to listen to what you have to say; hold your piece.

13. **E-nay-e go no whey; nat te-nite**------------*You are not going anywhere, especially   tonight.*

14. **Ah tell yo nah go pan ah plum tree cause it gat Wanga, but Oh Gad like yo break stick in yo Azs** ------------------------*I told you not to go on the plum tree because the plums are poisoned, but O my God, you refused to listen.*

15. **Ah see she dearder day**---------------------------------- *I saw her the other day.*

16. **Yo see them sugar apple whey Gussy dey-e-eat marning, noon, and night, mark   my   works,   she   go   get   ah   good   piece   ah shittings**..........................*Those sugar apples that Gussy eats daily will surely give her a diarrhea.*

17. **Who de baddy way he knack meh doe?** -------------*Who is knocking my door?*

18. **Kedrick, know yo damn place. Yo tink ah baun yesterday?** -------- Kedrick, **you must have some respect. You think I am a child?**

19. **She deh wid one ah Garfield Stroad bwoy**...............*She has an intimate relationship with one of Mr. Garfield Stewart sons.*

20. **Modder-wok, Minchude? Wah-mek yo nah come to school dis marnin?** -- Oh' my God, *Minchude, why didn't you come to school this morning?*

21. **Doan lay-too by the well yo no** ----------------------*Do not delay at the well, ok*

22. **Uhn nah e go no whey wid ah ghal, ah too damn wotlis** ------*I am not going anywhere with that girl because she is too damn worthless.*

23. **Ah warning yo eh-no, ah tell you to lee them Strode alone; yo know dey ain't too righted aready** ------*Take my advise and leave the Stewarts alone; you already know that they are not mentally sound.*

24. **Well Fethan, enna reach home yet? You want ah good cut-ass.** ----*Fethan, what took you so long to reach home? You need a proper whipping?*

25. **Alfred, you sure dat nat Icy bloomers yo have in yo hand dey?** ------------ Alfred, *are you sure that isn't Icy's underwear that you have in your hand?*

26. **Doh gee Sarah the clothes to wash because she doz do ting too vike-ah vike**----------------------------*Do not give Sarah the clothes to wash because she does things carelessly.*

27. **Ghal, doan eat nottin from Adelaide yo A'rrr; dat woman hand dutty ------** *-Ghal, do not eat anything from Adelaide, yo hear; she is an Obier woman.*

28. **De cattle full**--*The cow is pregnant.*

29. **Ah Kashie chook meh pan meh battam foot**................... *A thorn has pricked the sole of my foot.*

30. **Don't walk pan ah dotty** ------------------------------ *Do not walk on the dirt.*

31. **De bull jumped the cattle**----------------------*The cohabitation of the male and female cattle.*

32. **De pig drop urly dis marning; it mek nine**-------*The pig gave birth to nine piglets early this morning.*

33. **Ah been watching ah ghal fo Faith Coban since urly this marning, she look like she does ketch Malcady. Like she head does go and come?**--*I have been watching Faith Coban's daughter since this morning. She appears to be crazy.*

34. **Oh Gad! Well who dah e walk round ah house shut-tail so? Dat not Chezley fo Narma?** --------*Oh my God. Who is walking around the house butt-naked? Isn't that Chesley, Mrs. Norma son?*

35. **Yo didn't know Ce Margin gran daughter have three Pickney? Well Sid-down deh** ------------*Did you not know that Ce Morgan's granddaughter has three children? Well you are not up to date with what's happening.*

36. **Ah ghal fo Fegina raben eh? She ny'am all da vittle?** ----------------*Fegina's daughter is very ravenous. Did she eat all of the food (Victual)*

37. **Next year go mek three years now since McKay John and Goldstan nah-e --pull** -------------*Next year will be three years since McKay John and Goldstan are enemies.*

38. **Leh me gee yo ah la-lick** -----*Let me give you a lash at departure (not a whipping). La-lick was actually a last lick or final lash of gesture when children departed from school to their respective homes).*

39. **I ain't tink de last bwoy fo Susana is the husband own yo know; ah hear Festas name call**------------*Festus might be the father of Mrs. Susana's last son.*

40. **Ghal, well yo get it oh-toe-toe**------------*Girl you have gotten it in abundance.*

41. **Marva like too much ah damn commess, ley she go she way** --------*Marva*

is too contentious; do not pay her any attention.

42. **Help my Gad, if yo ain go and get ah bucket ah water, you ain gettin a drap a tea here this marnin** ----------------*I swear if you don't fetch a bucket of water, you will not have breakfast this morning.*

43. **Whey e call meh fah, whey e want?** -------*What are you calling me for? What do you want?*

44. **Ah tell yo to make de broth; you tellin me Guinea hen bring ram goat** -----*I told you to make fish broth, instead, you are telling me something unrelated.*

45. **O Gad, ah hear Ba Mindo tek-in again. Ah know them children go feel it when he close he eyes. Haas to ah whan whey name Henry. Ah bwoy look so phorr-me-whan** ---------*O my God, I heard that Ba Mindo is very ill again. His children will be saddened when he dies, especially his son, Henry. He looks rather pitiful and overly consumed with his father's condition.*

46. **Ghal, how yo gran modder? Ah hear she low.** ------*Girl, how is your Grandmother? I heard that she is on her dying bed.*

47. **O Gad, well wah mek ah bwoy fo Corn Do-Do phorr so? He look like he far from the kitchen**--------*O my God,* Corn Do-Do's *son looks extremely thin and emaciated, don't you think? It appears that he doesn't have much to eat.*

48. **Since them people come from Merica, Jasmine dey up and down behind them like Never-see Come-see.** --------------*Jasmine is always seen with those people that came from America. She acts very naïve. It appears that she is utterly inexperienced and simple in her behavior.*

49. **Tan Janey, dat is nat the kind ah creole to want in yo place eh nor. If them-dey so is to get inside ah fo-you house, yo have to dey foot, foot behind them, else dag ny'am yo supper** ------------*Aunty Janey, you don't need those kinds of people at your home. If they (unscrupulous) were to get inside of your house, you will have to scrutinize every move that they make or else they can steal from you and take your private business into the street.*

50. **Melda, ah buoy Chile fo Larry baun wid ah hand tite eh? Ah look like ah nah go gee ah we nottin**----*Emelda, Larry's son, is born with a closed fist; it signifies stinginess. He may not give us anything when he grows up.*

Yes! Only fifty years ago, these and many more colloquial phrases (listed below), were also prevalent in Union Island. To get a firsthand experience of these superstitions, one must be in the presence of two or three elders; such assembly will be an event to savor. Sadly, the remaining Silent Generation and Traditionalists on Union Island are few in numbers.

From the STIMULUS that led to the writing of "*Union Island History –Servitude, Metayage & Civilization (UIHSMC),* the author made mention of one of the folklore that was prevalent on the island during the twentieth century. It is imperative now to share the beliefs and customs of the ancestors because residual effects are still widespread throughout the Caribbean:

   a. Do not put your hands on your head because that can hasten the death of your mother.
   b. Always put a piece of red thread on the forehead of a baby because it keeps away evil spirits and prevents the child from becoming sick -Maljew.
   c. Never go to bed thirsty because your spirit will come out of you to get water while you are asleep.
   d. Do not sweep at night or open an umbrella indoors because these things can bring you bad luck.
   e. Do not sweep on someone's feet or they may never get marry.
   f. Whenever you are sick, you must wipe a wet egg on your face and immediately place it under your bed; this will hasten your recovery.

Here are some local idioms, which are home to Union Island. At worst, they can conjure up a tremendous amount of laughter.

   • When man dead...Grass Grow. ---------------Whenever the patriarch or father dies, the home is often neglected; this can result in the abandonment of certain rules, principles and customs. As a result, male intruders and the uninvited can feel unchallenged to take advantage of the female occupants of that home.

   • Speak of the Devil and the Imp appears --------- Speaking of someone unprincipled, dishonorable, deceitful and corrupt, and unexpectedly, he/she appears.

- Tek yo yam and gee me ma bag. ---------- I have done everything (job) that you required of me; therefore, I need payment right away.

- Annie go and Annie come, and if Annie go and Annie can't come, then to hell with Annie. ------------ Whenever you give to others (neighbors) who likewise can reciprocate, you are supposed to receive at some point in time, (whether now or in the future). And if you share/give indiscriminately to those neighbors, and cannot receive anything in return, then it is utterly useless to continue giving anything to those miserly neighbors.

*And this final one is for the road.

"WHEN YOUR HAND IS IN A LION'S MOUTH, YOU MUST GENTLY EASE IT OUT."

The above saying is universal in scope, but for Unionites who have a peculiar way of expressing their thoughts, feelings, and emotions, the above is uttered in such a manner that the only recourse is nothing short of a hearty laughter. This is how it is uttered from the mouth of a typical Unionite:

When e know e hand dey in lion mouth, e have to know how to tek it out.

In today's English, it means: Whenever you find yourself in a quandary or dilemma you must use diplomacy and tact, or exhibit intelligence and wit in order to get yourself out of the sticky situation.

This entire subject is primarily a reminder of Yesterday's language. And for the most part, it should be considered a souvenir to all Unionites at home and abroad. It is also a gesture of respect to the forefathers and foremothers (the ancestors), and lastly, to keep alive that which was, or has been the sole tongue of Union Island for several centuries. Please savor it with love.

Folks, you have come to the end of another appetizing segment, maybe one of the core topics of this book. Does the word Classic come to your mind yet? Well, the subject that follows takes you deeply into another intriguing topic -one of Union Island's premier custom that is quickly losing momentum as our feet are sunk deeper into this 21st century. Read on.

MAROON FESTIVAL

"Massa, me nah dead yet." He pleaded defenselessly for his life. But, the obdurate despot retorted mercilessly: "Carry um go bury um!"

In the Caribbean, the meaning of the word **Maroon** has evolved over the years and is now considered an event – a festive one. In the island of Jamaica, it has become a huge tourist attraction. In other countries, such as Cuba, Suriname, Puerto Rico, Brazil, Panama, and Carriacou, it is still kept alive. But on Union Island, it is safe to say that it is sagging listlessly on its last leg making its way into extinction. Let us now take a look at the original meaning of the name "*Maroon,*" how it came about, and what it meant to the Africans diaspora, but primarily the descendants of the Africans slaves of Union Island.

The word "Maroon" literally means runaway slaves – referring to slaves that were opposed to oppression and hence fled the plantations and escaped deeply into the rugged interior of the forest and hills rather than to remain in captivity. The word *Maroon* derives from the Spanish word 'Cimarrones', which meant 'mountaineers.' The slave's fight for freedom is the same struggle that the black Cimarrones of the Coast (Brazil, Panama) faced. After all, there were no alternatives for the slaves; they were mere chattel whose lives were doomed at the hands of their slave masters. Their only place of refuge was the dense forests, which, in most cases led to the highlands. Yet, these highlands were fortresses that were precarious. Life was very difficult for these people who had to start life anew under grossly inhospitable conditions –inclement weather in these highlands, white attackers, poisonous snake, predatory animals and the inability to obtain and grow food undisturbed. These were just a few of the challenges that they had to endure. Yet, even under these adverse conditions, life was better than the sheer brutality, misuse, and abuse at the hands of these evil "Massas" who rendered no form of recompense.

It is common knowledge that the treatment of African slaves on British sugar colonies was inhumane. The regular form of punishment for eating sugarcane on the plantation; stealing, or even being absent from the plantation for work often resulted in a fierce beaten with a stick (even to the point of breaking bones); having to wear a chain around the neck and ankle, and sometimes being incarcerated in dungeons. There were also more barbaric acts, such as the breaking of limbs, Buck Breaking, castration, and even beating out of the eyes. Not to mention the Darby's Dose method of punishment that was implemented in Jamaica on May 25th, 1756. Slavery produced cruelty and oppression rather than morality, decency, sympathy, religion or citizenship. A controversial verse in the Bible is 1 Peter 2:18-20 (New International Version). Verse 18. "Slaves, in reverent fear of God, submit yourselves to your masters, not only to those who are harsh." 19. "For it is commendable if someone bears up under the pain of unjust suffering because they are conscious of God." 20. "But how is it to your credit if you receive a beating for doing wrong and endure it? But if you suffer for doing good, and you endure it, this is commendable before God." Contrary to the above, the concept of Ma 'at, from ancient Egypt, represents the ethical and moral principles that Egyptians, and to a greater extent, the Africans, are expected to follow throughout their daily lives.

Again, contrary to the above, *What Color is your God?* -A book written by Columbus Salley & Ronald Behm stated: "The Bible and Christianity were the tools of White plantation owners to oppress and suppress the legitimate human aspirations of Black slaves. In other words, the above verses and others were incorporated into the bible during slavery with a single intent; that intent was solely for the cultivation of obedient and submissive slaves. Moreover, it is worth noting, that the second book of the Bible, Exodus 21:16 states clearly: "He that stealeth a man, and selleth that man, and if he be found with that man in his hand, he shall surely be put to death." With all of the above, the reader can now derive his own opinion.

There was nothing worthwhile about this wicked institution, and the only way to get out of this system of subjugation, misuse, and abuse, was to escape from the plantations. Quite a few slaves made that decision at the expense of their lives. Slave codes indicated that runaways who refused to be arrested might be lawfully killed. Slaves were forbidden to carry arms or to go off their masters' plantations without a written pass. Forbidden to lift a hand against their masters, even in self-defense; forbidden to beat drums, and to hold religious services without a white person present. Also, it was illegal for slaves to read or write; to gather in groups of more than five; to own property, and to marry. Nevertheless, some slaves still found the courage or cojones to flee the white man's plantation.

Even though Union Island is exceedingly small, the slaves of that day were not exempted from the sheer brutality, misuse, and abuse of this gruesome yet lucrative institution. Can you remember the story about a slave (mentioned earlier) that the late *Isabella Roache* had alluded to? It was during the early 20th century, a field-slave on a cotton plantation of Union Island was unable to work because he was sick. That made the slave master furious, and instantly ordered the burial of the slave in his current state of uselessness. 'Massa me nah dead yet,' (Master, I am not dead yet), the middle-aged slave pleaded hopelessly for his life, but the cruel slave master retorted angrily, "Carry him and bury him." The slaves interpreted in their dialect, "Carry um go bury um." Those were the worst years for the people of Union Island since the so-called abolition of slavery in 1834. Unfortunately, that ostensible document became lawful in Union Island in the year 1838.

It is regrettable that a slave who may have been severely ill had succumbed to an untimely death in that he was forcefully buried alive without remorse. The location of his atrocious burial site is under a huge Hog-Plum tree at Bajan Corner on Clifton Road. Bajan Corner attained its name from an old woman from the island of Barbados. Her named was Jestina Noel. Mrs. Jestina lived at that location for several decades; in her latter years, she was nicknamed Ce Bajan.

Because of this incident, and the location of this atrocious burial, many former residents had deemed that landmark as a haunted site. Even during the late 1980's, many residents feared walking alone at Bajan Corner during the late hours of the night.

Ta Muggy also made mention of another slave whose suffering was less significant. This slave, she said, had his small shack or living quarters on the cotton plantation. He did not show up for work for two consecutive days. The third day, with no question asked, the grass roof of his meager dwelling was viciously yanked off to send a message to other slaves. Looking back carefully, one can conclude that such occurrences would have been during the early years of 1901-1909. For a slave during the early 19th century would not have been permitted to have living quarters on any plantation. Instead, it was a watch-house that he had built on that farmland. But during such time, there was no significant difference between a slave and so-called free Negro 70 years after 1838. This condition existed because the atmosphere of the Massa-slave relationship had not changed. Unavoidably, black people (Africans) in Union Island remained almost as chattel for many years later. Slaves were not permitted to build proper living quarters; not because they did not have means to do so, but because it was totally forbidden. For the man whose roof was yanked off, his shack was located where Ms. Eldine Clouden of Clifton now lives. (The current location is adjacent to one of Mr. E. Richards's estate). This misdeed was one of the less destructive attacks on a chattel -a rare exception to the rule of that day. Sickness on the plantation was something that was not dealt with favorably; only the fit and healthy were needed. Hence, a slave who was unable to work was nothing but a liability to his owner.

Over a period of time, these runaway slaves -the Maroons, banded together to form communities after the strains of life had eventually been alleviated. It was their natural propensity to live in communities; it was their communal lifestyle that enables them to be recognized as a people, officially called Maroons. Maroons were present in Suriname, Jamaica, Haiti, St. Vincent, Grenada, Dominica, and Cuba. To date, there is no documented history available of slaves in Union Island, Bequia, and Carriacou that have fled their respective plantations for the hills. In fact, there is seldom any historical documentation about the cultural past of the slaves of Union island, period. Sad, but true! Equally so, there is no documented history of the annihilation of the Amerindians, the first people to inhabit Union Island. Certainly, the mountainous nature of Union Island is conducive for an escaped slave; he or she may not survive for a long period of time. Yet, no one can refute that the thought of escaping the white man's plantations never surface in the hearts and minds of the slaves in Union Island. Nonetheless, the original purpose of the Maroon celebration was freedom. This cannot be overlooked. The bulk of slaves who came from the motherland were primarily from the west coast of Ghana, Cameroon, Nigeria, Senegal, Sierra Leone, Liberia, Togo, and Guinea. They brought their cultures with them. The customs of the many tribes –the Yoruba, Ashanti, Kisii, Makoa, Adjas, Ebo and Fons were exhibited once per year on Union Island in that same cultural union that is called the Maroon, and later, Maroon Festival.

Up until the 1970s, older folks would speak candidly about the three major tribes that existed in Union Island –the Kisii Makoa, and Kanka tribes. Each tribe possessed certain salient characteristics; thus, they were easily distinguished one from another. One characteristic of the Makoa tribe is that they are rather reclusive and secretive. The Kisii tribe is said to have originated in Sierra Leone, Liberia, and Guinea, and members were said to have an intrinsic propensity for agriculture.

Let us now return to the Maroon Festival of the nineteenth century, and the first quarter of the twentieth century. The Maroon festival of Union Island and her sister isle Carriacou happened once a year after the island's harvest. Early that morning, everyone would gather at a designated area in the hills.

An abundance of raw foods was taken to the site to be cooked. With huge pots meticulously placed on three-stoned fireplace that was fuel with firewood. These Maroons usually prepare some of the tastiest dishes in the land. In retrospect, it was a competitive spirit that every cook exhibited on that special day. When cooking was finished, and the food was ready, it was blessed. Everyone would eat heartily and complimented each other on their fine dishes. "Aunt Caroline, ah Victual wid the rice and peas and jackfish eat good eh?" Then someone in the crowd may answer, "If you want to taste ah good wangoo pwah, step over here and have a mouthful ah mine." "Aunt Jane Ann, that is some nice Jack fish you have there, ghal," another person might whisper. Amazingly, with many of the older folks, the African dialect was very pronounced, and they spoke very little English. Everyone was totally immersed in the festivity, and they all had a great time.

Today, in the neighboring cay of Carriacou, the annual Maroon festival is much larger than that of Union Island and is celebrated during the final week of April. It is surely a cultural site to experience. The African attire is no different from that of the Afrocolombianos -the early African slaves of Colombia. It will be fascinating for first-time visitors to experience such festive event and atmosphere.

Unlike Union Island, where the African culture has dwindled significantly, the sound of the African drum and accompanying folk's dancers are still a force to be reckoned with in the sister island of Carriacou.

As mentioned earlier, the original maroon festival was held annually on the hillsides, or in the bushes; it was a huge event that lasted all day. During the later years, Clifton Hill became the principal spot for this festivity. This festivity involves the entire population. Foodstuffs consisting mainly of meats fish, rice, flour, cornmeal, peas, beans, ground provisions, and fruits were brought to the locations to be cooked. Some of the largest cooking pots were brought to the site and were placed on a three-stoned fireplace. Firewood was the only source of energy used to fuel the fire, for that was the custom of the natives. It was used at homes prior to the use of the gas and electrical stoves. Some homes still practice this cultural tradition today.

Cultural colors are evident in the African attire

Cooking, however, was preceded by a libation –the pouring of rum, wine, or water on the ground as an offering to the ancestors. There was plenty of food for everyone. Curry goat, Pigeon peas, and rice, fried Jack fish, Conch, sand potatoes, Wangoo and okras, stew chicken, green corn dumplings, Pelau, and wangoo pwah were available all day long. Everyone ate bountifully; no one was a stranger on that day. The Maroon's prime purpose, coupled with the libation, was to give homage to the Gods and the ancestors, and to ask for their blessings in the future. Yes, this was the crux of this mass gathering. And so, a huge portion of the food was taken to the local cemetery, where it was put into huge banana leaves and placed on the tombstones of the deceased. Some of this food was also tossed into the sea, for water in the eyes of the African, is the source of life; water represented life.

The African cultural dance that was performed after the cooking and dining is still prevalent on Union Island after a forceful divorce from the motherland some 260+ years ago. These cultural dances were done to the beat of the African drums, and out of these remarkable sounds came an intrinsic yearning that commanded the body of an onlooker to respond involuntarily:

Open la-la ah me whey dey, open la-la down dey
Open la-la ah me whey dey, open la-la down dey
Open la-la ah dah whey dey, open la-la down dey
Open la-la ah dah whey dey, open la-la down dey.

Sensual in nature, the large gathering sings with vigor to this local song. Meanwhile, the sound of the African dialect became flagrant as the African drum rolled simultaneously with conviction.

The matriarch takes command of the floor, dressed in long African attire, accompanied by two or three men attired in less conspicuous colors. Heads wrapped in a matching fabric; the women would dance in unison as the rolls of the African drum intensified. The tempo suddenly decreases but would pick up momentum again, enticing these women to dance with more vigor. Then instantaneously, one or two of the women would wave their wide skirts over the head of a drummer and dance as the crowd erupts with new energy.

The dancers danced gracefully with passion until it was time for another song. One female would sensually dance her way to the lead drummer and entice him to stop by placing her hands on his drum. The other drummers, immediately aware of her sensuous appeal, would instantly stop their drumming as well. She was in total command, dictating what she wanted, how she wanted it, and when she wanted it. Then almost immediately, the drum would roll again as another song was sung:

Too late, too laa-late, too late too laa-late,
Too late, too laa-late, wee mamma bell shango
Dem ghal laden, dem ghal laden, dem ghal laden
Leh ah-wee go ah Labay

Dem ghal may-may, dem ghal may-may
Dem ghal may-may, ley ah wee go ah Trespass.
Hezekiah don't care, Hezekiah don't care,
Hezekiah don't care, he love he Theo...Dora.

The transition from one song to another was carried out through the duration of the festival.

Ty runaway, Ty runaway,
Ty runaway, Ty run away O,
You nah have mamma,
You nah have papa a,
Ty run away.
Ty ran away, Ty runaway,
Ty run away, Ty runaway ah Batica
You nah have mamma,
Yo nah have papa a
Ty run away.

A typical Maroon night in Carriacou resembles that of Union Island.

These women controlled the streets where the Maroon activities were held with nonstop action. The incessant singing of African folk songs, drumming, and dancing continued with song such as *"Clear the way, clear the way O"* and *"I, I, I Sally-boo-leh,*

I boo-leh, I sally-boo-leh" into the late afternoon or night to end the Maroon celebration. Fortuitously, after each Maroon festival, the nights were never void of an intermittent shower, or at best, a copious rainfall.

Because of the likelihood of rainfall on the day of the Maroon activity, locals during the latter half of the 20th century have associated the annual Maroon festival as an inducer of rain. As a result, the Maroon of latter-date has assumed yet another connotation, which eventually derived an added appellation *–The Rain Maroon.* Today, amidst the Maroon's endangered stature, farmers and residents unwittingly welcome the gratitude of the ostensible Rain-Goddess. Consequently, everyone looks forward to many desirable rainy periods throughout the capricious months that follow this annual festival.

And with *Festive* being the last word, the subject that follows takes us into another Carnival-like atmosphere that was akin to this now archaic custom.

Robbed and deprived of their cultural expressions some 270 years earlier, the descendants of the Africans slaves exhibit their traditional dance during a Maroon Festival.

SHIP LAUNCHING

It is traditional for boats and vessels of Union Island to bear the names of the wife and daughters of the owners.

Called Boat Launching during its heyday is another subject of great importance, for it was an integral part of the lives of Unionites for approximately 130 plus years. Unionites were adept at this craft and did not only built boats, but large vessels were also constructed at the shipyard of Frigate, now called Top Yonder Bay. Before we delve into the meat of this matter, it is quantum sufficit that we once again recognize Union Island as the principal shipbuilding port in the region during the late 19th and early 20th Centuries.

Although Frigate Rock may have been a suitable site for building vessels, Top Yonder Bay was the principal shipyard for most boat builders of Union Island, period! The early years of the twentieth century give rise to the building of the Paragon, Priscilla, Pursuer, and Providence up until July of 1974 when the last significant vessel, the Unity, was built and launched. Moreover, it was during the first half of the nineteenth century (1839) that the first, and largest vessel was built in the region. This huge ship, which was named Katherine, was actually constructed on the soil of Union Island approximately 180 years ago. Now, that is historical!

Let us now take a detailed look at Boat-launching (Vessel) - one of the island's premier cultural practices that suffered a metaphorical Cardiac arrest almost four decades ago.

When any boat or vessel is to be built on the soil of Union Island, the most difficult part of the entire project was to procure the lumber. And the lumber must be brought to the site of the boat-building yard on time. Fortunate for the local shipwrights, the boat-building lumber came from the dense forest of Colon Campbell, Union Island; this area was rife with multiple Cedar trees. Even today, almost two centuries later, lumber can still be got from this densely neglected area of the Island. After the construction of a huge boat or vessel at Top Yonder Bay or Frigate, the logical thing that follows is the launching. Because of the tedious nature of this undertaking, the owner makes it his greatest endeavor to see that everything is meticulously put into place to facilitate a smooth outcome.

The boat/vessel –launching day is an entire day's activity that is wrapped up in festivity. On that day, the entire island descends on Top Yonder Bay or Frigate to perform the traditional ceremony and custom that is related to launching in Union Island. Like a newborn child, the prospective boat or vessel is assigned a godfather and godmother. The owner, priest, or minister, along with other important personnel, proceeds to bless the craft. Praying and singing of hymns are done on site, followed by a libation that is performed at the stern of the craft. The libation is the sprinkling and pouring of rum and/or water on the craft, asking for the guidance and protection of God and the ancestors whenever the vessel makes its first and subsequent voyages at sea.

A designated female places on her head, the cake that was baked for that special event. Her hands are glued to her hips, while she dances to the beat of the African drum and/or other instruments –a spectacle indeed! A collection bucket is made available for anyone who can make a financial contribution or donation. After the dance, the cake is cut into many slices and distributed on the spot as everyone partakes.

As in any home in Union Island that has just lost a loved one, foodstuff, liquors, gifts, money, and livestock is showered in abundance at the home of the vessel's owner ahead of the launching date. The cooking part of this ceremony is the women's responsibility, and they are the absolute best in the region. Elaborate cooking is done to feed the entire village of participants and onlookers who assemble at the launching site. The food is taken to the location of the craft. In only a few more hours it will be shoved and pulled into the water by every man, woman, and child. The entire launching process is fully accomplished by the cooperative efforts of the mass gathering at Top Yonder Bay/Frigate. It is phenomenal for a first-timer to observe the entire activity. This activity entails, the craft being pushed and pulled from the site where it was built until it reaches its final destination – the sea, where it will remain afloat.

It is traditional for boats and vessels of Union Island to bear the names of the wives and daughters of the owners. A typical example is the vessel Sylvia E. M., of the 1970s, which was owned by three locals: Paul, Peter, and Mano. The letter "S" stands for Sylvia, the wife of Mr. Paul Wilson. The "E" stands for Elizabeth, the wife of the late Peter Wilson, and the "M" stands for Mary, the wife of Mano Hutchinson. The latter two are now deceased.

The flag, which bears the name of the boat/vessel, is folded, tightly wrapped and placed on the deck of the ship. The large gathering is eager and impatient to find out the name that will be given to this new craft. All eyes are fixated on the owner, who stands way above on the deck, ready to announce the name of this virgin craft. He unwraps the folded flag and prepares himself to broadcast the name to the huge gathering. The eventual announcement is met with joyful pandemonium by the fleet of onlookers. The blowing of conch shells, the cheering, and the beat of the African drum bring more awakening to the already lively morning.

The vessel/boat must now be placed in a ready position before the entire process of launching can be performed. The vessel is kept upright with many long poles attached to its side and wedged firmly into the earth. Each pole is numbered so as to facilitate the smooth transmission of this part of the activity. A male with a sharp ax is assigned to each pole. He stands alert, while awaits the instruction to chop without floundering; this can be a tense moment for this assignee. With myriad instructions being shouted in this ruckus-like atmosphere, the enthusiasm of the onlookers grows with clapping, cheering, and hollering. The chopping of the pole is meticulously done; to falter at this stage can render severe damage to the craft. The point of culmination arises when the last pole that carries the enormous weight of the craft is chopped, turning the craft on its side and in a ready position for the eventual launching.

A long rope is extended way into the sea to an anchor, which is placed exactly in the vicinity where the boat should be able to float without its keel touching the floor of the sea. This anchor should be sturdy enough to endure the strenuous task of the pulling. A line of people is tethered to the other end of the rope, with a block and tackle placed midway to ease the process of launching (pull the craft into the sea). Under the keel of the craft are tree trunks or logs lined up as rollers to aid its smooth transition into the water. These rollers are placed slightly ahead of the craft, to the spot where it is supposed to move. The stern of the boat is also secured with ropes to prevent it from leaning and sliding out of control and incurring injuries. With authoritative instructions given, men, women, and, children grab the rope firmly and begin to pull, but in the opposite direction of the craft; others literally shove the craft in the direction of the sea.

The pulling and shoving continued with lulls after each effort so that participant can rest during such a tiresome task. When the vessel reaches the water, a loud cacophony erupts as everyone is jubilated. The atmosphere becomes a gala as the crew is energized to push the boat further into the water. As soon as the vessel begins to float, a few bottles of liquor are smashed into its stern. This symbolizes a task well done.

Ashore, the bacchanal climaxes with elaborate eating, drinking, socializing, and dancing to the beat of the African drum and other instruments brought for that special event. This entire day's activity continues until sundown, and everyone happily goes home. Later on, in the street of Union Island, the feeling of community is still evident as residents can be found fondly discussing the success of the day's event.

Sadly, this major event is approximately four decades removed from the soil of Union Island, for the last ship, The Unity was built and launched at Top Yonder Bay in the year 1974. Today we can only crave the renaissance of Boat launching in Union Island. Gone are the days of these major social activities that retain the semblance of cohesiveness of Unionites on Union Island.

Such is the case with another annual event that is festive in nature but has long met its demise at the hands of evolution. That annual event is **The Union Island Carnival** of yesteryear. Let us peruse the contents of this, another defunct event that is meticulously defined in the pages that follow.

THE UNION ISLAND CARNIVAL

"Boy you is ah Stroad! I can't tell exactly what side ah the family you belongs, but I know ah Stroad is ah Stroad."

For well over two decades the annual Easter festive season of early April is called Easterval, a combination of the word Easter and Festival. This season is drenched with a myriad of activities that encompass a Carnivalesque atmosphere. These activities attract mass regional attention as well as residents of Europe and the Americas. Lots of people find their way back home for a full week or two of thorough enjoyment, entertainment, and play. During the earlier years, the annual carnival festivity was very artistic and cultural. It encompassed many bands with elaborate costumes that were skillfully displayed in the streets of Ashton and Clifton. Today, Jouvert (Jump Up) begins very early in the morning as masqueraders dance in the streets to music that is played loudly on trucks. This "jump up" as it is called, starts at the basketball court, travels to Cross Road, Bordeaux, and on to Richmond Beach where it ends. Every segment of this now archaic festive event (Union Island Carnival) was meaningful and possessed a great deal of cultural significance.

For the carnival of yesteryear, all of the costume bands would make their way to the Magistrate House at Clifton Hill. There they would perform at their best, exhibit their artistic skills and prowess, and subsequently be judged. Calypso competition was another activity of note. Young men and women of Union were very competitive for each year's calypso crown.

The atmosphere then was thick with excitement as residents crowded the streets in droves, eager to be a part of this annual celebration. Many can still remember the 1969 carnival of Union Island when the street of Ashton was alive with the melodious sound of Trinidad & Tobago's "Road March Queen" Calypso Rose. Everyone was gleeful as they sang along to her song, "Fire, Fire in me Wire, Wire."

Carnival of yesterday dates back to more than eight decades ago, for that atmosphere was rife with numerous activities. The History Mass of Union Island was phenomenal; every onlooker's eyes were glued to these characters. The historical rendition of European history and speeches were performed by older men that were dressed in elaborate kilt-like costumes, coupled with adornments that resembled those of a knight. They danced with an extremely long whip while intentionally projecting a mean-spirited appearance. Valuable characters such as Ernest McTair, Claude Ambrose, James Stewart and his brother Henry Stewart, Peter Alexander, and the flamboyant Willie Edwards (the grandfather of Mrs. Merle Ackie) were all integral players of this artistic legacy. These were the key players in this once noteworthy History Mass of Union Island. The generations of today have lost interest and do not exhibit the same level of skill or dexterity. The badge of honor once held by these players, whose profound knowledge of British history was unrivaled, is now archaic, for want of a better word.

Traditionally, the History Masses of Ashton and Clifton had to exhibit some form of make-believe rivalry among each other before they could make a pact among themselves. The site of this eventful gathering was Ce Courtney Bridge. You may ask, where is Ce Courtney Bridge? It's the same bridge that lies some seventy feet east of Cross Road in Ashton, which is now called the Dry-River Bridge. Ce Courtney Bridge attained its name from a native of Barbados named Mrs. Courtney Wilson. She was the grandmother of the late Augustine Cox, who has lived in that area for many years. So, this location was where the two factions of the History Masses of Union Island would meet. The Clifton faction needed permission to cross Ce Courtney Bridge, so the Ashton faction would engage them with numerous questions of European origin, taunting with their whips. Satisfactory responses usually resulted in an immediate pact and free passage over the bridge. An unsatisfactory response might result in a gesture-like whipping. In reality, this gesture was more of a custom and formality than an authentic rivalry.

Everyone descended on Cross Road Junction (Green Corner), and around the Small School area, which was the center of this mass gathering and all other carnival activities. The Crossroad location was home to the popular Allan Scrubb, the grandfather of Mrs. Icena Wilson. Bah Allan, as he was popularly called, once had a shop exactly in the location that his great-grandson Kendall Wilson now occupies.

Many of these History Masses could approach any onlooker and demand money. The late Henry Stewart was famous for his two-line rendition: "Hezekiah give me meh Cora, Hezekiah give me meh Cora." No one seemed to understand what he meant as he shouted loudly while brandishing his huge whip. The victim would become scared and reach into his pocket to dispense the pound, shilling, pence, or ha'penny (whatever he had); he then would hand it over to the masked man (Henry) who would quickly take his fee and retreat quietly to sort out another victim.

The pound, shilling, pence, and ha'penny were the monetary units that were used back then. The smallest unit, the ha'penny, was worth half of a penny. They all were a part of the British monetary system still used in the Caribbean more than half a century ago. These coins have since been replaced by the Eastern Caribbean dollar, quarter, nickel, dime, and penny.

So yes, the carnival was practically a whole day affair that encompassed numerous activities. Older folks can remember the late Cornelius Jones of Canouan Island, the father of Reginald Jones of Clifton. Cornelius was well known for his colorful Indian attire; he participated annually in the Indian Mass with singing and dancing that depicted the East Indian culture. The East Indian culture became pervasive in the Caribbean after Indians from the country of India were brought to Trinidad and Guyana as indentured servants. We can see clearly that all of these cultural attributes and elements that were interpolated into this eventful Gala did have their rightful place.

The numerous activities that are associated with the annual Easterval gala resurrect the feeling of homesickness each year in the hearts and minds of nationals that are living abroad. Returning home to a slower lifestyle, every visitor tends to let his or her guard down just to relax and take it easy. The white sandy beaches are readily available, and no one knows these beaches better than a returning native. They are ready to assume ownership of the island that they left decades ago without fully acknowledging the changes that have occurred. The conch, fresh fish, crabs, goat, and locally grown chicken are accepted and savored with joyful readiness. The corn-fish is relished; the roast corn, green-corn dumplings, wangoo and okras, sea moss, and a host of local delicacies are treasured like never before.

The Easterval celebration is indeed a time to shake a leg. A returning native won't be hesitant to do so; he or she is always in the thick and thin of all activities on the roster. Though there's not much nightlife in Union Island, during the evening, visitors are amble everywhere in the streets. Everyone knows each other, remember? So, a feeling of cohesiveness enables everyone to feel at home once again. And amazingly, the visitor reverts to the dialect of his youthful years. You are never a stranger there, for there is always someone who can clearly identify your bloodline and speak profoundly about your ancestors. "Boy, you is ah Stroad! I can't tell exactly what side ah the family you belong. I know ah Stroad when ah see one; ah Stroad is ah Stroad. Boy, you not Rodwell? Incoman, not your father? Ok then." (Stroad is a local name used in Union Island that refers to the family name Stewart. Older folks today still used that name regularly).

Basketball completions, Queen Show, and parties make up the night's activities while boat racing (Regatta) and other sporting events are done during the daytime.

Lennox Charles, a Unionite now living in Europe, revived the Steel Pan orchestra in Union Island during the early 1970s. As a result, the band was able to compete against other steel band orchestras in St. Vincent during Carnival festival. His little orchestra was judged and attained the second position. Lennox also introduced basketball to Union Island during that same period.

Union Island is definitely the place to be during the active month of April each year. It is a month that is rivaled by no other time of the year; even the famed Christmas holiday of today is pale in comparison to the numerous activities of April.

FISHING

Remember when many fathers and young men would descend on the shores to meet these fishermen to help haul the catch ashore?

¥ou the reader will observe that the history of Union Island commenced with the French during the latter years of 1750, followed by the English, and the Treaty of Paris in 1763. In researching the history of Union Island, you will also observe that every event during such time is inappropriately centered on the year, 1763. Why? Is it because of the enormity of the above mention pact that brought closure to the Seven-Year War between Great Britain and France? Surely, it is! Therefore, it is prudent to enunciate that any history that was not inclusive of the European presence on Union Island was considered non-historical, negligible or at best, or peripheral in nature. The original people whom the French had met on the island were never considered a part of the human family. And so, it must be acknowledged that fishing in the waters of the Grenadines is an old industry; it did not start during the time of the French intervention, and later the Treaty of Paris, which ushered in the British in the islands. Instead, it has been in existence many, many centuries before the European's presence, point blank.

The Amerindians who were the inhabitants of this region some 5,400 years BC used fishing as an integral part of their livelihood and for survival. The French, during the 16th Century too, made a fortune in the Grenadines, a region that is rife with turtles and a wide variety of fishes and the Humpback whale. The French in the region, exported to Europe via Grenada and Martinique, the shells and preserved meat of the turtles. They, in turn, made a fortune from this business. During the 16th, 17th and 18th centuries, Union Island was a hub for the French privateers that traversed the waters of the Grenadines on their multiple voyages to the larger islands in the region.

During the latter part of the 19th century, onward to the first quarter of the 20th Century, Richard Mulzac made fishing and whaling an essential part of his entrepreneurship on Union Island. The cotton industry, on the other hand, had seen its better days and was quickly declining into oblivion. During those earlier years, fishing was done on a very large scale as opposed to what is now referred to as *grossly insignificant* in recent years.

The absence of a viable fishing industry in the Grenadines represents a significant loss of Union Island's livelihood and culture; and not just Union Island, but today we will speak primarily about Union because it is the center of focus. Thus, this island is now experiencing a drastic reduction in fishing-related activities along the once-trafficked shorelines. As a result, it now appears that the last sound of the conch shell has gracefully made its way into total oblivion. Well... almost. Esteem names such as Aaron Douglas, Woodley Cox, Sylvan Hutchinson, David John (Gayman), Willy Daniel (Santas), Ozias Paul, and Gifted Wilson were the vertebral column of the fishing industry that existed in Union Island for many decades. These names were household names to every resident who lived on Union Island during the 60s, 70s, and 80s. After all, the island is small enough that everyone knows each other.

Is there really a shortage of fish in Union Island? Just two decades ago, such a notion could not have been conceived. But time has changed drastically. Residents of Union Island are now living in a time when old ideas are superseded by new ideas. Somewhat. Can Unionites realistically believe that they can erect a protective covering over their culture, and that shell will safely shield it from extinction without employing adequate maintenance? Absolutely not! For these kinds of changes are contingent on the evolutionary forces of nature.

There is a complete shortage of home cooking along the local fishing grounds. So, where does subsistence come in? Subsistence always meant a lot to Union Island and the rest of the Grenadines. For the records, a subsistent economy is an economy in which enough food is grown, hunted, or gathered to provide for the people. A surplus is grown only if a community desires or need to trade with neighboring communities. But to the dismay of many, even subsistent fishing has dwindled to an unprecedented low. Of course, it is unrealistic to expect things to remain one way forever, but isn't it baffling that it is now status quo to be buying fish regularly from the neighboring islands? Of course, there must be a feeling of guilt and inadequacy. After all, Ashton Bay, Basin, and Chatham bays were large breeding grounds for Jackfish that once made up a major part of the gross domestic product of the island. And jackfish, in particular, was once prevalent in their diets. This begs the question: Why haven't the Wangoo and okra been mentioned as Union Island's national dish?

Remember long ago when the aforementioned fishermen cast their large nets at Campbell and made huge catches? Remember when many fathers and young men would descend on the shores to meet these same fishermen and to help haul the huge catches ashore? Remember when these fishermen, after spending numerous hours at sea, would return with their catch to be greeted by an elder? These fishermen would, in turn, give a small portion of their catch to such elders? Remember when the sound of the conch shell was the only means to alert the community that fish was available and being sold? Are the Silent Generation, the Traditionalist and baby boomers the final bearers of these memories in that whenever they transition, these priceless memories will die as well? O well.

The calf of a Sperm Whale, trapped in the lagoon of Ashton Harbor while lurking in the calm waters of Union Island (2010 photo).

These fishermen were rather determined and purposeful with the little that they started out with. Their fishing techniques increased over the years out of necessity and through an increase of knowledge, awareness, skills, and determination. After all, they were the patriarchs and were responsible for providing food, clothes, and shelter for their families and the communities. These were some of the cogent values and customs that were etched into the cornerstone of the culture of Union Island, and these fishermen had known it no other way.

Out of big catches, boatloads of Jackfish were transported to Grenada on a regular basis for sale; the island of Grenada was the sole market for these huge catches. When the fishermen could not sell all of these Jackfish, they would employ the bartering system. They would exchange for ground provision, mangoes, and other fruits, the unsold quantity of Jackfish rather than returning with them to Union Island. The same boats that left laden with fish a couple of days earlier would return laden with mangoes, fruits, and other ground provisions. Remember when these fishermen would freely give some of their mangoes to the children standing by watchfully? Today, the island's fishermen have abandoned the use of seins and trammels. Unfortunately, the art of fishing or the legacy of fishing at such high scale has come to an unprecedented low.

Were there no fruits of youthful industry planted in the hearts and minds of the younger generation? The author mentioned earlier that many baby boomers and subsequent generations had immigrated unwittingly to other countries in search of a better life; that, of course, has become a trend in itself. Nevertheless, the question must still be posed: Where are the knowledge, beliefs, morals, laws, arts, and customs of Union Island's society? The values? These, and many more important issues that pertain to the island's demise are worth considering; Like the Silent Generation and Traditionalist, the Baby Boomers are also convinced that the virtues and backbone of the island's culture are nearly lost. Which do you like better, the environment of yesterday or that of today? Do you love the Union Island then, or now?

TURTLES IN THE REGION

The Grenadines are home to these four species of turtles, which are seen in abundance at the Tobago Cays Resort

Seen in the distant are four beautiful islands of the Tobago Cays.

For centuries, the coral-filled waters of the Grenadines have been home to the Hawksbill (Eretmochelys imbricate), Leatherback (Dermochelys coriacea), Loggerhead ((Caretta-Caretta), and Green turtles (*Chelonian Mydas*). Residents know very well that the beaches of Big Sand, Point Lookout, Ms. Irene, Ms. Pay, Chatham, Bloody Bay, and Queensbury Point have been safe havens for these reptilian wonders that come in annually to give birth to hundreds of their offspring.

During the mid 17th Century until the arrival of Antoine Rigaud and his compatriots, Grenada & the Grenadines have been a huge hunting and fishing ground for the French. The most sought-after was the shell of the proliferous turtles in the region. These turtle shells (primarily green turtle) were a excellent source of income for these Frenchmen who exported them to Europe via Martinique and Grenada. Today, surprisingly, the Loggerhead is not frequently seen on the sandy beaches of the Grenadines as much as they were during their gestation period in the past.

Regional fishermen seldom see the Loggerhead even at sea. It is said that this species of turtle is endangered internationally. During the month of March –gestation period, these reptiles approach their place of birth three times in forty-five days, eager to bury their fortune under the densely fine fossils. There these secured embryos take approximately two months to hatch. To poachers, the demand for this seasonal commodity is insatiable; the freshly laid eggs of these turtles are a delicacy when boiled. Long ago, poachers were adept at identifying the fresh tracks made by these creatures whenever they came upon the land to lay their eggs. Some poachers were clever enough to determine the age of the turtle by carefully observing the texture of the freshly laid eggs. They could also determine whether it was the first time that a turtle had returned to the place of its birth to lay its eggs.

But turtle hunting is not novel in the waters of the Grenadines. It has been a legacy that dated back many, many years ago. In fact, Antoine Rigaud and Jean Augier, the French used turtles as a source of food during late 1750 when they first laid foot on Union Island. And as mentioned before, the shell of this reptile was also a valuable commodity for trade. But even before the existence of the French, the Amerindians used the meat of turtles as one of their principal food sources. Today, although there is a decline in numbers, generally, turtles are still plentiful in the region. Thanks to Tobago Cays Marine Park, a national park and wildlife preserve of St. Vincent & the Grenadines. The Tobago Cays are an archipelago of five small-uninhabited islands, namely: Petit Rameau, Petit Bateau, Petit Tabac, Baradal, and Jamesby.

The Grenadines are home to the four species of turtles, which are mentioned above. These turtles are seen in abundance at the Tobago Cays Resort all year round but are more proliferous during their gestation periods. The Carib Grackle (blackbird) and the iguana are also native to four of these pristine islands (Tobago Cays). This is a spectacle for tourist and visitors.

For centuries, the natives of Union Island have considered the meat and eggs of these reptiles as an invaluable commodity compared to the meats of other sea animals. For that reason, no one would pass up the opportunity to unearth these delectable eggs and then catch the turtle fifteen days later. Fortunately, the Union Island Environmental Attackers, a nonprofit organization, has assumed the vanguard in hopes of preventing the extinction of these reptilian wonders. They are also engaged in the servicing of other meaningful projects on the island. Those other projects range from quarterly island cleanups, which addresses sanitation and garbage removal, to health talks at schools, adopt-a-tree programs, and a host of valuable undertakings that are meaningful and productive for the island as a whole.

The Union Island Environmental Attackers patrol numerous beaches to promote the successful nesting of these endangered sea creatures. Because local poachers are the number one predator, the organization monitors the eggs until the hatchlings are born and heads to sea to face yet other predatory challenges. It is estimated that an average of one out of every thousand Leatherback turtles, (largest species) survives to adulthood.

To discourage poachers and inquisitive hands from unearthing these embryos, the Ministry of Fisheries implemented a maximum fine of $5,000 EC for anyone that is caught. Seldom has anyone been found guilty of such infraction since this legal enactment. Through seminars, the people must be informed and educated about the plight that these turtles face to keep their population alive when the odds are stacked highly against their survival in the wild. On a turtle watch of March 2011, one of those ageless wonders (Leatherback turtle) inherited the European name Analese. This successful tagging was conducted by the Union Island Environmental Attackers under the stewardship of Mr. Roseman Adams, an entrepreneur of Clifton. We hope that with other successful tagging in the future, prospective turtles will bear names that are native to these shores -names such as Lydian, Janie, Annie, Sheila, Serena, Norma, Caroline, Virginia, Susana, Leah, *Isabella* and Thelma. The myriad of sentiments that accompany these familiar names surely wouldn't hurt either.

To aid in maintaining a safe haven in the region for all marine life, the ecology of the region must be protected. Protection encompasses the preservation of mangrove coastlands, shallow reefs, and beaches that engulf this skimpy landmass. A landmass that is equivalent to a mere 3.5 sq. Miles, a source of life and home of the turtle and other valuable resources.

◆◆◆□*Chapter Four*

SUBSISTENCE FARMING

In the year1931, exactly one year after the death of Richard Mulzac, there was a grave mishap at the cotton gin.

It cannot be overstated that the long dry season experienced annually in Union Island is the sole reason why Unionites are inclined to use water very sparingly. In short, water conservation is paramount on the island to prevent water shortage. There is not much difference between the conditions today and those of a century ago, or even two centuries ago; Union Island has a semi-arid climate, and the island can be exceedingly dry during the relentless dry season that begins in the month of November and lasts throughout April. The island is disadvantaged in that it does not possess a rainforest or rivers like the mainland (St. Vincent) do; hence water conservation is integral to the life of the people. Water shortage is not exclusive to Union Island and the rest of the Grenadines Islands; it extends to the mainland of St. Vincent when there is an extremely dry year.

As mentioned before, in Union Island, there are no rivers, public desalination plants, or major reservoirs to provide, supply, and distribute water throughout the island to the people. Hence, the island remains devoid of water pipelines and may remain that way for another couple of generations. Unfortunately, the only source of clean drinking water is the water that has been conserved in cisterns and water tanks during the intermittent rainy season. The rainy season begins in the month of May and lasts until late November or December. Recent notions had it that a vibrant rainy season is contingent on Unionites successfully ingratiating themselves to the rain-god during the annual Maroon festival. Unfortunately, this perception is far removed from the truth and is facetious at best.

Unlike the mainland, St. Vincent, whose principal crops are

bananas, plantains, breadfruits, sweet potatoes, etc. The main crops of Union Island are now corn and pigeon peas. For decades, corn and peas were grown extensively throughout the island but decreased immensely during the early eighties and nineties. Unfortunately, the level of cultivation has never returned to its previous form. Acres of land that were once cultivated with vast quantities of corn, pigeon peas, cassava, okras, potatoes, pumpkins, watermelons, and peanuts (groundnuts) now lie barren to the ever-present shrubs and some species of trees that are deemed nuisances to the vegetation.

Cotton was the principal crop that generated a substantial sum of money over the years when the landowners did not have to pay for its production. Cotton met its ultimate demise in the late 1960s–70s, but in reality, the cotton industry was impacted negatively after the abolition of slavery in 1834. There were two types of cotton in the region; they were Marie Galante and Sea-Island Cotton. The latter supplanted the former because the plant was not as huge as its counterpart (Marie Galante) and was much more productive as well. Yet, one of the impediments of Sea-Island Cotton crops was that they were more prone to worms than their cousin (Marie Galante). As a result, inspectors made sure that new plants replaced old plants annually. The main advantage of doing so was that the smaller plants made the cotton much more assessable during the period of harvesting. During its heyday, it was said that the cotton crop generated an average of about £250.000 per annum; this is quite a substantial amount of income, but it could be attained only under the auspices of chattel labor.

Several years after Charles Mulzac assumed command of the cotton industry, a cotton gin was introduced on the island. It aided in the cleaning of the product before export. This very useful machine supplanted manpower, a process whereby sharecroppers struggled to separate the multiple cottonseeds from the valuable fibers, which was used for fabrics. The ever-present seeds of this plant were useful for the production of cottonseed oil, a vegetable oil widely used for cooking. The cholesterol content of the cottonseed is very low compared to that of many edible oils. The foods fried in this oil maintain a long shelf life because of its antioxidant qualities; this was a plus when conservation was of concern during those earlier days.

Observing his father's health declining rapidly, Richard Mulzac assumed command of the challenging cotton business. A few years later, he handed the responsibility to his son Irvin so that he could focus his attention Fishing & whaling, regional marine trade, and on the large herd of cattle that they reared. He also conducted extensive marine trade in the region. Like Richard, Irvin was a shipwright by trade, a profession that he inherited from a family of boat builders. His extraordinary skill in boat caulking placed him on a pedestal way above everyone who caulks boats on the island. The cotton gin that he operated was located in the vicinity of the Sunny Grenadines Hotel, which was located above the home of Mrs. Adela James, a resident of Ashton Village. The steps of this ancient building are still visible today, many years after the building was razed.

In 1931, exactly one year after the death of Richard Mulzac, there was a mishap at the cotton gin. This sudden accident caused a young female worker to lose one of her arms. Dora Campbell of Ashton Village, a female in her late twenties, was employed at the Mulzac Cotton Gin. She was an excellent worker, in a position that Mr. Irvin Mulzac and his wife Esther, the younger sister of Edith Alves, thought she had been well fitted to, and might even be irreplaceable. One morning while she was feeding the raw cotton through the spinning cylinder of the cotton gin, her left hand got caught in the teeth of the machine. Mr. Gifted Ramage, her coworker who was stationed at another part of the factory, heard her screams but misinterpreted the sound of her voice. He later saw the bloody discolored cotton and surmised that something drastic might have happened to the young lady. He tried to alert other workers of his finding, but the words of the stuttering young man were uncharacteristically vague and unclear. Without help available, the young mother's left arm was severed all the way up to her shoulder. She received medical attention later that day.

This young lady immediately assumed the name "One- hand Dora. "But the loss of her arm did not prohibit her from doing her daily chores or living a normal life, for she was still able to cook, wash, and use her garden hoe proficiently. The name "One-hand Dora" stuck with her for the rest of her life. She died in her sunset years in 1972.

Three decades after the injury at the gin, a continual decrease of cotton production on the island coupled with other commercial problems resulted in the permanent demise of the once lucrative cotton industry. Subsequently, the factory was rendered out of commission due to inactivity. In essence, it marked the death of an industry that lasted well over 170 years.

Now with corn and pigeon peas being the principal crops on the island, were they the staple of the natives' diet? Many may be inclined to say, "Was," but time will be the litmus test as this crop delves deeper into the twenty-first century. Up until the late 1980s, every family was engaged in the planting or sowing of seeds. Secondary crops such as cassava, okra, sorrel, and pumpkin were also sown simultaneously.

A typical garden in Union Island. Corn & Pigeon peas are the principal crops.

The seeds or kernels of corn are sown in holes twelve inches wide by four inches deep, which are approximately three feet apart. Six or seven seeds are then scattered into the dug holes and covered with soil. Pigeon peas, on the other hand, are planted in smaller holes about eight inches in diameter by four inches deep parallel to the corn. Four seeds of pigeon peas are scattered into these holes and covered with dirt. Then four or five days later, new plants emerge from the earth. The corn germinates a little faster; it is a member of the grass family. It is wise to soak the seed of both the corn and peas in a container of water ahead of time to accelerate germination. The seedling at this stage takes minimal a amount of time to germinate. Two days and they are up out of the earth.

The seedlings of the pigeon peas take a little longer - emerging in another two days. The fresh seedlings are in their vulnerable stage and can easily fall victim to worms and the ever-present blackbirds. Every Unionite is familiar with the destructive nature of the ubiquitous Blackbird. Children often hear their parents and older folks talk about how they were not allowed to attend school as often as they should because they had to stay at home to guard the seedlings against these notorious birds, whose proper name is the Carib Grackle. As small as the Tropical Mockingbird (Parka Change-Jay), this Blackbird of Union Island is notoriously destructive by nature. It cuts the shoot of the young germinating corn in its quest to gain access to the seeds under the earth. And it continues, incessantly cutting each young seedling from hole to hole and then scratching the ground for the seeds until it has its full. Then it flies away to a neighbor. That is why six or seven seeds are put into one hole with the expectation that one or two may fall victim to the blackbird or fail to germinate. Sometimes many corn-holes are void of corn because the Blackbird is the first visitor. In many gardens, corn is replanted over and over because some holes may be short of two or three plants as a result of the Blackbird's undoing. This is just one of the hurdles that the farmers of Union Island have endured to get the crop from one stage to another.

At one time, the Scarecrow (Bwar-Bwar) was used to deter the Blackbird from its incessant destruction on the cornfield, and it did work for quite some time. After a few weeks, however, it appeared that those Blackbirds had done their careful observation and analysis and realized that these humanlike figures didn't move except when the wind blew. They began to land and defecate on them for good measure. As a result, the problem of the Blackbird was back where it started and remained a permanent one for many years.

Everyone disliked the blackbird; young chaps would set numerous traps to catch them alive.

Fortunately, the problem of the menacing blackbird on Union Island during the rainy months is no more. Is it because of the vast reduction of corn cultivation that was once practiced throughout the island? Or is it that the diet of the blackbird has evolved over a period of years? Whatever the reason is, it is clear that some other type of food has replaced this bird's affinity for corn.

"Long ago, blackbirds were lethal enemy number one to every gardener, but they are almost domesticated these days. They land a few inches away from us, unconcerned about the presence of humans as they make their pursuit for the same cooked food that we eat." These were the words of Kenneth, a resident of Ashton as he explained the disparity between the Blackbird of today and those of yesterday. "Long ago, they were fiercely hunted down, almost into oblivion," Kenneth continued. "In fact, we used to set traps for them, and whenever one was caught, its feathers were drenched with kerosene and lit on fire, and it was allowed to fly to its instant doom."

Picture of the ubiquitous Carib Grackle (Black Bird) on a mangrove twig.

During the heyday of the corn & peas crop of Union Island, no one was remorseful about the brutal death of a blackbird at the hands of a farmer. The children who were the watchdogs of the gardens sang this song.

Ay, ba Nattie blackbirds pass straight and go your way,
Mapu ripped ah Banta pick em up and say poo
Ay, ba Nattie blackbirds pass straight and go your way,
Long way for you to go, Mapu ripe ah Banta,
Time fo ah-we go home.

Children throughout the island sang this song in their gardens during the early hours of the morning to stave off the Blackbird while it was most aggressive. They also had to be attentive during the late afternoon because these birds were not easily deterred. They actually thought that the Blackbird in some way understood the song that they sang and would eventually go away. Mapu, as mentioned in the song, is a small purple-black fruit that grows on an evergreen tree, the Mapu tree. It was a favorite fruit of the local birds, especially the Blackbird.

The name Ba Nattie, from the above song, speaks of one of the sons of William McDowell Stewart. The notorious blackbirds often attacked the freshly germinated corn on his plantation.

Another significant problem related to the corn crop in Union Island was the infestation of worms. These worms, or caterpillars as they are called, feed greedily on the corn leaves before they make their long transformation into the pupae stage to complete their metamorphosis. So, there were quite a few problems and challenges before the people could even get to the point of harvesting a drum (barrel) or two of corn and pigeon peas.

Corn took approximately three months from the time of sowing to harvesting. And although the plant didn't require much intensive care, corn and its immediate sibling, pigeon peas, had to weather the storm of challenges met by grazing animals. Cows, goats, sheep, and even pigs could not resist the temptation of lush green cultivation. Animals caught inflicting damage on any plantation could be pounded (seized until the owner paid a ransom for the damage wreaked by his livestock). In most cases, these animals were returned to the owners without charge because people during those early years had a very strong sense of cohesiveness that transcended beyond monetary value; it was a condition that is almost nonexistent today, unfortunately. Communal lifestyle was the order of the day and was one of the strong values that existed decades ago.

During the time of corn harvesting, some are picked while the bulk remains on the plants to dry a couple of weeks later. They are later harvested, and the corn stalks are carefully cut to make room for the pigeon peas to grow. The harvested corn is then placed on caucus bags or canvas and left out in the sun to dry while still on the cob. After two weeks of drying in the sun, the corn is manually removed from the cob (shelled) and placed on

These same caucus bags or canvas to further dry in the sun; at this time, 80 percent of the liquid has been extracted through the sun's heat. By then, the entire drying process is completed, and the corn is then poured into huge steel drums for storage. Many local farmers take pride in growing huge amounts of corn—more than two drums. Farmers during the old days were actually dedicated to agriculture and would put in the labor and sacrifice to gain the best yield possible. At the end of a good corn season, every farmer would have enough corn to last beyond another year of harvesting. After one year in these huge barrels or drums, the corn was referred to as old corn. During such time, a new crop would again be harvested.

Corn had multiple uses. One major use was as feed for the poultry that was present in everyone's homes. A significant amount of these fowls is reared for poultry and fresh eggs. Chilli-Bibbi, another product of corn, is a powered-like candy that is made from ground patch corn (popcorn). Sugar and spices are added to embellish its fine taste. This candy, of course, is every kid's delight.

Every home had two grain-mills; one for making cornmeal while the other is used for grinding the pre-dry corn to make green-corn dumpling. Cornmeal is used for making Wangoo and Wangoo-Pwah, which every native relished. The latter is a recipe in which pigeon peas are integrated into the cornmeal to make a very delicious dish. This recipe for both dishes and other delicious dishes can be found in *The Stewart Cookbook of Union Island's Favorite Recipes.* The unfortunate issue that stands today is: Every generation that came after the early baby boomers of Union Island are unable to cook efficiently, a native dish of cornmeal. And this encompasses Green Corn Dumpling, Wangoo & Okra, and the inimitable Wangoo Pwah dishes.

During the months of December through February, the peas crop is ready to be harvested. While the green peas are relished by every Unionite, the bulk of the peas are left on the trees for several weeks to dry. When the peas are harvested, the farmer will cut the old plants from the plantation and heap the shrubs into several huge bundles. Several weeks later, each huge bundle will be lit on fire; the fire-mass is locally called a *Buccan* -a word that is derived from a wooden frame on which the Tainos and Caribs slowly roasted or smoked their meats.

The women of Union Island are undoubtedly some of the best chefs in the region -second to none in local culinary art. Mrs. Eileen Stewart, Mrs. Jenny Charles, and many others have migrated to North America but attained their cooking skills directly or indirectly from Union Island and have kept the legacy alive. Having a dish of Pelau with locally grown pigeon peas from the kitchen of Mrs. Norma Thomas of Ashton Village will evoke a severe feeling of longing. If a stranger is served this dish, he/she may be tempted not to leave without having acquired the recipe. The sad truth here is, it is not what is done, but how it is done. And indeed, cooking in Union Island is done with passion. Again, *The Stewart Cookbook of Union Island's Favorite Recipes,* dedicated to the late great **William McDowell Stewart**, the patriarch of the Stewart family of Union Island is now available to all. Every Unionite should own a copy of this book; in fact, it should be in everyone's kitchen if they are adamant about keeping the legacy alive for their children and the children of their children.

Pigeon pea, as mentioned, is another predominant crop on the island. This crop, like corn, assumed the position as the chief crop from its ancestral predecessor, cotton. While these two crops may not be extinct on the island, it is believed that they will meet their demise in the near future. Sweet and bitter cassavas (yucca) are yet another crop that was home to Union Island. It made its way to the island as a crop to feed the slaves due to its rich content of carbohydrates. This gave the slaves the required energy to work hard and long hours on the plantation. Sweet and bitter cassavas are distinct in color; the stem and leaves of the sweet cassava have a pinkish color while the bitter is darkish green. The bitter cassava was used extensively by the local women to make farine and cassava bread even into the 1970s. Today, this practice is archaic. The women of Union Island were the rulers of the land, the homes, and the garden while the men were the rulers of the sea. The women of that day played a major role in the production and manufacturing of food.

Well then, what has contributed to such a massive decline in agricultural production in Union Island? Did the ancestors err in passing on the baton to the current generations such that it has significantly impacted the culture of the island? As mentioned before, the aversion to working the land, which has spiraled down through generations is a very critical factor that should be looked at carefully. Today's generations have willingly relinquished some essential building blocks, particularly in agriculture. This entailed abandoning the hoes, cutlasses, and plows, and disassociating themselves from the laborious task that accompanies gardening. From their perspective, they have never experienced or witnessed the gains of the land translated into dollars and cents. Another important consideration is the ever-present force of technological transformation that youngsters are unwittingly swayed into. It is here to stay. And now, the big question, "The Exodus Factor." Is it so consuming that masses of Unionites cannot resist its gravitational pull? Is it because of Union Island's size, coupled with its daunting semi-arid climate, a dearth of jobs, educational opportunities, and the legacy of governmental disenfranchisement that the island has inherited since the time of Charles Mulzac? These issues and much more must now be looked at objectively.

Natives will accede that Subsistence Farming is a thing of the past, for they are now inclined to frequent the stores and supermarkets for all of their staples. They regularly visit the neighboring island of Carriacou for staples that were present in their backyards just a few decades ago. During the golden days, rain represented productivity, which rendered lots to eat, stock up, and sell. It was at that time that every household took up their garden hoes, cutlasses, forks, and rakes to till the land in preparation for farming.

ENDANGERED ARTS & CUSTOMS

Fire on Top; Fire Below   *Roast Bakes*

With the debacle of the cotton crop during the late nineteenth century, this new atmosphere has given way to other means of survival on the island. The Mulzacs were owners of many vessels, and they transported cargo regionally to other Caribbean countries. They fished extensively in the waters of the Grenadines and also had numerous livestock. This legacy is one that was handed down through the years and had become a way of life for the people of Union Island. There were also other means of livelihood that the people practiced. Regrettably, they were struck violently by the hands of evolution and had since met their demise. These other means encompass the corn & pea crops as well as the exportation of tamarind, Cornish, Divi-Divi, crabs, chicken (fowl), sea moss, and sugar apples to Trinidad. Their absence represents a significant economic loss to an already frail economy.

There are some practices that once were a dominant part of the culture when subsistence was integral to the lives of the people on this little island. The following are just a few:

Corned Fish

Fish catching has always been fundamental to every fisherman in Union Island, and although there isn't a huge market on the island for the freshly caught product, no one can dispute its immense contribution to the diets of every Unionite. Corn fish is the fish that is salted and dried in the sun, a method of preservation that is used for centuries by the natives. With this method, the fish can be kept for several months before use. It is similar to the salted codfish or Bacalao that is used universally.

This is how corn fish is done on Union Island. First, the scales are removed from the fish, and then the head is sliced in half, all the way through the dorsal fins to the tail. The fish still remains in one piece as the intestines and gills are removed. Numerous vertical incisions are made in the flesh so that the salt, which is used as a preservative can penetrate rather easily. A dose of salt is meticulously sprinkled into every incision of the fish's flesh. The fish is then folded and placed in a container for at least an hour so that the salt can penetrate further into the flesh. It is then placed in the sun, on a galvanize roof to dry. Long ago, the choice location was the roof of the external kitchen, where two days of drying would extract 90 percent of the water. This dry, salted fish could then be stored in a cool, dry location for months before use.

Though this art of Corning fish is still practiced on Union Island, it hasn't been properly bequeathed to the younger generation. As a result, this fine art and skillful method of preservation are not utilized enough throughout the island.

Dried Okra

The okra crop is very important in Union Island and has multiple uses in many dishes, but its primary purpose is to make kalalloo—a well-known dish that is home to the Caribbean. Due to the perishable nature of the okra crop, its shelf life is no longer than a week, at best. Because of the single rainy season experienced in Union Island, this important crop cannot be available all year round. Therefore, the drying of okra is simply a process of preservation whereby it may be available for use during the severe dry season. A huge quantity of freshly picked okra is sliced into 1/2-inch rings and placed on a canvas or caucus bag to be dried in the sun. The drying process takes approximately three days, and the okra is subsequently stored in a container to be used at a later date. The combination of corn and okra, both locally grown products, makes up the once cherished and tacitly acknowledged national dish, Wangoo and okra.

This is how it is done: The dried product is placed into a large pot on a fire and is baked dry. The content is then placed into a mortar and pestle, where it is thoroughly crushed or pounded fine and subsequently sieved. The sieved content, though brown in color, is very potent when used with ground sesame seeds (locally called Benna). The end product is used as a substitute for freshly picked okra. A tedious task, eh? Yes, it is, but that is what was done with passion when the refrigerator was nonexistent. Obviously, this art of preserving Okra is not practiced anymore in

Union Island. Instead, other vegetables and fruits that are available all year round are now obtained from St. Vincent.

Local Coffee (wild coffee)

The wild coffee plant—a small, leafy plant that is approximately two feet tall—is grown extensively throughout the island as a wild menacing shrub. The tiny seeds, which are almost rock-hard in texture, are extracted from their long, skinny pods. They are baked very dry to remove approximately 90 percent of the liquid. This makes the seeds relatively brittle and very easy to grind. They are then ground fine in a grain mill and packaged in an airtight container and ready to be used as a beverage. It is ground much the same as regular coffee and has a pleasant odor that commensurate its fine taste. During the first half of the 20th Century, this product was made at almost every home on the island. This fine, appetizing product, though marketable, was never sold locally or regionally. The roots of the wild coffee plants also have medicinal value. They are scraped, boiled, and used for severe bellyaches and pain. This locally made medicine is very bitter but effective.

Okra Seeds (beverage)

In this case, the okra is left to dry on the okra plant for several weeks. The dry pods are picked, shelled, cleaned, and then placed in the sun for further drying. These tiny assorted okra seeds that are half the size of the pigeon pea are carefully baked dry in a wide pot to a dark brown color. Finally, they are ground in a grain mill—the same mill that is used to grind the pulpy kernels of corn. This fine, powdery product is then placed into an airtight jar to maintain its shelf life. It is said that this now archaic coffee-like beverage was considered second to none, especially when mixed with milk. Rumors have it that it was a better-tasting product than the above-mentioned coffee drink. This product and the wild coffee beverage can also be used as a marketable commodity both locally and regionally.

MAKING FARINE

Farine, as it is called in most English-speaking countries, is a product that is known throughout the Caribbean and the world. It is made from the roots of the Cassava plant. Its origin is South America, and it is widely used in Brazil. Cassava—or yucca, as most Spanish-speaking countries call it is the greatest starch-yielding crop in the world. Farine is mentioned here because its once hefty production in Union Island has now dwindled down to zero. The process of manufacture entails removing the skin of the cassava by scraping. The cassava is then washed with water, preferably seawater. This brilliant white product is then grated with a large, locally made grater (metal or tin punched numerous times with a nail) and then squeezed dry of all its liquid. The liquid is collected to use as starch, and the fiber-like product is sieved and baked in a huge copper pot. The end product is the *farine.*

But there are two types of cassavas that are grown in Union Island: the bitter and the sweet. The bitter cassava is poisonous if eaten raw. The harmful component of the bitter cassava is hydrocyanic acid (HCN). When ingested, hydrocyanic acid impacts the respiratory process negatively, which results in asphyxiation and ultimately death. The good news is that the harmful component in bitter cassava can be removed by extracting the liquid through squeezing. In that case, the valuable starchy liquid can be collected and used for starching clothes and other uses. Boiling is another means of removing the poisons when there is a need to consume it immediately. There is no need for alarm here; the ancestors that date back to the West Coast of Africa have used this product for centuries. They are quite adept at their craft.

Uttermost attention must be paid to loosen animals in the vicinity during this entire farine-making process. If any animals were to drink of the squeezed liquids of the grated cassava, they, too, would surely die. During the 1950s, several residents have lost their domesticated animals in that manner. When there is a large quantity of cassava to process, this tedious method usually takes the residents an average of three to four days to complete. When the bulk of work has been too much for one day and the grated cassava must remain overnight, the green leaves from the lime tree are placed with the mixture so as to prevent it from fermenting or spoiling. That was the sole means of preservation during those early days.

Making farina was important on Union Island. One major site of production was at Clifton Village, in the vicinity of Mrs. Amutel's Supermarket, a supermarket at Clifton Harbor. Residents of Clifton would gather around the Almond tree at Clifton Harbor, scraping, grating, and straining the contents to make the farine. Food to feed everyone was cooked on site, with dry wood used to fuel the fire—a common practice among the early inhabitants. That was the true definition and spirit of community in Union.

Churning Butter

Making butter in Union Island? Yes, that was done too. The milk used for churning butter was milked from cows. A cow won't give up the bulk of its milk unless the calf is allowed to suck first. Now a milking cow can be milked twice during a half-hour period. So, the calf is allowed to suck while the cow relinquishes 85 percent of its milk in the first milking. The other 15 percent is collected after a two or three-minute hiatus when the calf begins to suck again. According to older folks, that final milk is richer, so it is this portion that a small quantity is taken for the purpose of making butter.

The fresh milk is placed into a wide container such as a soup bowl. The milk is left overnight, and the cream, which settles at the top, is carefully removed and placed into a narrow-necked bottle like a regular wine bottle. The cork is then placed firmly over the bottle and left in a dark area until the next day. This is done every day until the bottle is almost full; then it is left for another three months before the churning process can begin. When this product is ready to be churned, local sea salt is placed into the bottle to activate the churning process and to aid in the washing procedure. The neck of the bottle is held tightly and is continuously stricken into a soft pillow-like material until the content of the bottle is consolidated into a single mass.

The content that now looks light yellow in color is carefully poured into a container where it is cleaned and washed with additional salt and water. The end product is a fresh jar of homemade butter—free of all chemicals and preservatives. Almost every household that reared cattle during the better part of the twentieth century made this fine product, and it lasted as long as they wanted it to. Margarine usage in Union Island is alarmingly high and is consumed much more today than butter. According to a recent newsletter by Dr. David Williams, a renowned physician, indicated that the consumption of margarine by humans is much more dangerous than smoking cigarettes. Yet cigarettes smoking is said to be the major causative agent of lung cancers-80% to be exact.

As we can see, the product of the milk's cream, butter, was

quite a collective effort. Tedious? Yes! But enjoyable at a time when there was not much to do; it surely was time well spent.

If the question "How is the local butter made?" were asked of generations X and Y, they may not know anything relating to this local custom. Alas, this is gone, too; yes, it is a thing of the past.

Guava Jam

Like many other fruits, guava was abundant on Union Island during the twentieth century. Children tended to favor it more than any other fruit except plums. Amazingly, this delicious yellow fruit contains more vitamin C than most citrus fruits. There were two species of guava in Union Island during those earlier days. The interior of these two-species found in Union Island and the Caribbean were red and white, locally called "red gut" and "white gut," respectively. Almost every home had at least two guava trees, and besides being eaten ripe, this highly aromatic fruit was used to make jam (jelly), cheese, and other confections.

During the rainy season, Guava Jam was made in every home in Union Island; it was a treat for children. Below is a curtailed version of how guava jam was made in Union: Selected ripened guavas are placed into a large pot with clean drinkable water. The contents are thoroughly boiled to a pulp and sieved meticulously to remove the numerous seeds. A large amount of brown sugar is added, along with spices, lemon juice, and other condiments, and the liquid is again boiled so that more than 60 percent of the water evaporates. The lukewarm content is poured into a jar-like bottle and allowed to cool. The result is numerous jars of homemade jam, which is children's delight.

Fire on Top; Fire Below

The author would be remiss if he failed to mention roast bakes in this section. This is bread that is baked in a particular way by the people of Union Island; Creativity is the keyword here. Every Unionite utilizes a steel pot for the purpose of baking bread, locally called "Bakes. "These bakes are cooked in a huge pot and covered with a flat, circular cover that is a slightly larger than the circumference of the pot. A mild fire is placed on top and also under the pot, giving ample time for the bake to rise slowly and to be baked proportionately without being burned. Get the idea? This is something that Unionites are noted for: *Fire on Top-Fire Below.*

Roast bakes and a cup of Santa Maria or Jumbee-Bush tea with fresh cow's milk. Yes! We got that a few minutes before we left for school. We got it most mornings for that matter. We came home after grazing the sheep, goats, or cattle or after toting water from a nearby well or the public cistern only to be greeted with a couple of hot roast bakes. The butter that was placed in the Bake would sometimes melt and run all the way down our elbows. Well, not only can we remember those early days; the fact is we cannot forget them. They are the salient memories that stay with us forever. Was mention made of the highly favored "Coconut Bakes? "I will stop here and promise not to conjure up any more of these provocative memories. Natives can only hope that this custom can remain and make its mark as Union Island's breakfast of choice.

But baking was not restricted to pots, as described above; a homemade oven was at every home. I can still imagine the smell of freshly baked bread, sweetbread, cakes, and a variety of pastries coming out of these concrete ovens every Saturday afternoon. The only homes that are void of this unforgiving aroma were those of the Seventh Day Adventists, whose baking was done primarily on Fridays before sunset. The average size of these ovens was 5'x5'x6'. They were built of Portland cement; sand and selected stone that was referred to as firestones. These firestones were used because they retained the tremendous heat made by preheating these ovens at high temperatures. Firewood was used to fuel the fires for preheating these ovens before placing the bread and pastries inside.

Mr. Hardy Ackie, a resident of Ashton, was one of the typical oven builders of those days, and he knew his craft pretty well. These ovens, which supplanted their predecessors, the clay ovens, were dome-shaped (or like a "U" turned upside down) with a large door. Indeed, these archaic ovens were ideal for baking bread, even for commercial purposes. Their retention of heat was enormous. The right side of this oven had an outlet for cleaning the ash after preheating. Unfortunately, these ovens are no more; the modern-day oven has supplanted this ancient work of art.

Fires

Long ago, our ancestors kept their fires burning constantly. The presence of a fire burning at one's home was meant to keep out evil spirits and insects. Fires were always burning on a large tree trunk or stump in one's yard somewhere. If for any reason a resident were without fire at her home, she would send a bearer to her neighbor's home to get a fire stick. Because of the community spirit, that good gesture of response was not considered much; it was common -something that was expected in this close-knit community.

Tobacco Pipe

Unlike today, where cigarettes' smoking is prevalent throughout every community, the Tobacco pipe was the choice gadget for smoking. Cigarette lighters and matches were not used then; a small fire-stick did the job; it lit the pipes. Older folks (men as well as women) could be seen with this device at the corner of their mouths puffing the freshly dried tobacco. As soon as the sun went down, so did the garden hoe, and then the pipe will emerge from a ledge or a hidden corner near a water goblet. It was routine. It's like the televisions that have become an indelible part of our daily lives. A minuscule few would be able to remember those good old days, or golden old days if you will. As happened with many other customs that preceded this current generation and vanished, the Tobacco pipe is almost obsolete on Union Island. And mind you, there were no records of lung cancer among the ancestors. How fortunate.

The Unionite

The year 1975 marked the birth of Union Island's first newspaper. The founder, Mrs. Cleo Scrubb-Kirby, was a Unionite by birth and had just returned home after spending numerous years abroad. This remarkable paper she named the Unionite, was a sign of patriotism that she was proud to exhibit. She was both the editor and publisher of this tabloid, which the residents saw once each month. Every month when the paper was published, many excited citizens made door-to-door visits to every nook and cranny of the island to ensure that the paper was sold. To date, it is the first paper to have been manufactured and on the island.

This newspaper kept the natives apprised of all local activities and occurrences and also featured community development in the rest of the Grenadine Islands. In the Unionite, Cleo stated that the intention of the newly founded paper was to help Unionites at home and abroad stay in touch. It also offered news on historical and current events by promoting community development while featuring people who had helped to develop the island in the past. She went on to say that the paper offered an outlet for local expression and cultural creativity and that she hoped that Unionites, wherever they were, would get the message. All the writers were residents of Union Island. The paper encouraged the writing of short stories and other contributions from neighboring islanders as well as other countries. Each edition featured outstanding personalities in the community.

In one of the editions of 1975, The Unionite featured the centennial anniversary of the St. Matthias Anglican Church, celebrated on Sunday, May 11, 1975. The paper also featured the late Mr. Tyrell Harvey, his venture abroad, and the first means of transportation, which he made available to his people.

Unfortunately, this vibrant young woman (Cleo) left Union Island a few years later to reside in England. Regrettably, this led to the imminent death of the *Unionite*; regrettably, this once promising newspaper had never resurfaced. It is reputed that this vivacious woman (Cleo) died in 2008 at her home in the UK.

Another newspaper that attained notoriety during its brief tenure on the island was the **Daylight.** Lennox "Bomba" Charles, a Unionite, who is currently living abroad, introduced this paper a few months after the final publication of its predecessor, *The Unionite.* Unfortunately, this paper lasted little more than one year.

The people of Union Island are thankful for these two visionaries: Mr. Lennox "Bomba" Charles and the late Mrs. Cleo Scrub-Kirby. These valued literary contributions to the island during the final quarter of the 20th century were a sure sign of upliftment; it represented development and growth.

HERBAL REMEDIES

Hour Grass was placed on the belly of a dead to prevent it from rising.

The above subject, 'Remedy,' during the good old yesterday denotes, "an herb that cures or relieves a disease or bodily disorder, a medicine, or a treatment for a disease or ailment." The adjective, 'Herbal,' determines the source of the remedies or medicines. So how do we define 'Medicine?' Simply put, it is the science and art that deals with the maintenance of health and the prevention, alleviation, or cure of diseases. To add to this, it is also that branch of medicine that concerned with the nonsurgical treatment of diseases.

Who is the father of medicine? Does this title belong to Hippocrates, the outstanding ancient Greek physician that existed during the age of Pericles? Or is it Imhotep, a physician that lived approximately 2600 years before the great Hippocrates? Imhotep, who lived during the Third Dynasty, is also credited with being the founder of ancient Egyptian medicine and the original author of the *Edwin Smith Papyrus*, detailing cures, ailments and anatomical observations.

These are noteworthy feats by two giants that existed during their eras. Nevertheless, the authenticity of this information is worth optimum attention and should be mainstreamed to the world at large. Thus, such a debatable subject and concern is more fitting for a forum of greater magnitude but is necessary to bring closure to the widely diverse opinions that exist.

Called the Father of Modern Medicine, another ancient philosopher, Dr. William Osler C. (July 12, 1849 – December 29, 1919) stated, "It is much more important to know the patient who has the disease than to know the disease that the patient has." Really?

Well, it is safe to state emphatically that the tradition of folk medicine has played an indispensable role on the little cay of Union

Island for centuries. Some medicines may have been invented out of a desperate search for relief from ailments that plagued their communities. We are also aware that the Africans have brought some of their herbal traditions with them during the Transatlantic Slave Trade. Plants, the only source of all medicines during such time, were abundant in every nook and cranny of the island. The unfortunate truth is that the uses of herbal medicine on Union island have been in severe decline since conventional medicines have gained a footing in this society. Medical pharmacology is a rapidly expanding field of study because new drugs are being developed nearly every day. Most drugs in use today come from three natural sources, and plants, are the principals of these three.

Once upon a time, a long, long time ago on Union Island, the kitchen was the hospital, clinic, or medical center –a place where grandmothers, mothers, and aunties would quickly concoct a remedy for many ailments. The Seed-Under-Leaf plant was for cold and fever, prevention and disintegration of gallstones and kidney stones. The Santa Maria was used for gas removal and settling of the bowel. Many of the locally grown herbs have healed the sick, cleansed the leper, recovered the sight of the blind, and of course, set at liberty those that are bruised—a short draft from the Bible.

A typical Aloe Vera plant in Union Island

Aloe Vera, known by the Egyptians as the plant of immortality some 6000 years ago, is a native plant of Africa that grows very well in St. Vincent & the Grenadines. It is reputed that

Aristotle (the father of comparative anatomy and physiology) asked Alexander the Great, his most illustrious pupil, to conquer the island of Socotra so that his army would have access to the abundant fields of aloe. This plant is a member of the Lily family; the juice or gel from the leaves contains powerful healing compounds. It is widely used to treat minor skin irritations, wounds, and hair loss. Aloe Vera is one of the best stomach cleansers in the entire herb kingdom; it is well known for its ability to eliminate common gastrointestinal problems and shows promise in treating Type 2 diabetes. Its value both orally and topically is incredible; this plant has been used for centuries and has remarkable healing properties. The obnoxious taste, mind you, may be daunting to even the hardened users of this plant, but its exceptional value supersedes all deterrents. The cliché "no pain no gain" applies in this instance; anything worth achieving will be difficult. Many users attest to the powerful rejuvenating properties that stimulate the body's repair mechanisms and aid most health problems. Aloe taken first thing in the morning does the body wonders. The fleshy part of the plant can be blended with fresh orange or pineapple juice and other favorable condiments to embellish the taste.

Topically, Aloe Vera does a magnificent job in healing the skin of burns, scars, shingles, warts, acne, and even wrinkles from aging. Internally, aloe is said to help cancer patients. For sufferers of lung cancer, it is said that the continuous use of aloe activates the white blood cells and promotes the growth of noncancerous cells. Aloe is highly alkaline, and in medical science, it is well known that cancerous cells cannot survive in an alkaline environment. Aloe is also good for patients that are afflicted with the following: Asthma, Epilepsy, Arthritis, Rheumatism, heartburn, Diabetes, Liver and Kidney problems, Intestinal worms, Prostate problems, Urinary tract infection. The rhyme, or Aloins, in medical terms, has been used as a local laxative for many, many years ago. To many, it is considered an irritant laxative; it may have adverse effects if consumed irresponsibly. But like any over-the-counter or innocuous drugs, prescription is absolutely necessary. All herbs, if taken in excess, can impact the body negatively. Therefore, one must be particularly moderate and discrete in consumption of Aloins. These excellent detoxifiers have been grossly under-used by the people in the Caribbean.

Here are many of the local herbs with significant medicinal value. These were the only solution in a time when doctors and medical facilities were not in place many years ago:

1. **Hypertension (high blood pressure):** Hour Grass, Trumpet Bush, Aloe Vera, Celery, and Carailli.

2. **Diabetes:** Aloe Vera, Carailli, Mauby Bark, and Seed-under-leaf, Avocado with raw honey, Papaya leaves.

3. **Blood builder:** Black Sage, Log wood, Crattah root, Coconut root.

4. **Asthma:** Wild Calabash (fiddle wood)

5. **Cold remedy:** Snake weed, Dog Bush, Christmas Bush, Seed-Under-Leaf, Trumpet Bush, and Mini Root (Mini Root induces sweating.)

6. **Cools the system:** Water grass, Vervane, Love Vine (Purr mattress), Cactus (Ratchet, Pickle Pear).

7. **Biliousness:** Seed-Under-Leaf (Very bitter herb) and Aloe Vera

8. **Sleep inducer:** Sour-Bop leaves, Vervane.

9. **Expulsion of worms:** Paw-Paw seeds, Vervane, Wormgrass, Seed-under-leaf, Aloe Vera.

10. **Belly Aches and Menstrual pains:** Mayan Roots (very bitter herb), Seed Under Leaf, Aloe Vera.

11. **Cleanser (female reproductive organ):** Caster Oil, Crattah root, Seed-under-leaf, and Cassava Grass (The boiled root of Cassava Grass is an excellent remedy for childbearing women).

12. **Calcified Stone Removal:** Seed-under-leaf, lemons

13. **Tea Bush:** Santa Maria, Vervane, Lemon grass, Baby Bush, Sugar Apple Bush, Jumbee basil (bush), Christmas Bush, Black Sage, Sweet Broom.

13. **Aphrodisiac:** Branner, Seed-Under-Leaf (Also on the

reefs lives the Long back—a sea crustacean creature that attaches itself to the rocks (The natives normally ate this delicacy raw), and of course, the people choice (Sea Moss).

14.   **Carminative:**   Senna Pods, Aloe Vera, Seed-under-leaf, Castor oil.

15.   **Abortion:** Jumbee Basil (bush), Black Sage, and Seed-Under-Leaf combined with other herbs.

Honorable mention must be given to another local herb that is prevalent in our backyards. Hailed as a food seasoning (condiment), Big-leaf thyme (Spanish) is an herb with antibiotic properties that fight bacteria. It is helpful where a cough, bronchitis, asthma, and other respiratory ailments exist. It is also a digestive stimulant and is helpful in promoting blood circulation.

The reader will observe from the above list of herbs that Seed-under-leaf and Aloe Vera are the two most commonly mentioned. Near to being called panaceas, these herbs were widely used in every household in Union. Once upon a time, the Seed-under-leaf herb was widely used for jaundice because it detoxifies the liver; it is also used for hypertension and will eliminate gall & kidney stones from the digestive and GU systems.

The Seed-Under-Leaf plant, (seen above) as mentioned above, is almost an elixir in its own right and can be found in every nook and cranny of Union island. This herb is a natural stonebreaker; it disintegrates gallstones, kidney stones and eliminates calcification in these organs.

The **Hour Grass** is another herb that was regularly used during the earlier years when the island did not have a mortuary to preserve the body of the dead. This herb was not used as an oral medicine but instead was placed on the belly of a dead person to prevent the stomach from rising.

Although the above herbs can be found in every nook and cranny of the island, they have not been used by the most recent generations. Well...they have been used but sparingly, at best.

Dry Juice (Joy Juice)

Unlike the aforementioned medicinal herbs that have their salutary impacts on the population of Union Island, Dry Juice is a relatively common plant that can be seen in any locality on the island. Because it is not known to possess any remarkable value, there is no widespread use of this herb. Jimsonweed, as it is called internationally, can be a source of a powerful hallucinogen, a drug that is capable of producing hallucinations, or changes in the perceptual process.

And lastly, let us take a look at the Papaya plant. The leaves of this fruit-bearing plant can be used for the prevention and treatment of gastrointestinal tract disorders, intestinal parasite infections, and as a sedative and diuretic. Papaya leaves are also used for excruciating nerve pains (neuralgia). In the kitchen, we have noticed that the green papaya fruit has been used as a meat tenderizer for many years. This is because of the presence of Papain, a chemical that is found in the fruit.

HARVESTING SALT

Many years ago, Sea Salt was the only kind of salt that the natives used.

Harvesting salt, or salt picking as it is called locally, has been an annual event for the people of Union Island for quite a few centuries. Prior to that, (17th century) the French used the salt from these salt-filled ponds of the Grenadines to preserve the meat of the turtle, which was later exported to Europe. Two salt ponds were located in Union Island; Palm Island, and Mayreau has one apiece. Each year, from the months of March through May, the

Salt ready to be harvested at the Belmont Salt Pond, Union Island

people of Union Island looks forward to taking a casual walk on the mud-filled salt-pond of Belmont to engage in their rightful obligation of the island's legacy -picking salt.

Currently, Union Island is not the only salt producing island in the Grenadines; the tiny island of Mayreau is also large in the production of this fine product. The Grand Turk, another island in the Caribbean was also noted for its mass production of salt during the early 20th century. The salt pond on the tiny island of Prune (Palm Island) has succumbed to numerous guesthouses and tourist resorts as it gives way to a rising tourist industry in the region.

Because of the semiarid climate of the Grenadines, Union Island may experience severe droughts during its annual dry season, which starts from the month of November and ends in May. The island has two salt ponds that are situated very close to the shoreline, next to mangrove patches. One is located at Ashton Village, south of the island, and hence is called the Ashton Salt-Pond. The other is located at Belmont, north and slightly east of the island, and is called the Belmont Salt-Pond -the only salt producing pond of the island. The Ashton Salt-Pond, the larger of the two, hasn't produced any significant amount of salt for the past eighty years.

It is during the severe droughts on the island that the sea level descends at alarming rates and water evaporates rapidly at the pond. This impacts the level of saltwater at the salt pond, resulting in a wide plane of crystals. Crystal in these ponds at any given point of time is salt that is ripened and ready to be harvested. **Picking salt** is the local expression for harvesting this fine product. If the crystal were covered with a thin layer of water, another day or two would be required for that overlying water to evaporate thoroughly. From an aerial perspective, this glittering plane of salt below gives the appearance of a wide football field of diamond; it is a magnificent picture to behold.

The entire country is collectively engaged in this exciting process of reaping this important natural resource. On a good salt-picking day at the Belmond pond, the youngest child to the eldest can be seen physically partaking of this rich legacy. First, there is a twenty- to thirty-foot walk into the muddy pond to reach the line of the salt. A container must be taken on site and filled with the raw material. One must always take the size of container that he or she can carry when it is filled. Because of the compactness of the mud, the containers remain firmly upright without tilting or overturning even when filled. Most people undertake the task barefoot; others use water boots, in which it is much more difficult to maneuver because of the suction of the mud.

On reaching this wide plane of crystal, the pickers stoop, put both hands together, and open them up, fingers pointing outward and palms facing upward. Then they push gently under the layer of crystal and raise their hands slowly; the salt easily separates from its bond. This process is very easy, requiring little energy. The average size of these layers is 8' x 11' in dimension, and they are composed of numerous fragments that disintegrate like a shattered windshield of a vehicle. These layers of salt are repeatedly placed into the containers or buckets until they are filled. The full containers are then taken back and poured into a large porous bag so that it can be drained of any liquid it may contain. Then off the pickers go again into the pond to collect another container of this valued product. And on it goes. It is unbelievable how easily these salt crystals can be separated into single blocks of approximately 1/2-, 1/4-, or 3/4-inch squares, depending on the thickness of the salt patch. The size of the block of salt increases further into the pond and then decreases again at the end. The color also varies depending on the water content. The whiter the salt is, the lower the percentage of water contents.

The harvested salt from these regions are called Natural Sea Salt and may be harvested twice per year on a good year.

Seen here: A white plane of crystal at the Belmont Salt-Pond

Many years ago, that was the only kind of salt that was used by the natives. Today, Unionites can buy packaged, refined salt; it may be much more convenient but can have an adverse effect on their health because of the deficiency of numerous natural elements. It is reputed that eight- two important elements of sea salt have been extracted and sold at exorbitant prices, rendering the salt less effective for good health.

"Natural sea salt, when taken with the consumption of lots of water, will only impact your health positively," says the renowned physician, Dr. Batmanghelidj, internist, and cardiologist. It is imperative that the natives and persons that suffer from hypertension (high blood pressure) use natural sea salt rather than refined, packaged, iodized salt, which is deficient of its other natural elements. Many hypertension sufferers are inclined to eliminate the consumption of salt from their diets. However, as Dr. Batmanghelidj also warns, such action is not salutary to the sufferer's health in that it weakens the urinary bladder. The result of salt deficiency in one's diet, Dr. Batmanghelidj cautions, may lead to a somewhat embarrassing condition that is called Urinary incontinence.

◆◆◆□*Chapter Five*

RELIGION, LANDMARKS & THE BIRTH OF THE GOSPEL HALL CHURCH

Tastelessly, in recent years, some important buildings that were landmarks have been razed and rebuilt into modern structures that bear no resemblance of their former selves.

The predominant religion in Union Island is Christianity. Should this be surprising? Absolutely not! The Catholic, Anglican, Seven-Day Adventist, Baptist, Pentecostal, Gospel Hall and Church of God in Christ are quite a few religions for a small community, not to forget that most of these religions had their genesis in Europe. Each church practiced Christianity from a relatively different perspective. And although Islam may have been the religion of most Africans that were rooted out of Africa and brought to Union Island as burden bearers, today, there is not a single trace of its former existence. Hare Krishna, Buddha and other religions of the East have not been prevalent in this region thus yet. After all, with the population of this seemingly insignificant landmass, one would surmise that the majority of the population would have swayed to a single religion. Tactlessly this is not so. Should it be questioned whether the people of Union Island needs a bible revival for the black's survival? Surely! With some of the stringent customs that once governed the manner that Christianity was taught and practiced for centuries, we must admit that the church has come a long way over the last four decades. But even with such state of evolution, there are still lots of strides to be made. Nevertheless, this interesting subject will be dispensed with for the time being, for it may be suited for another occasion.

The churches and municipal buildings that were built in Union Island during those early years were well structured and finely designed. These public dwellings stood out conspicuously among the multiple Wattle and Daub structures that housed the growing community. From an infrastructural standpoint, lots have happened over the years; the island, in turn, takes on a different appearance as many modern brick houses replaced the ubiquitous thatches of yesterday.

What is rather disturbing is that there are some significant buildings that were landmarks; some of them had been razed and rebuilt into modern structures that bear no resemblance of their former selves. The Gospel Hall Church is one of the best examples. This church that is located pivotally between the V that is formed from the distribution of the Main Road into the Valley and Bordeaux Roads was laden with decades of history. This attractive building stands conspicuously in its location but bears no semblance of its originality -80 years of precious memories and sentiments have been thoughtlessly ruined and washed down the drain.

Another significant building and landmark is the former post office of Clifton that was destroyed by arson in 1997.

The well-known Clifton Clinic is another typical example; this was the only medical clinic in Union Island at one time. Regrettably, the absence of these landmark buildings signifies the death of an era and the emergent of another.

The rebuilding of these monumental structures subtracts greatly from the image of the island historically, the feeling of nostalgia, and the sentiments that accompany our formative years of growing up. Instead, considerable efforts should have been placed in the restoration process so as to keep the physical aspect of our history alive.

The former structure of Gospel Hall Church was particularly mentioned because it meant a lot to several generations that frequent that building, it spoke volumes and conjured lots of youthful memories. During our formative years, they had been an integral part of our lives; unfortunately, we are not where we ought to be regarding the protection of valued assets what we are fortunate to have. We should be adamant at undergoing painstaking renovations in restoring the originality and details of these buildings, and to preserve their charms and architectural integrity of the few structures that remains. The Anglican Church that was built in the year 1875 is one of our oldest buildings that can be seen on the island today. The architectural integrity of this dinosaur is well intact and stands out as one of our premier landmarks. The names Charles Mulzac and John Louis Archer are synonymous to this institution; they have played significant roles in the maintenance and up keeping of this church.

Another of our landmarks is the United Friendly Society Hall. This aged building is situated at Ashton Salt Pond, (non-arable land) close to the current police station. This dinosaur was built in the year 1936 by a group of fine workmen under the stewardship of Mr. James Simmons, Charlie, and Mr. Daniel Ackie. The latter was the grandfather of Donald McTair; one of Union's finest carpenters today. This building is well intact but needs restoration like any old structure will, over a lengthy period. Though this structure appears small to our evolved minds, it was the chief entertainment and recreational center for most activities in Union Island. Dances, concerts, play, raffles, meetings, etc. were held in the confines of this building. It supplanted the old Anglican Church School of Ashton where most social and recreational activities once took place. But most importantly the United Friendly Society, as its name implies, maintaining fraternity while making provision for the dead. Not only did this society aided in the burial of its members, but the community as a whole. Funding and materials to build caskets at the time of the death of a loved one are of paramount importance. In this interest of tradition, I hope that I will one day be laid firmly into one of these wooden boxes that are built by the skillful hands of another Unionite.

Although time has changed, the United Friendly Society Hall it still provides funding to members of the community who needs it, but unlike yesterday, caskets are instead bought rather than built locally. Building caskets is an art that everyone once valued. Onlookers were often mystified by the artistic prowess and cheerful readiness exhibited by our carpenters during those former years. Everyone will concur that it did serve very well in its heyday. Maintaining its originality during restoration will also mean conserving our sentimental attachments.

Look again at the pictures on page's 42 and 109. These pictures will one day become the sole physical reminders of the first and oldest building that was constructed on the soil of Union Island. Like the aforementioned structures in the previous paragraphs, this dinosaur, once referred to as *Big House*, too, have ill advisedly met its demise in the year 2015. This is the latest act of stupor that successfully aided in the annihilation of Union Island's history. It is said that bits of harvested cotton were found in the ruins of this 18th-century edifice during its futile demolition.

Two principals who were largely responsible for the above-mentioned Gospel Hall religion being in Union Island were the late Phillip Evan Stewart and his sister, Ann Mariah Stewart, (the grandchildren of the renowned William McDowell Stewart). During the early half of the 20th century, a Christian minister by the name of Lardy Questelle (Ba Lardy), his wife, Alcina (Ce Elsie) and son Walter were fond of Ashton village and found kinship in two individuals who were also God-fearing people. These people were Mr. Phillip Evan Stewart and his sister Ann Mariah Stewart, locally called *Miss*. They had no building to teach the gospel at the time, so they made use of a huge Mango tree that was situated in the vicinity of their father Robert's (Ba Nattie) land. Ann Mariah being undeterred by such inconvenience and inclement weather condition continued her teaching under the huge Mango tree even after the Questelle had left the island with intent to return some time later. The Questelle did return to Union Island, but not without other Christian members such as the Huckster family and other missionaries. Mr. Huckster came with his wife Bertha and their son Walter. The Questelle who were now residents of Ashton, Union Island, were neighbors of Joseph Alves (Daddy Alves). With such friendly turnout from the locals, the need for a church instantly became an important issue. Mr. Archibald Thomas (Old man), the grandfather of Minister Leroy Thomas, being a fervent believer in the Christian teaching himself, immediately became a member.

Observing the gross inconvenience that the Christian ministry was undergoing, coupled with his fervent desire to help with the development of the new church, Mr. Robert (Ba Nattie) Stewart, the father of Phillip collaborates with Louisa Joseph (Ce-Julia). They both were in legal contracts to lands that share a common border with lengthy amortization plans that lasted for well over two decades. In 1929, both parties made out a deed for a small portion of land that is situated at a pivotal location in Ashton. That land was donated to the church. Subsequently, a wooden structure of the Gospel Hall Church was constructed. Today, almost nine decades removed from those earlier years, a modern concrete structure replaced this once priceless landmark that has served as an educational institution for both the young and old. The deed for this land was documented to the steward of the Gospel Hall Church whose nucleus is located in London, England.

The construction of this edifice began in 1929 when Mr. Phillip (Evan) Stewart, a resident of Union Island, with the help of his wife Rosalyn, brought the prefabricated parts of the Gospel Hall Church from Baltimore, Maryland, and shipped it all the way to Union Island. Because land transportation was a major challenge in Union Island during those early years, the prefabricated parts were brought in at the nearest port, Ashton Harbor (via Frigate Rock). These parts were manually transported to the intended location of the church and were assembled on site. Today, vehicular transport is available for this purpose. It is believed that Mr. Tyrell Harvey - an entrepreneur of Ashton Village brought the first vehicle to Union Island in the month of December of 1958.

A 2009 picture of the Ashton Gospel Hall Church under construction. This building was constructed in 1929. Mt. Parnassus and Mt. Tabor can be seen in the rear.

Another noteworthy figure was the aforementioned red-skinned Canadian of German parentage, Mr. W. B. Husker. Mr. Husker was also played a significant role in maintaining and keeping the dreary Gospel Hall religion alive. The Christian congregation referred to him as Brother W. B. Husker. Husker later became a resident of the Richmond area of Union Island, and he lived in a secluded manner. And although some residents were skeptical and distrustful of him, they never rendered a single word of disdain. As a preacher of the Gospel Hall Church, he was said to be a man of clout in the mainland of St. Vincent. This Canadian native arrived in Union Island and immediately made it his home. Unlike many foreigners, he never returned to the land of his birth. Although many people were suspect of his commitment to the Christian religions and the church, he did keep the seats packed with locals, foreigners, and also people of authority. Mr. March, Little John, the Eustace family of St. Vincent and Brother Lennox of England were some of his affiliates who frequent the new church. After many years as a clergy, Mr. Husker became very ill and needed medical attention. Battling his illness for several years, Mr. Husker was taken to St. Vincent where he finally caught a stroke and succumbed to his illness. This period was during the latter years of the Great Depression (1930s). Residents of Union Island later learned that this man was a heavy consumer of alcohol, and drinking may have impacted his health negatively. Berta, the wife of the deceased, was also ill; she was suffering from varicose veins stricture. A year later, she migrated to the United States of America.

Several years later, (the 1940s), Mrs. Elsie Questelle, the wife of Ba Lardy died and was buried at the Ashton Cemetery. Keeping his promise to his wife Elsie, that he will never marry another woman if she dies before him, Ba Lardy took the family bed and placed it on the grave of his wife. The remains of the bed were visible in the cemetery up until the year 1970. Ba Lardy remained one of the central figures of the church during his latter days.

During the 1950s, a young Caucasian man from England called Brother Lennox assumed control of the Gospel Hall. In absentia, he conducted the affairs of the church until the early 1980s. Brother Lennox, who lived in England, would visit the church as often as he can (one per year). Most of the older folks knew Brother Lennox very well, and whenever he visited Union Island Gospel Hall Church, he was well-accommodated by the residents. He was well received, and the brothers and sisters proffered the best treatment to him. They will endeavor to make sure that his needs and wants were totally satisfied. Even when eggs became a scarce commodity on the island, he was sure to have his fill; in short, he was well catered to. In 1981, he died in his hometown in England.

Brother Jonah Stewart, a devoted Christian minister of the

Gospel Hall church, played a significant role in up keeping and maintaining the church up until his later years. His physical affinity to the house of the Lord had tacitly placed the onus of responsibility squarely on his shoulders. He was the go-to person, not merely an artery, but Aorta through which oxygenated blood supplied the entire system of the Gospel Hall Church. Like the adage: Those who stand still and watch from the sideline of life only partially live, we must choose to participate...Brother Jonah participated his service to the Gospel Hall Church and the people of Union Island. Consequently, his contribution and service to this institution are permanently etched into the cornerstone of time.

THE REVERED ELDERS & A WOMAN'S ROLE YESTERDAY

Unfortunately, any desire to excel academically was fervently met with disapproval from their husbands

Long ago our parents referred to the elders in the community as "Bah, Ce, Ta, and Nennie. "Bah" for the males and "Ce" for the females. The names Bah Archer, Bah Fection, Ce Chamnie, Bah Mindo, and Ce Catharine were just a few of the names that my memory has allowed me to conjure. Ta is the short form of tanty (aunty) and Nennie for the Godmothers. But during the 20th century, even up to the late 70's these titles were still assigned to the names of our elderly. In my formative years as a child growing up in Union Island, I often witnessed my parents using these names as they paid respect to our noble elders and ancestors. Ce Mary, who once lived above the Union Island Secondary School, was the aunt of my father, Garfield Stewart. Bah Purgin, another elder, and father of the late Robert Wilson were the two of the last residents of Ashton to bear those titles with pride.

What was the origin and meaning of these two venerable titles? Computers have become the staple of every home and business the world over, and obviously, it has become my first choice to explore for this kind of information. Well, to date I have been unable to locate any information that can lead us to the etymological root of these two words. For one thing, we all know that these two words are of African origin, but that is about it. What I have derived over the years through these prevalent usages is that the word Bah may have been curtailed from the word Abba, which according to Dictionary.com, is the Aramaic word for father that had been used in the New Testament by Jesus and Paul to address God in personal intimacy.

You could also hear the introductory song of the famed Gospel Hall Church "Abba Father We Adore Thee" each Sunday morning as the melodious voices of Sister Florence Forde, Yolanda, Joann Gellizeau and Yvonne Harvey resonate through the streets of Ashton. This was the very first song that came from the book, Gospel Hall Hymnal. The late Brother Tom, father of Mrs. Joann Gellizeau, also had a compelling voice – that of bass, which he exercised with maximum capacity as he led the church every Sunday morning with his rendition of that song. To bring more clarity to the word "bah," we can say that it actually equates the title "Don" in its meaning in the Spanish language.

Now "Ce" on the other hand speaks to the distaff or female side of the human family, the African family that is; the matriarch, the mother of civilization, and we can amicably add, "The Goddess of the Universe." Search engines are unable to give a definitive understanding of both words Ce and Bah, but our ancestors were precise enough to give us their clear denotation through the use of our culture.

These titles are alien to the new generation, and will soon be extinct from our memories. As the saying goes, "What you learn and don't use, you'll lose." Indeed, this is of the past. But let's take a keen look at Union Island's women of yesterday, or better said, our noble women of yesterday as compared to the contemporaries -our noble women of today.

The women in early communities had diverse responsibilities. In Union Island, the average size of a family was eight members. The wives were solely responsible for the upbringing of their offspring. They had to wash, starch, and iron the clothes as well as cook, clean, garden, do the dishes, and shop. And all of the above was done in time to keep a functional home. Not to mention that these wives' circumstances were filled with the usual, sometimes overwhelming stresses associated with being a mother, doctor, nurse, teacher, counselor, and an arbitrator in sibling rivalries, wife, and love, and the responsibility of satisfying their husbands at all costs. These young women of grace and beauty were vibrant and strong both physically and emotionally.

Unfortunately, any desire to excel academically was fervently met with disapproval from their husbands, and if, before marriage, a woman held a job as a teacher or public servant, they were discouraged from doing so upon entering the marriage vow. So is it is safe to enunciate that The Yesterday Woman's Role as a wife concluded her educational advancement, but brought on enormous responsibilities with great self-denial. Her principal function was childbearing, parenting, and all of the attributes of a housewife, but again, futile little in the way of academic advancement.

Those responsibilities of the grandmothers, mothers, aunts, sisters, and daughters were tedious compared to those of the marriages of today. The patriarchs' responsibilities were to bring home the bacon, which they did dutifully on most occasions. However, they provided little to no help to his mate with the endless household burden that was bestowed upon her by tradition. Nevertheless, an amicable marriage relationship remained intact for an average of six decades, indicating that the women honored the phrase "Till death do us part." The question must now be posed: Is the women of today willing to emulate the women of yesterday in regards to the enormous responsibilities that were placed on their shoulders? Many will respectfully think otherwise.

Having said all of the above, I feel obligated to mention the matriarch that I have known throughout my entire existence on this planet. I use the word matriarch because she exemplifies the true meaning of motherhood. She is the stem wall, the pillar of the home, my strength yesterday and more so today because of what she permanently ingrained in me. And in many instances, when in adversity, I hold on tenaciously to my belief because of her teaching.

I can say emphatically that she is largely responsible for who I am and what I am becoming. I honestly do not think there is another person who truly knows the might of this soft-spoken woman as much as I do. To me, my mother, **Sheila** Roache-Stewart, epitomizes the rock of Gibraltar. She has been such a great inspiration to us (children). She raised us with sheer determination and hard work, and she believed firmly in herself and the methods she implemented while raising us. As a youngster growing up, I always looked up to her, not only because she fed, clothed, and kept us soundly within the guidelines of ethics and morality, but also because her presence meant the world to us. From my mother, I learned how to wash, cook, bake, garden, and the art of being an animal farmer. The latter I crave limitlessly. But let's face it; does anyone really love you the way your mother does? The answer here may be relative, but I can say categorically that **Sheila** was and is my first love because of the love that I received from her in abundance. She also has been the first hero and role model in my life. And for this, I can state emphatically that the best in me I owe to her. I love you, Mom.

A 1968 photo of **Sheila** Roache/Stewart @ Port of Spain, Trinidad. Here, she looks like a descendant of the Ebo tribe of Ghana.

In looking back at her total contribution to my life, I inadvertently aspired to seeing those kinds of qualities in my relationships with females with whom I shared my affections, but to no avail. That is how much she affected my life; she left a greater indelible mark on me than on any of my siblings. Today, there is a degree of void or lack of fulfillment in my life; here in America and miles away from the Equator, I am unable to implement some of the customs and traditions that had richly made my life a resource in the Caribbean. **Sheila**, to this day, is very passionate about her agriculture and animal husbandry, which she does dutifully every day. She rears her sheep, goats, and fowl right in her backyard with fervent passion and exhibits the same desire that she has always had since I have known her.

I mentioned earlier that we had a large herd of goats stationed at the pastures of Ms. Irene —by far the largest herd on the island. **Sheila** was responsible for this creation and was one of the most noteworthy agricultural farmers of her time at Campbell. Thank you, **Sheila**; I love you dearly!

YESTERDAY'S MARRIAGE

The male flag lies on top of the female's flag; this exemplifies dominance of the man or submissiveness of his mate.

To take a phrase from the preceding subject, it says: "An amicable marriage relationship remained intact for an average of six decades, indicating that the women honored the phrase *Till death do us part."* But did the men of yesterday honor and represented the embodiment of that phrase? We will pause now and then dispense with such a question, for it may be more appropriate for a different setting. More importantly, we will carefully follow the steps of a typical marriage of Union Island during the good old days of yesterday, or better said, THE GOLDEN DAYS.

A young man sees the woman that he loves, or yearns to have, and desires to make her his wife. To make this a reality, he must immerse himself fully in the marital traditions. Dating is short-lived at all costs, for all roads hastily lead to the altar -the tying of the knot, the marriage. The first step is to inform the parents of the prospective bride that he has an interest in their daughter. This is done by visiting the home of her parents on a late evening to disclose his affection for the young lady and his intent to take her hand in marriage. Writing a letter that asks the parent's approval of his marriage to their daughter is also another way. Now some parents will go as far as to select mates for their children without first consulting with their children. In this particular situation, the parents of the prospective bride and groom subsequently develop a closer rapport among themselves. In many cases, the parents of sons may go as far as to become a watchdog over the prospective young lady to protect their son's interest.

Now in some cases, a young man and woman may meet and express affinity toward each other. But when this does not meet the approval of his/her parents (mostly the sons), who may be prejudiced against the girl and her family, the parents may express disapproval of his intent. They might fear that he will disparage himself by marrying into a lesser family. This may take place in the girl's family as well, especially if the young man doesn't seem to have a decent job or has much going for him financially. The parents of yesterday had a lot of clout regarding the choices that their children made; that's the way it was then, and even today; if we look carefully, we may be able to spot some residual impacts. Because of this parental issue, many young couples were dissuaded from relationships during their early years but later reunited after they had experienced the turmoil of unsuccessful marriages. Many, many older men, in particular, can attest to that.

The process of visiting the home of the young lady or writing a letter to ask her parents' permission to take her hand in marriage is locally called "Going home for girl X, Y, OR Z." And that young lady may bear any of these common names listed: Doris, Odette, Elvina, Agatha, Gertrude, Florence, Violet, Pandora, Dorothy, Melvina, Bettie, Gwendolyn, Agnes, Elmina, Mildred, Eunice, Faithful, Sarah, Emilie, Icena, or other name that relates to that time, age or era. Young men, on the other hand may bear the names listed below: Alfred, Milton, Oscar, Festus, Russell, Jonah, Samuel, Hudson, Percival, Nathan, Eldon, Theopolis, Egbert, etc.

Some young men were confident enough to visit the young lady's parents and request her hand in marriage without the young lady being aware of their affection and intentions. Others who were a bit squeamish or did not have the self-confidence would seek the assistance of a noteworthy person in the community to accompany them to the parents' home.

In rare cases, if a young man who sailed on National Bulk Liners was called out to sea before he could approach the parents, he might write a letter to communicate his intentions. The approval of the parents (liner employees were hardly ever denied) brought closure to one chapter. He was now privileged to call on the young woman at home and to occasionally take her out for a walk to the beach or the pasture amid the inquisitive and watchful eyes of the community.

The logical step that follows is the official engagement as the courtship picks up momentum. Next, an engagement ring is placed on the finger of the bride-to-be. This is done in the presence of family members and a few close friends. During such time, the parents of the prospective bride amicably inform the suitor in no uncertain term that the engagement term will be brief. Consequently, all plans and arrangements for the wedding intensify, and the momentum again shifts into higher gear. With little time to waste, a date is set for the day of the wedding, which happens only on a Tuesday. The onus or responsibility now rests on the shoulders of the prospective bride and groom's parents. The choice of wedding gown and outfits for the groom, bridesmaid, chief bridesmaid, flower girl, honor attendant, bride's escort, best-man, and officiant (minister or priest) must be put into place. So must be the flowers and seating arrangements, cake, and the big cookouts to feed the community. Welcome to the institution of marriage.

The groom-to-be, honors tradition by voluntarily refraining from seeing his prospective bride for the seven days leading up to the wedding. The day that precedes the wedding (Monday) marks the first of a pair of cookouts for such a momentous undertaking. "The Parents Plate," a sumptuous dinner that is designed particularly for the parents and elders, is done in the highest order. A cow, goats, sheep, pigs, and fowls may be slaughtered to provide enough food to feed the community for the entire day. Cooking is done in huge copper pots placed on three stones while firewood is used as energy to fuel the fires. Elaborate cooking and dancing fill the atmosphere with glee as residents descend on the home of the bridegroom to celebrate this forthcoming event. Singing erupts in anticipation of a long, happy marriage for the bride and groom. This local song, which was sung in the African dialect, is surely a favorite for the occasion; it was composed by **Isabella Roache**. A faction of the huge gathering sings a question while another faction responds, also in singing. It is sung and danced with the beat of the African drum.

Ah we want peace and unity
All ah we ah whan
Ah we want peace and unity
All ah we ah whan
Ah we want peace and unity

All way Mama want?
Mama want peace and unity
All way Mama want?

Mama want peace and unity

All way ah we want?
Ah we want peace and unity
All way ah we want?
Ah we want peace and unity
All way ah we want?

Ah we, which means "all we" in the old dialect of Union Island, is interpreted in clear English as "Us or Everyone." Sharply, the African drum again rolls as the West African customs resurface and is expressed once again through dancing and singing.

Open the door leh me man come in
All ah we ah whan famileee.............
Open the door leh me man come in
All ah we ah whan family.

This gala, which offers much to eat and drink as well as lots of laughter, extends far into the night. While the kerosene lamps are lit inside of the house, the Flambeau or Massantow are ablaze outside, providing light for the event through the dark of night, until sunset.

The day of the wedding is the birth of a new celebration. The location will now be at the bride's home, where cooking commences just after sunrise and is accompanied by other activities. The points of interest that precede the actual tying of the knot are the "Meeting Up" and the "Dancing of the Cake."

On the day of the wedding, very early in the morning, the families of both the bride and the groom convene at a central location with a large following of spectators on site to witness this grand event. Cultural music begins with the beat of the African drum while designated dancers take center stage to exhibit their prowess. These dancers are elegantly adorned, with long, wide, frilly floral skirts that lend mobility and grace to their dexterity. The large gathering of spectators surrounds the continuous dancing and singing but gives ample room to the dancers. The crowd is almost wild now as the decorated mothers of both bride and groom assert themselves at center stage; this is a true expression of the island's culture. With the mothers becoming the center of focus, all eyes are glued on them.

A competition ensues as fierce dancing between the two mothers begins. This activity is rightfully referred to as the Meeting Up. The mothers of the bride and groom firmly grab the right and left sides of their skirts and motioned them in and out, up and down with reckless abandon. Sensual whining follows this dancing activity and brings this social event to the point of culmination. The spectators themselves are unstoppable as they repetitively sing the favorite two-lined song. The first line is sung as the question is posed, "All way ah we want?" Then the second part is an ecstatic response: "Ah we want peace and unity." The heat is so intense that some excited onlookers are provoked to join the dancers at center stage, but are restrained. This liveliness is the central part of this function; it sets the tone for the eventual wedding ceremony later that day.

Almost as soon as the whining simmers to a snail's pace, two dancers emerge with wooden trays on their heads. These wooden trays are placed on a firmly wrapped or folded cloth that is positioned under the trays on the heads of these female dancers. They dance elegantly with these trays that are balanced on their heads; hands almost glued to their waists and never seeming to be uncomfortable while their prized possessions are unattended.

This artistic skill that is bequeathed from the West coast of Africa is a practice that is common in Union Island. Heavy loads are carried in baskets, trays, buckets, and so on by balancing them on their heads—which African women can attest is by far the best way to carry their heaps. Some West Africans call the cloth that cushions the weight of the object on the head an "Akartne." In the Akan tribe of Ghana, it is called Kahyire. In Liberia, it is known as Cala, and in Union Island, it is called Karta. The contents of these embellished trays on their heads of these women are the wedding cakes and their fine adornments of flowers. These cakes were baked and decorated ahead of time for this significant event. While the cake of the bride is highly decorated with multiple layers, that of the groom remains a single layer, according to the dictates of tradition.

The dancers of the cake must now make way for the final episode of the morning, the dancing of the flag. The fingers of the drummers are never too tired to evoke the sound of the African drum whose beat reflects the regularity of a metronome. The presence of these final two dancers of the flags epitomizes the authenticity of the culture from the motherland. Two flags are held aloft on entrance and waved rhythmically to the beat of the drums. It is done with such dexterity that one might assume that a sword fight was about to ensue. This dancing continues at center stage as the flag bearers circle the ring several times and then stop abruptly. The poles of the flags are then carefully placed across each other, forming an X while the flags themselves are turned toward each other. The male flag lies on top of the female's flag; this exemplifies the dominance of the man or the submissiveness of his mate. This, of course, is ritualistic in scope and has its salutary significance. Such vibrant activity marks the end of the morning session, which lasts approximately one hour.

The crowds disperse at the end of the dance while some members descend at the home of the bride's family. It is another big day of cooking, and everyone is eager to do his or her part to make this event a success. Everything that has been planned since the initial evening visit by the prospective son-in-law to the marital ceremony must now come to fruition. Every effort is geared toward this event being impeccable. From here on, everything that transpires into the actual marriage resembles that of common Christian marriage. You already know the sequence of activities in this revered engagement, so there is no need to bore you with the details. Therefore, we will stop here, for nothing beyond this point is unusual. Till death do us part? I do!

With the completion of the marital bond, the niceties, and the novel experiences, it is safe to surmise that, in a few months, the young bride will be in the family way. The parents of the married couple again take on the responsibility of guardianship; the do's and don'ts are handed down in such a way as to leave no alternative. The young couple, having no experience, does nothing but accede to every word of command. The months are swiftly flying by. It is now seven, eight months and the pregnancy is quite visible. As with the wedding, elaborate preparation is made for the unborn. Someone unfamiliar with the culture might be baffled as to which or how many of the females are pregnant. These precautionary measures are the action of overly concerned mothers and in-laws; nevertheless, everyone means well.

Thus, a youngster becomes part of a new generation in a population that must succumb to the metamorphosis that has become a culture in Union Island.

THE STEWART'S FAMILY

Sickness within the family was never considered a secret; hence the sick received the best care because every hand is usually on board.

Numerous natives have been mentioned that bear the ever-present family name STEWART. It is common knowledge that the Stewart family is the largest in Union Island—much larger than any other family. But how did that happen when the Spann family was widely established and recognized from its inception? The Mulzac family, who for the most part supplanted the Spann, was at one time the chief architects on the island as well as the principal entrepreneurs, fishermen & whalers, shipwrights, vessel owners, and landowners. They too are meager in numbers today compared to yesterday when the onus of government in Union Island was squarely etched on their shoulders.

The Stewart family name is by no means of African origin. Instead, it is of English derivation, and so are the many family names that Unionites have bared for centuries. Studies have shown that "Stewart" is an occupational name for a steward or manager of a household or estate, or one who had charge of a king's or important noble's household. These names were given to the Africans during slavery. Though not by their own choices, they bear the names of their slave masters with pride. It is important that bearers of these names now study the roots or origins of the numerous names that they are identified by. They should also have a thorough understanding of the meanings of these last names. It is equally important that they recognize that their ancestors were stolen from Africa, so they have basically lost their way. In jeopardy since their exodus from the motherland, they have lost their names, languages, religion, culture, folkways, mores, and norms. Nevertheless, they have earned the right of ownership after 260 years of existence on Union Island.

But from where did the Stewart's family name of Union Island came? And when did it arrive in this little rock? Let us carefully discuss the genesis of the famous Stewart's family of Union Island. Earlier in this book, mention was made of Samuel Spann, the S & J's interisland slave trade and their proclivity for piracy in the region during the 1770s. Mention was also made of the tension that existed between Great Britain and France before and after the Treaty of Paris in 1763. Because of these factors, S & J's, and many other ship owners have suffered tremendous loss at the hands of other savage pirates and privateers. This resulted in the loss of several of their valuable cargo ships. Some ships were attacked and sunk; others were viciously robbed of their cargo, which made up of slaves, gold, silver, rum, or anything of value. During these attacks at sea, many pirates refused to surrender their ships and were killed at the point of capture and their ships were taken with all of its cargo.

During the slave trade in the Caribbean region, several merchants lost their cargo ships in the waters of St. Vincent and Grenada. While some of these disasters were recorded, (1611, 1653 and 1675) many went unnoticed. During the early 19th century, a cargo ship laden with slaves had run aground and later sunk into the waters of Mayreau, Palm Island and Union Island (Page 221-222). This disaster was undocumented. While many slaves had succumbed to their watery graves, many were also fortunate to survive the ordeal and landed on both Clifton and Richmond bays of Union Island. Among the survivors was a young slave who later had a son named William McDowell; his last name "Stewart," depicted that he was the property of a Scottish slave master whose last name was Stewart. Evidently, during those years, it was mandated that every slave is branded with the name of his/her master. As a result, the father of William McDowell immediately became the recipient of the family name *Stewart*. Like William McDowell's father, many other black families on Union Island have attained their names in the same or similar manner. With the sinking of that ship, S & J Spann and Company, under the Stewardship of Samuel Spann became the recipient of many more slaves at no cost. This enlarged the S & J Spann and Company workforce on their plantations. Approximately two decades later, the Spanns relinquished the cotton industry and sold the island to Major Collins. But by such time, the historical foundation of the Stewarts clan was permanently set into the cornerstone of time.

As indicated above, the observed patriarch of the Stewart family was Mr. William McDowell Stewart, a sharecropper who had firsthand experience as a slave. Because childbearing was widely encouraged among slaves, William had quite a number of children. As with numerous ancestors of his time, there is no documentation available to indicate the date of his birth. Mr. McDowell and his wife, Louisiana Wilson begat quite a number of children back then. Some of their names were Robert, Peter, John, Aaron, Emanuel, Hughwith, Violet, Artine, and Vashtie. They were the generation of first landowners; it was during that time that the British Crown subdivided the island, giving the residents the pride of ownership. During this time, the cotton crop, still the main source of income was grown throughout the island. But corn and pigeon peas had already made a mark and later supplanted it to become the chief crops on the island, and it has remained so even until today. Corn and peas are further discussed in another part of the book.

The proliferous nature of these descendants of Africa was evident throughout Union Island, especially in the Stewart families. The children of Mc. Dowell Stewart had an average of nine children apiece—except Emanuel, whose count was in the vicinity of twenty-plus. So, like Jacob of the Bible, they fathered lots of children who were undoubtedly their pride and joy. The Stewart families were very close-knitted and valued bloodline as sacred; they also believed in a strong social support system among themselves. Sickness within the family was never considered distasteful, nor kept as a secret; hence their sick always receive the best care, because all hands were on board. Committed to making life better, Stewart's young men took to both the land and sea to take care of their huge families. The women, being housewives and mothers, remained true to the use of the land. They were very supportive of their husbands in making life possible and were able to effectively communicate and work together as a team amidst numerous challenges. In short, they loyally remained in love and faithfully honored their noble responsibilities, and the phrasal definition: "Till death do us part."

Although the mass exodus of young men from Union Island during the turn of the twentieth century and onward has affected the population tremendously, the Stewart influence was still significant. Later, there were three major concentrations of the Stewart families on the island. The central village of Ashton (Frigate) was the home of 80 % of the black population on Union Island since their arrival from Africa. This location was where the Stewart family of Union Island started and proliferated immensely.

As mentioned before, the high level of fertility was not

exclusive to the Stewart families; many other families were there too. Other family names that made-up Union Island's population were: Wilson, Mulzac, Richards, Scrubb, Douglas, Thomas, John, Hutchinson, McIntosh, Roache, Clouden, Ambrose, Cox, Jones, Simmons, Alexander, James, McTair, Williams, Lewis, Joseph, Paul, Regis, Harvey, Daniel and the Spann. The entire human family of Union Island is intertwined enough that it is said locally, "All ah we ah whan family" (We are all one family).

As with the Spann and Mulzac families, these huge concentrations of Stewarts have diminished considerably, especially in recent years. The culprit, of course, is the ever-present Exodus Factor. With that being said, it is safe to surmise that the dilution of the Stewart's bloodline has also led to the demise of many-valued and treasured principles that this family was noted for. Regrettably, this already shrunken family name (Stewart) of Union Island will give rise to another family name that has little or no historical significance to the island. Distressingly, the unending transformation continues.

◆◆◆□*Chapter Six*

UNION ISLAND'S VESSELS

Locals used the flour bags as fabric to make frocks, shirt and trousers for their children to attend school.

Since the late 19th century, until the last quarter of the twentieth century, many vessels that were owned and operated by Unionites have circumnavigated the waters of the Grenadines, and by extension, the Caribbean. Remarkably, many of these vessels were built on the soil of Union Island. And although shipbuilding was not fully established during the time of the Spanns, the first and largest vessel, The Katherine, was built in Union Island in 1839. Later, many other large vessels were built at the notable shipbuilding yard of Top Yonder Bay. The names of these vessels are: Spartan, Ocean King, Lady Osprey, Wanderer, Wild Rover, Paragon, Priscilla, Pursuer, Providence, Franklin D. R., Princess Louise, Utah, Radel, Lady Jestina, Lady Sylvania, United Kingdom, United Glory, West Indian Eagle, Zena S., Olanda, Champion, Speedy Queen, Federal Queen, The Asco, Faith H., Adelta, Aloma, Yvonne Marie, F.S. Elizabeth, Sylvia E. M, Virginia, Flanders, Seamang, Angela, Kelvin & Clyde, and Armour Marie. The gold medal for the largest boat owned by any Unionite went to Mr. Augustus King Mitchell. That boat was The Triton (Aloma), which he purchased in St. Lucia.

Then there were the United Pilgrim and United Brothers, two vessels jointly owned and operated by three brothers: Gurry, Eastman, and Evan Stewarts (excellent shipwrights). The feat of partnership among brothers is nonexistent today, for the concept of collaboration is more likely to be met with these choice words: "A partnership is a leaky ship." Regretfully, a competitive, contentious spirit has replaced that strong feeling of cohesiveness and cooperation of long ago. This new level of divisiveness or discord has contributed to the demise of many business ventures that would have benefitted Union Island greatly.

Many of the vessels mentioned above have frequented the Gulf of Paria and the mouth of the Demerara River on a regular basis. Most of them were called Windjammers (operated only by sail). Motorboats during those earlier years were scarce commodities. The men and patriarchs effectively governed Union island in a unique way that alleviated it from many strains and challenges and helped to alleviate the state of abject poverty and wants.

Many can now reminisce about the jetty of Clifton Harbor, how it was trafficked with commercial livelihood when these vessels made their way into the harbor after they had engaged in interisland trade and transportation. They returned laden with cargo through the hostile seas that engulf Jamaica, Trinidad, Cuba, Puerto Rico, Dominican Republic, Haiti, Barbados, and Grenada. These vessels were the lifeline, the aorta upon which the people of Union Island depended for oxygenated blood because the regional trading was important both commercially and as a food source.

Basic foodstuffs such as rice, sugar, flour, cooking oil, canned orange juices, powdered milk, and the like were regularly imported from Trinidad. They were sold, not just to the natives of Union Island but also to other nearby Grenadines' islands such as Canouan, Mayreau, and Carriacou. Clothes and regular household goods were obtained from this regional trading, primarily from the island of Trinidad where there was a wider array of manufacturing industries. During such time, St. Vincent, the mainland, was in its infancy regarding the manufacturing clothing and similar commodities.

Long ago, the flour imported from Trinidad was brought in 100-lbs white canvas bags that were very sturdy. Locals made use, not only of the contents of those bags but also of the fabric that the bags were made of. They were used to make shirts and pants for children to attend school. And they were washed, thoroughly starched and ironed every week. A school child back then had but one uniform and was quite contented with it.

On Union Island, local produce was exported to generate income. Exported commodities included tamarinds, sea-moss, crabs, fowl, corned fish, and Devi-Devi. The exported Devi-Devi was used in Trinidad for making soap or glue. Foodstuffs, textbooks, and other needed school supplies that were boxed and tied with yawn-rope (a type of rope) were bought in Trinidad and shipped back to Union. Portland cement, rebar (steel), nails, blocks, and screws constituted to additional cargo that made its way to Union's hardware and shops.

Many of the local crafts sank, or in some cases ran aground, at nearby reefs. The last of these vessels was Speedy Queen, which was part owned by Mr. Mills Mc Intosh, the late Milford Mc Intosh, and Ifield Pope of Clifton. It is alleged that this vessel sank between the unfriendly waters of Trinidad and Grenada— "the Bocus," as it is locally called.

The Speedy Queen was built in 1964–65 at the harbor of Calliaqua, St. Vincent. After attaining all the information and expertise he desired, Mr. Mills McIntosh left the North Coast of Colliers Wood, England, in the London Borough of Merton, having determined how he wanted this craft to be built. "We needed the best lumber to build this ship," said Mr. Mills Mc Intosh, the mastermind of this whole venture. "At the end of the day, the consensus was to import from Guyana and Surinam all building material, chiefly the lumber that these countries are renowned for." He went to the town of Calliaqua, St. Vincent, where two local shipwrights nicknamed Mr. Gudgy, and Building Hucot took to the harbor to complete their new assignment.

This boat took exactly two years of painstaking time in the shipwright's yard of Calliaqua before it was ready for sea. Gudgy and Building Hucot were very committed and excellent at their craft, and they did deliver as promised, after two years of meticulous work. Upon completion of this arduous task, the bottom of the ship was cast with a special type of concrete for extra stability. Then two Rustan engines out of Lloyds, England, were installed, containing four cylinders each, and a gearbox of German origin, the Hurth. These engines gave the boat the kind of power needed to travel the rugged seas of Trinidad and Tobago, Guyana, Surinam, Venezuela, and the Windward Islands.

"Things were happening financially," said Mr. Mills. "We had constant revenue that was showing significant signs of prosperity. I captained the vessel for its entire life except for that one voyage on October 3, 1970, when it went missing. Things do happen at sea," Mr. Mills, whispered dejectedly. "My heart is telling me that those poor chaps were asleep when disaster met them that Saturday night." On that vessel were the other part owners: Milford McIntosh and Ifield Pope, the husband of the late Princess

Pope. Seventeen other passengers and sailors were a part of the voyage. They all perished at sea.

Earlier I made a note of some personalities that have grazed the soil of Union Island. Their contributions and legacies have left an impact on the island. But I would be remiss if I did not mention the true cornerstone and bedrock of this little island, Mr. Augustus King Mitchell. He was the owner of the most vessels in Union Island during the 50's and 60's. His empire extended into numerous small businesses, from hotels to real estate. His formative years at the Anglican Church School were indicative of his aspiration not to settle calmly into the status quo of "just getting by, or coping. "It was clear at an early age that he had entrepreneurship written all over his psyche. And like Captain Hugh Mulzac, his hunger to excel could not be satisfied within the confines of the Grenadines waters. He wanted more than what was proffered to him, and he was bent on attaining every ounce of what he aspired to.

Died almost two year ago, Mr. Mitchell, like many other vessel owners were indeed an essential part of the development of Union Island. With the use of his numerous vessels that transported cargo throughout the Caribbean waters. Many young men were able to obtain jobs as sailors, and chefs on these crafts. They were also able to provide the adequate support and care for their families.

Today, the multiple activities that once existed at the Clifton Harbor because of the frequent arrivals and departures of these crafts are drastically reduced to a single digit; that single digit referrers to a single ship that traversed the waters of Trinidad & Tobago, and an infrequent visit to the nearby island of St. Vincent.

Gone are the days of the vessels that were owned and operated by the men of Union Island.

MARINE TRAGEDIES

Both men stood for a while waiting for him to resurface, but he never did.
Unfortunately, he was never seen again.

When you look at the above topic *"MARINE TRAGEDIES,"* what comes to your mind? Does bliss, happiness, joy, excitement, thrill or an amicable feeling inundate you? Certainly not! This subject implies precisely what its name says, (Tragedies) and perhaps it is the most touching segment of the entire book. This subject evokes a feeling of pensiveness, sorrow, sadness, despondency, anguish, and grief, and justifiably so, it is solely because of the distressful result of each event that is listed below. Let us take a keen look.

Even before the turn of the 20th century, numerous Unionites have lost their lives to the unforgiving waters of St. Vincent & the Grenadines, Grenada, St. Lucia, Dominica, Barbados, Trinidad & Tobago, Jamaica, Guyana, Antigua, Martinique, and many other Caribbean islands. This subject, (Marine Tragedies) reminds us of the numerous disastrous outcomes that have befallen many of our young men and women at sea. The chain of events that are listed below is worth relating in details for a number of reasons. The principal reason is that these marine occurrences were never documented; hence no information on this subject is available to be read at any archive or institution.

In the years 1611, 1653, and 1675 respectively, three large cargo ships, which were laden with slaves, sunk in the waters of the Grenadines. The former fell victim to Spanish enemy ships that took the slaves and destroyed the crew. The latter, (1675) was a slave ship that came from the west coast of Guinea, Africa, with a large cargo of slaves. It was wrecked in the vicinity of St. Vincent and the island of Bequia. As a result, a large number of slaves were rescued and thrived into the forest of St. Vincent. These slaves later intermingled with the native Caribs and hence produced notable black Caribs that were once prevalent in St. Vincent. Then, during the time of the so-called emancipation, approximately one and a half centuries later, another ship ran aground during the night, in the reef-laden waters of the Grenadines. It was said that this undocumented accident took place in the waters of Mayreau, Palm Island, and Union Island. Some old folks refuted that location and indicated that this marine accident instead took place between the waters south of Frigate Rock, between the tiny islands of Palm Island, Petit St. Vincent, Petit Martinique and Carriacou (approximately 1.5 miles' disparity). Although many lives were lost, the survival rate far outnumbered the death toll.

The survivors swam and later walked the shallow reefs of Union Island to safety. Unluckily, these slaves immediately became the chattel of Samuel Spann –the owner of the island. These tragic incidents may have set the tone for the countless black lives that succumbed to watery graves many years later; this, a seemingly inescapable, yet morbid future for the Union-man, who desires to make his living at sea. Still, another one and a half centuries later, September 1921, John Mulzac, an older brother of Captain Hugh Mulzac, with a crew of several black sailors lost their lives in the Caribbean Sea. At that time, he was taking his vessel, The Evelyn Guy, back into port.

Thursday, June 19, 1989, is unquestionably a night to remember. It affected me both positively and negatively, but by and large, there is something worthwhile to be learned from such a tragedy. At that time, I was living at my brother's home in Washington DC. That evening, I was at home taking care of some personal things. Earlrick, my brother, and his wife, Lucille had left for church. A few hours earlier, I was sitting in the living room looking at the TV for approximately twenty-five minutes. Nothing seemed to grab my attention, so I kept changing channels rapidly. I was about to put down the remote when suddenly a strange feeling came over me. My body began to shake uncontrollably. I looked at one of the windows facing the street, and immediately a commanding voice inside of me ordered me down onto the carpet. There I remained for several minutes as my body continued its shiver. Then, almost instantly, a burst of energy inundated me. I rose without delay as though nothing had happened. Little did I knew that my brother Urias was breathing his last breath at sea during those few moments while my body was unable to contain itself.

Back in Trinidad, my mom, **Sheila**, had a disturbing dream one week prior to Urias' tragic death. She was at the Bethesda Gospel Hall Church, Port of Spain, where she attended the Sunday service. **Sheila** fell into a brief nod and dreamed about the roaring of the sea and its many waters. Among the waters, she saw knives and other sharp-edged weapons as they moved violently to and fro. "It was a slumber that sapped the energy out of me." She said, "I woke up gasping for breath; I was exhausted."

Two days later I received a call from a very close friend out of Trinidad named Gracie Ford. She relayed to me that seven men, all from Canouan, except my brother, Urias, had left Union Island on a small boat that was laden with beverages. They all were heading to Canouan but sadly they did not get to their destination. It was an incredibly sad time for us as a family, but my Mom and I already had a spiritual experience; it alleviated the stresses of the inevitable. This was a tragedy that we had to deal with nonetheless. It impacted us greatly. Nevertheless, this personal loss could not compare to the countless Union-lives lost at sea through negligence, bravado, and a hefty percentage of ignorance.

Over the years, the native fishermen or cargo boat owners of Union Island did not use lifejackets at sea. This practice of nonchalance was handed down from one generation to another. From every corner of Union Island, the shoreline has been available to every resident: "It's just a hop, a skip and a jump away" as we say colloquially. And for that reason, 99.9 percent of the people knew how to swim. That may have hindered their sense to use of precautionary measures to avert the dangers at sea. Here is a detailed account of many undocumented events of Unionites who have lost their lives at sea then, and in recent years.

Mid 1940's

Mr. Benjamin Hypolite and his little son Simon, Jobe Alexander, Mr. Albert Lewis and wife Elizabeth, Elnora McTair (child of the late David McTair), Howe Wilson, Ms. Flora Douglas and Mrs. Newly Harvey (the first wife of the late Tyrell Harvey and mother of Nimrod Harvey) all residents of Union Island, perished in the seemingly benign waters of Union Island and the sister island, Carriacou. La Lena, a sailboat owned and captained by Mr. Benjamin Hypolite (Christmas) of Union Island left the jetty of

Hillsborough, Carriacou, on a late Monday afternoon on its voyage back to Union Island. It never got to its destination. It is believed that the little craft was midway between these two islands (Carriacou and Union Island) when a sudden windstorm or twister got the better of them. The captain, along with the other eight passengers, did not stand a chance; the boat was not fortified with life jackets or any other reliable facilities that could have saved lives. They disappeared almost instantaneously.

One young man from Ashton Village claimed to have seen the little craft moments before it's unfortunate disappearance. He did not notify anyone until the following day. This lad was the son of a trafficker from St. Vincent named Ms. Locus. She once sold her produce, or ground provisions, at the well-known Meldon shop of Ashton Village. Mr. James Cox formally owned this shop and later sold it to Mr. Meldon John of Campbell. The chap left Union Island immediately as residents expressed their displeasure at him for withholding such critical information. Had they known that the boat was seen that afternoon, help would have been sent out in search of survivors.

Another small boat from Union Island almost encountered the same fate several years later. This little craft left the calm waters of Hillsborough, Carriacou, where many residents make regular visits to their doctors. They had lots of groceries, ground provisions, and fruits. The captain and his boatload of passengers were well on their way home, but before they arrived at the deeper blue waters, a sudden gust of wind capsized the little craft. The bulk of their groceries, along with the ground provisions and many bananas, floated everywhere. Everyone held on tenaciously to the semi-submerged craft. Fortunately, some fishermen that were in the area saw the incident and immediately rescued them. Two individuals who experienced this close call were the late Mama James and Ms. Wilhelmina Adams. The latter was well known throughout the island as "Dune." It was reputed that one woman, despite the severity of the situation, found it necessary to have her fill with the ripe bananas that were floating around while awaiting rescue. Nevertheless, all lives were preserved, and they were able to get the boat back into working condition almost immediately. The boat and the entire crew got to Union Island later that day.

Friday, February 18, 1966

The words of Hugh Mulzac, "Even when planned activities

are conducted with the best intentions and skills, they don't always turn out as expected." Such is the case with Mr. Theophilus Longdon of Ashton, whose commercial journey to the island of Grenada was derailed by the seemingly calm waters of that region; he was with a crew of four young men.

It was about 9:00 P.M Friday, February 18th, 1966; a small boat laden with conch left the quiet harbor of Ashton on a journey to the commercial seaport of St. Georges, Grenada. The captain, Mr. Theopholus Longdon, with a crew, which includes: Stanley Davis (Tall Boy), Lovell Eustacious Scrubb, Cecil Longdon, and a miner named Tyler Thomas. Everyone was quite excited about his trip to Grenada. It appeared to be a smooth, comfortable voyage as they sailed through the exceptionally calm waters. They had long since passed the little island of Carriacou and by then had completed over 70 percent of their journey. A discussion related to Mr. Nicky (Tin Dada), a seaman from a previous trip to Grenada, who was reported to have been relieved of his entire purse of $60. Members of the crew began to bicker among themselves and were probing to determine whether someone on that crew might have been responsible for the offense; the discussion escalated into an argument.

One member of the crew, Stanley Davis, felt he was disrespected, and took umbrage when some members were insinuating that he might have been responsible for the misdeed. In disgust, Tall Boy stood up and pointed his hands in the air and shouted, "If I took the money, this boat ain't reaching Grenada." Instantly, his words came to reality.

All eyes were fixated on Tall Boy's hands in the air, and as he took his hands down, the boat became submerged with the cargo of conch. Miraculously, his words had become a reality, Tyler Thomas explained, "It was around midnight; I don't know what had happened. That was something else, and it still bothers me today; every so often when I remember it. Everyone was in the water just like that. Lovell's feet were on my shoulders, and he pushed me right under the water, causing me to scramble about. I still remember the sweater I had on. The tide was very, very strong and moving up in an easterly direction. It swept us up immediately. From the beginning, Tall Boy started to complain about cramps in his feet. I heard him moving in the distance. I did not hear anyone else except Theophilus, so I started to swim until I caught up with him. Boy, we kept swimming together for a while, and suddenly Theophilus said to me that he didn't think he could make it. I was shocked to hear that, so I said to Theophilus, 'Pray Theophilus, just Pray.' Then I started to sing 'Rock of Ages cleft for me, let me hide myself in thee.' that was all I could do: swim and sing; that was my only hope."

Tyler Thomas, the youngest of the crew, was the son of Mrs. Norma and William Thomas. He swam with the old man thirty-one years his senior and took a proactive stance in motivating his older compatriot never to give up. Without sight of land in the dark, Tyler had a sense of what direction they should swim. He encouraged his elder as they swam blindly through the hostile current. Five hours later, they saw land. It was early in the morning, way before the sun came up from the horizon, and there lay a cay that they later learned was Big La Tantes. La Tantes are three small cays that are located approximately 5 miles off the north, northwestern coast of Grenada (map on page iv). The tide by then had changed direction, but it was so strong that it prohibited them from reaching land almost until midday.

"Well we reached Big Les Tantes and rested on the sand for a while, but there was no form of help for us there," Tyler said. "We looked around and saw another small island with smoke coming out of its bushes; the island was Little Les Tantes. We decided to swim to that island to get some help. Boy, it took us another 30 minutes to get there, but the smoke was still at a distance away from us.

The curious sixteen-year-old then shouted at the top of his voice for help. Realizing that help was in the distance, they both climbed onto the rocks and went over to the other side where they would be able to discover the source of the smoke. They went to explore and sighted a couple of campers.

Excited that help was available, he told the two men of the horrendous situation that they had endured. The campers served them breakfast. They started eating, but because the older man had drunk a lot of seawater while swimming, he vomited profusely. They finished their breakfast, rested for a short while, and then decided to climb the rocks in search of their fellow crewmembers. They got to the other side of the small island and immediately Tyler saw his tired friend Cecil (Sagga) very close to a rock, just about to climb to safety. In excitement, he said to Theophilus, "Look Sagga." The older man hastily looked and saw his son as

Tyler cautioned him not to call him. But the elated dad couldn't contain himself upon seeing his beloved son on the cusp of safety. He shouted "Cecil!" and immediately Cecil turned his head in the direction of his father's voice. Suddenly, a strong wave rose above the tired youngster and instantly he was washed under the water. Both men stood for a while waiting for him to resurface, but he never did and was never seen again. They wept bitterly.

The campers later took Theophilus and Tyler to the port of Sauteurs, north of Grenada. There they attained much-needed help, and the news was later broadcast to Union Island via St. Vincent. The men were then transported to Granville, another small town of Grenada. They spent the night there, and early the next day they boarded a boat that safely transported them to the port of Hillsborough, Carriacou. In Carriacou, a small boat from Union Island titled Zag, captained by the late Cecil Regis (Drifters), was patiently awaiting the two men. Cecil weighed anchor, and off they went to Ashton Harbor, where 90 percent of the residents of Union Island awaited their arrival.

At about 2:30 P.M., the little craft sailed into Ashton's Harbor, where a thousand plus happy residents mobbed them. "It was like a melee that afternoon; everyone was happy to meet and greet us." Tyler said, "Unionites really turned out that evening, Josiah; they did, and I felt a sense of oneness. I felt loved."

Lost on that voyage were Cecil Longdon, the son of Jessita and Theophilus Longdon. Stanley Davis, the husband of Mrs. Faithful Ackie. Also lost was Lovell Eustacious Scrubb, the son of Pablo and Rosa Scrubb.

After witnessing the disappearance of his son on February 19th, 1966, Theophilus Longdon's heart remained heavy with grief and pain for the rest of his life. The end came when he was finally relieved of his prolonged burden of grief; he was buried on Monday, March 20th, 1995. Theophilus Longdon was the husband of the late Harriet Longdon and father of Winston Longdon. Tyler Thomas is the only surviving member of the crew that left for Grenada on that late Friday afternoon exactly fifty-two years ago.

Sixty-one years later, the unforgiving waters of the Grenadines were hungry once again. On a stormy day, Monday, July 17th, 2017, Winston Longdon 67, and his aid, Sheldon Gellizeau 17, left the sheltered harbor of Ashton on a small fishing boat. For both men, it was just another routine day of fishing. But for anyone at sea that is not armed with the relevant marine equipment that is necessary for a time of disaster, it can be chaotic. And chaotic it was for the small craft with the duo; they were never seen again.

Tuesday, June 25, 1985

Nelson John and Sherwin Wilson, two young teenagers, lost their lives on a small boat (Top Gun) between the waters of Grenada and Carriacou. They were returning home after a successful trip to Grenada and were never seen again. No physical evidence was ever found. It is believed by many that the severe rough waters of this region swamped this crew. Nelson John was the son of Jessie and Thomas Polson (Uncle Tom), while Sherwin Wilson was the son of Emris Wilson.

Friday, August 5, 1983

A crew of four from Clifton Harbor—Glenroy Alexander, Julian Adams (Huggins), Kenroy Alexander, and Johnathon Snagg (Ranking lost their lives at sea on a journey from Martinique back to Union Island. This boat, Wandering Star, was captained by Kenroy Alexander and was on its weekly voyage back from selling fish and shrimp and then buying non-perishable goods to be sold locally in Union island.

It is believed that they were met by a severe storm on that dark, rainy morning, and the boat overturned. This conjecture was reputed by some based on a few unusual occurrences that preceded its disappearance. Holden Regis, the captain of the vessels Sweet Memories, was also engaged in the same maritime venture. He had left Martinique one day earlier but did not encounter any abnormality on the water. "The water was nothing out of the ordinary. It is not that it was entirely calm, but nothing to lose sleep over." And even though we believe they became victims of the capricious weather and the rant of an unrepentant sea, it remains a solemn mystery. Many questions whether foul play had occurred. But even if that was the case, we still must pose these questions: Did they have lifejackets? Did they have a radio whereby they could have communicated for help on such a regretful night? These are some of the unanswered questions that haunt us whenever we have losses at sea, especially the precious lives of our loved ones. Below are some of the events that led up to the disappearance of *Wandering Star.*

One day after Wandering Star had docked in the port of Fort de France, Martinique, the crew of five observed an unusually pungent scent coming from the deck of the boat. The scent was so obnoxious that it was impossible for them to remain on the craft. Everyone was uneasy and wondered where the scent came from, but no one had a clue or an answer. The crew collectively questioned whether a pungent liquid had been intentionally poured on the ship in their absence. Maybe someone was trying to dissuade them from returning to the boat, they pondered. But the question is, by whom? With the help of friends, the crew worked feverishly to rid the boat of such intolerable odor, and they did. Ready to return home to Union Island again, they pulled anchor and set sail on the voyage back to the little Grenadine Island. A couple of hundred meters off the harbor, another unusual occurrence, grabbed the attention of the crew. This time it was addressed, and early the next morning the boat was ready to sail again. One member of the crew, Reynold Mills (Tamboo), was rather disgruntled and chose to remain ashore rather than sailing the following morning with his compatriots. It turned out to be a prudent decision on his behalf. It was the last time that he had seen the faithful ship Wondering Star. Reynold later returned to Union Island on another craft, *Good Fortune*, a boat that was owned by his brother, Newton Alexander.

Monday, June 19, 1989.

On June 19, 1989, Urias Stewart, and a crew of six young men, all from the island of Canouan—Trevor, Dannie, Chris, Curtis, Boyie, and Byron—sailed from Carriacou, where they had bought beers and other strong drinks earlier that day. They stop on Union Island on their way to Canouan. Urias could not resist the opportunity to travel with them he wanted to attend a party that night in Canouan. Urias was excited to celebrate with his friends on this sister island. His friend at the jetty of Union Island tried to discourage him from traveling late that evening, but Urias could not be dissuaded. It was already dark in Union Island. Urias was the last to board the boat. They left quietly that evening and were never seen again.

Earlier that year, there was litigation against Urias by a foreigner and that the foreigner was dissatisfied with the outcome of the lawsuit. Some think that may have sparked some reprise from the foreigner who knew that Urias was about to travel on the unguarded waters; the foreigner seized the opportunity for revenge.

Did these six young men meet their end because of Urias' presence on that little craft? Did they? This is some food for thought.

A minuscule few believed that the little boat, laden above its legal capacity with liquor was easily swamped in the somewhat choppy waters between the islands of Mayreau and Canouan.

Friday, March 15, 1991.

The death of Denzel Stewart struck home very hard. This gentleman died in the same ostensibly shallow waters that appeared to be only a stone's throw between Union Island and her sister Isle Carriacou. Many residents refused to accept the news of the death of this community-minded youngster. *"But I talk to him yesterday. Now you telling me he dead."* *"He say, he was coming back in Point Lookout tomorrow to look at ah job I have fo him. He was so nice."* *"Way the arse is this? Is so people does dead now? Jest so?"* These were some of the sentiments of a few residents as they voiced their varied opinions on the streets of Union Island. Could this tragic incident, and incidents of similar nature be avoided in Union Island? Let us take a detailed look at this single occurrence.

The festive atmosphere of March was quickly approaching, and everyone was rather uneasy as they eagerly awaited the famed Easterval Celebration. Rumors had it that Denzel Stewart and his friend Junior Coy were drunk yet had still embarked on a journey to Carriacou nonetheless. Residents later learned that the above was inaccurate. This is what had happened as was reported by Junior Coy aka (Ground-E).

It was approximately 12:30 A.M. on Thursday, March 14, 1991, at the Ashton Harbor. These two gentlemen may have had a drink or two, which was quite normal. Denzel expressed in no uncertain terms that he wanted to go to Carriacou and would like Coy to take him there immediately. Coy, however, was not too happy to leave Union Island at that time of the night and tried to dissuade his friend. Denzel was not taking no for an answer, so Coy's appeal seemed to fall on deaf ears. To keep his friend happy,

Coy acquiesced. And without preparing for the journey, both men got into Top Gun, the little boat that was owned by his brother Jacob Coy (Lassie). Without checking the capacity of the gas tank, they started the engine, and off they went into the dark of the night. But with such level of negligence, it is prudent to enunciate that the seeds were already sown for disaster.

They had barely reached the midpoint of their journey when the outboard engine that they depended on to take them quickly to the port of Hillsborough suddenly shut off. They tried for approximately fifteen minutes to get the motor back in working condition but to no avail. Their patience was swiftly diminishing with every unsuccessful effort they made. Realizing that the little boat was drifting quickly, Junior decided to swim to Carriacou to get help, for its lights appeared not too far away. Denzil decided to stay on the small craft in hopes that "help" would be available shortly. Quietly, Junior got into the water, and off he went swimming towards the lights of Carriacou. But two minutes had not yet passed when he heard Denzel's voice shouting, "Ground-E, wait for me, wait for me."

Ground-E did just that and swam hastily towards him. Without lifejackets, both Denzel men swam together for approximately 30 minutes supporting each other amid the raging waters. They were quickly succumbing to exhaustion because they had not rested the preceding day. Denzel, the bigger of the two, began to show signs of helplessness but persevered at a slower rate. Seeing that his friend Denzel was in despair, Junior asked him to hold onto his shoulder in an effort to alleviate the strain of his tiring arms. The heavy boots on Denzel's feet were a gross disadvantage; it made swimming more difficult.

"In the beginning, the lights from Carriacou appeared to be close, but the more I swam, the less improvement I saw," Junior Coy recollected. "I was so tired that I could barely keep my head up. The weight was keeping me down, and Denzel appeared to be drinking water." Relieving Denzel from his shoulder, the fight for survival came down to a war against the relentless water. "I was a little ahead while Denzel with gallant effort swam slowly behind."

Junior became emotional "All I know is the sea Josiah, it is all that I know." As the light of the morning brightened, he lost sight of Denzel. Cold, tired, and exhausted, Junior remained hopeful that help would come to him even if he had to make it to the shores of Carriacou swimming, which was still far away. His hope became a reality at about 9:00 A.M. when Jasper H., a small engine boat that was owned by the late Festus Hutchinson of Ashton Harbor rescued him. Denzel, on the other hand, was nowhere to be found. Neither was Top Gun, the little boat belonging to his younger brother.

Friday, January 24, 1997.

On Friday, January 24, 1997, Captain Ledger Alcide (54), his son Otway Alcide (21) of Union Island, Bertram Daniel (65) of Mayreau, A young man 23 years of Union Island, and Dallo (35) of Lower Questelle, St. Vincent, all perished at sea. These entrepreneurs engaging in commercial trade with the French island of St. Maarten left the sheltered harbor of Kingstown during the wee hours of the morning, heading towards the harbors of Phillipsburg and Marigot. The craft never made it to its destination and was never seen again. Although not much can be said in conjunction with this boat, enough time has passed to bring us to a consensus on this one. Mr. Ledger left behind his wife, Millicent Alcide (Liz), and children, namely: Curtis, Yolanda (Pinky), Joy, David, Raymond, and Lavern.

It is believed that this boat sank in very rough waters, where help was unattainable. Mr. Ledger Alcide, who was well known as Dick Richards, was the hardest-working young entrepreneur on Union Island. Dick had recently sold a vessel and had migrated to the United States of America, where he lived for a short time. Dick's livelihood was etched in the Caribbean, and he loved the Sea with a passion. He later left America and reverted to what he knew best: marine life. Well, he wasted no time, and again he was the owner of another vessel that he bought. This time he named this new craft Flying Lobster.

Armed with a crew of four (mentioned above), Dick immediately immersed himself into a friendly trade relationship with the cosmopolitan island of St. Maarten. His cargo was ground provision, plantain, bananas, and a wide variety of young plants that he sold to a market that was tailor-made for him. On his return to the islands, he would bring with him refrigerators, TVs, VCRs, and so on, to be sold to the locals of Union Island. He also brought back cooking oil in large quantities, knowing that there was a local market for that product as well.

After eight months of inter-island trade, Dick knew his way around this new frontier. As a result, business appeared to be doing fine, and he and his crew took advantage of every opportunity that presented itself. One week earlier, they had been scheduled to make a trip to St. Maarten, but because of the inclement weather in the region, they were forced to remain on land until the weather condition subsided. On January 24, they eventually pulled anchor, and off they went into a calmer sea to the great beyond, never to be heard or seen again.

Friday, February 14, 1997.

Coincidentally, disaster struck twice that year, and on the same day of the week to boot. Friday, February 14, 1997, is another date that Unionites can commemorate with the burning of candles. This time the culprit was the roving water of St. Vincent and the Grenadines. Rupert Polson, (Jah-Pot), as he was amicably called, left the port of Kingstown late one Saturday evening, between 4 to 5 P.M., heading for Ashton Harbor. Two other young chaps—Rocker and David—accompanied him; they both were from the mainland, St. Vincent. Another sailor on his way to St. Vincent claimed to have seen the boat as they both traveled in opposite directions. The time had passed when these three young lads should have been back. Relatives and friends became more concerned with each passing hour. With their eyes affixed on the once-narrow passageway that separates Frigate Rock from Union, everyone hoped for a propitious sighting, but unfortunately without success. The early morning swiftly turned into noon, and noon made its way to another sundown. The optimism that had been exhibited twenty-four hours earlier suddenly evaporated. A strange feeling of sadness arrived and lingered, as everyone was forced to accept defeat. The island had lost another battle to this aged enemy and friend, the sea. Once again, Union Island wept.

Saturday, December 21, 1968.

One of the most gruesome accidents in the waters of the Grenadines in recent years was the sinking of the small passenger/cargo vessel, Federal Queen. And although numerous black lives had been lost in this vicinity during the catastrophic African Slave Trade, the death toll of Black lives was never documented or made available for the records or history books. The disastrous events that are mentioned during the earlier years (pages 221 - 222) are some typical examples. Although the Federal

Queen accident occurred some forty-plus years ago, it is still fresh in the hearts and minds of Unionites and Vincentians, especially the families of those loved ones that perished at sea.

The late William Stewart and Wickliffe Hutchinson of Ashton Village, Union Island, were the owners of Federal Queen. On December 21, 1968, Captain William Stewart weighed anchor of this small vessel and set sail for the mainland of St. Vincent. As it left the harbor of Clifton, Union Island, onlookers quickly lost sight of this little craft as she disappeared into the darkness of the night.

William Stewart, nicknamed *William Toast*, had a boatload of people who were from the mainland but they had been employed in the Grenadines. That December evening, they boarded the little craft in the hope of returning to their homes for the Christmas holidays. Rumor had it that the boat was laden above its legal capacity, and was unsightly to the eyes of some onlookers. It had approximately eighty people onboard, and some people had reluctantly come off the boat a few moments before it left. Of the many people who came off the craft, two notable persons were: the late Jonah Stewart and the aforementioned Dick Richards, the latter, will finally meet his death some twenty-nine years later on a commercial voyage to St. Maarten. It is alleged that one mother literally pushed her son onto the loaded craft to ensure that he did not miss his opportunity to travel. Oh! What a mistake that was. Nevertheless, everyone knew that this caring mother had meant well.

Everything seemed well when the vessel left the choppy waters of Union Island, but it immediately became an uphill battle for the captain and the crew as the craft entered into deeper waters. The island of Mayreau immediately became visible as small spots of light were seen in the not-too-far distance. These spots represented kerosene lamps—the only source of light other than flashlights that were battery operated. But as the island of Mayreau instantly became visible, after another thirty minutes, it was totally out of sight. They cruised by the island of Mayreau and were in the vicinity of Canouan as they continued into the darkness of the night. The shadow of Canouan, too, was out of sight when they trespassed into the unfriendly waters that led to the Bocus. The Bocus, which is sometimes called Pateau, is the roughest part of the sea in the Grenadines. The boat was far from this seemingly volcanic-like wave when a gush of water swept across it. The large crew moved frantically from one direction to another, and down the boat went. One survivor indicated that while he was sitting fast asleep, he was awakened when he felt his bottom drenched in water. "A few minutes later, he said, the boat went down with everyone."

The sea was now flooded with a wide array of disoriented people. They began to panic in the dark of the night. A lighthouse in the distance caught everyone's attention, and immediately they began swimming toward it. Unfortunately, their swim was away from land and safety. Some, however, did have a sense of direction and swam where they thought the island of Canouan was situated. Susan, the lone female survivor, was a resident of Georgetown and was among the first to swim to the island of Canouan. She once lived with Mrs. Lucita and Robert Joseph (Arthur Gale) of Union Island. William (Toast) Stewart, the captain, Alston Ramage, and Jeffers Jones (T-Nana) of Union Island also made it safely to the island of Canouan. Ken, another native of St. Vincent, the mainland, was also among the few survivors. Though they knew very well how to swim to land, they were far from being prepared for such a Herculean task.

Forty-one lives were lost on that early morning of December 22. Most of the deaths were from St. Vincent, the mainland. Of the death toll, one name that stands out was a resident of Georgetown by the name of Envy Pitt. Two others from the mainland are John Mike, Clifford John, and Tyrell Lynch of Biabou. The deaths from Union Island were Cecilia Alexander, Ottley Jones, the son of Mrs. Rosalyn Jones; Alfred Gellizeau aka (Din-Din), the son of Priscilla Gellizeau; and finally, Norris Dickson, a friend of the late Stella Badnock. It is reputed that a young woman (Sheila) was found alive in the water the following day. She was rescued but later died of dehydration and exhaustion.

A wave of sadness inundated Union Island that morning when the news was dispersed. That day, the wind refused to blow on a day that was relatively cloudy. Residents spoke in very low tones as if they were whispering so that the next-door neighbor would not hear. The truth is, everyone felt the pain of his or her collective loss in a country that was far more community-minded than it is today. It was a period of sorrow that touched every life in St. Vincent & the Grenadines.

Frederick A Fender was an expert American canoeist that once sailed alone in the Caribbean with his Yakaboo during the early 20th century. He frequented the waters of the Grenadines and was familiar with many of the cay. This is what he stated:

"May 1st, 1909. – A whaleboat with a crew of five men left Sauteurs for Union Island; not since heard of. The men were not drunk; neither was the weather out of the ordinary. During the short year since I was with them: four of the men I whaled with have been lost at sea. With the Negro, carelessness is always a great factor, but here the wind and current are a still greater one. Here the trade always seems to blow strongly and at times assumes gale force "w'en de moon change."

Over the years, many more young men have lost their lives at sea. Listed here are names of a few: Godwin Wilson, Medford Wilson (former judge of Grenada), Reynold Gellizeau aka (La Beau), Hayden Hutchinson, Terrence Joseph, Edmond John, Peterson Cox, Tommy Coy, Lyndon Stewart, and Matthew Alexander.

"Marine preparedness" and training can, and should be implemented and enforced in St. Vincent & the Grenadines by the relevant ministry. The training process should be standardized to ensure that all seamen (sailors, fishermen, etc.) are guided by the same information and in the same manner. Hence, every seaman will be absorbing and learning the same essential methods of safety. Ongoing training, In-services, educational facilities & aids should be provided annually. To further enhance the efficiency of this industry, competency testing must be performed every three years to ensure the efficacy of marine preparedness. Notwithstanding, the utmost concern here, is the safety of our seamen, but equally important is the preservation and maintenance of these sea crafts –their sole source of income. Hence, with training and education comes competency -a Level of proficiency that will safeguard lives, and in some cases, saves these valiant young seamen from their bravado selves.

BASIN POND (BASKET)

"Boy, I couldn't even pass too close to Basket and make my mother know about it."

It is well over 100 years since the old name "Basin" was supplanted by the more requisite name "Basket." This pond attained that nickname because of its inability to retain water for an extended period. "It can leak like a basket sometimes; before you know it, it is dry again," said the late Henry Stewart of Campbell. At the location of Basin Pond, there is a caption that is posted on a tourist information notice board; it reads as follow:

"This pond is part of the most extensive complex of the eighteenth-century ruins on Union Island. Jean Augier, one of the island's first French settlers, built it sometime around 1760 when he landed on the island. Basin, which is considered one of the largest of the island's ponds, stored and provided water for the plantation slaves. It was entirely paved with local stones and cemented with heated coral and conch shells. After emancipation in 1834, Basin Pond continued to be a main source of water for the local people." The caption went on to say, *"Up until the 1950s, it was still used for washing and 'watering' animals."*

The last sentence of the above paragraph is not only misleading but also inaccurate; the residents of Ashton Village, and to a greater extent, Campbell, have used this pond for watering animals up until the 1980s. During the entire decade of the 70s, many residents did their laundry at Basket Pond. During slavery, this pond or waterhole as it was generally called, was used to water the slaves and animals simultaneously. The cows were led directly into the pond to drink water, but after having their fill, they generally defecate into it. This turbid water nevertheless, was still used by the slaves for drinking and laundry purposes.

Currently, this pond is almost intact, just in need of some

cleaning to remove shrubs and dirt that have been accumulating at its base, the result of many years without proper maintenance.

"Basket" is a very old name that is known to everyone on Union Island. Yet, the name "Basket" was not mentioned once on this noticeboard that exhibits the history of the pond. Now, this may sound like a trivial issue or outright caviling, but knowing the proper name is necessary for the maintenance and preservation of the island's history as it continues to evolve. Residents ought not to be cavalier, innocent, or ignorant regarding what the preservation of the island's history, legacy, and heritage means. In bringing this to light, every citizen of Union Island should be exhorted to be vigilant in keeping the island's history alive and intact. To partially paraphrase the current Prime Minister, Dr. Ralph Gonzalves on a similar issue, "Every square inch of Union Island's his-story and her-story is our story."

Basket, despite its long history of usefulness, has been tainted by a single unpleasant moment, which to this day continues to be more pronounced at this historical landmark than its sheer purpose and usefulness. Although this unfortunate event transpired more than sixty-five years ago, it is still alive and vivid in the minds and hearts of many residents.

During the rainy months of the year 1950, two young sisters (Patient, age 10, and Agatha, age 11), accompanied by their friend, Zennie, age 10, were about to leave for the pasture of Ms. Irene, where their animals were reared. Their younger sister Elitha, age 3, had wanted to accompany them on their journey, but they were not interested in having her company that morning. Agatha put her wide straw hat on, and with the two other girls, they journeyed on foot all the way through Campbell road to the dense vegetation of Ms. Irene's. On reaching Basket Pond, they saw two people on the opposite side washing clothes. They appeared to be wrapped up in their chores and were oblivious to their surroundings. Zennie left the two sisters to take care of her animals that were tied at her mother's plot of land situated a few hundred meters away. Patient and Agatha were fond of sailing boats, and they seized the opportunity to sail their small coconut boats at the pond. They sailed their boats from one end of the pond and retrieved them at the other. Racing coconut boats at Basket was a custom that every youngster had partaken of for many years. In fact, this art was done almost every day, especially during the months of June through October, when the pond was filled with water. Now Basket Pond was filled with water, and the girls were anxious to sail their boats in the calm of the morning. All that the girls needed then was a light breeze on the grape leaves, which was used as sails on their boats. That breeze makes the boats accelerate to the other side of the pond in a short period of time. Patient and Agatha loved every ounce of it.

Meanwhile, approximately twenty-five minutes had passed, and Zennie, who had left the two sisters earlier, had finished her chore and headed back in the direction of the pond. Immediately, she saw a straw hat floating aimlessly on the water. Something seemed awry she thought, as she observed a small crowd gathered around the pond frantically looking everywhere. Instantly, she went to investigate and observed that the hat had belonged to her friend Agatha. She also observed a long stick floating alongside the hat. Her two young friends were nowhere to be found. Zennie shouted the names of both girls several times, but there was no response from either. The frantic crowd dispersed around the pond and made a brief search of the nearby area, but all efforts made that morning turned up empty. Suspecting that something had gone tragically wrong, the small group frantically yelled out for help. The alarm was so intense that it drew the attention of others in the vicinity that had been taking care of their animals. Everyone gathered around the pond, looking for any sign of life. Others left the scene terrible troubled but headed for their respective homes nonetheless.

Meanwhile, at Ashton Village, Ms. Siderlyn, the mother of the two sisters, was quite uneasy. She had expected to see her daughters back at home about an hour earlier. Quickly she placed her slippers on her feet and started off for the pastures of Ms. Irene. On her way, she fetched a whip, intending to give the girls a physical reminder on their behinds that in the future, they would not spend such a long time at Ms. Irene's Pasture. (And she would have made use of her whip no matter where she met those girls on their way back home.) But before she got anywhere close to Ms. Irene's, she was greeted with the sad news that her daughters were missing, and may have drowned at Basket Pond. Unable to contain herself, the dejected mother wept the entire journey to Basket Pond, where onlookers consoled her.

It is conjectured that a breeze may have blown Agatha's hat into the pond. Anxious to retrieve her hat, she quickly fetched a long stick and stretched over the pond to reach it. The light object instead, sailed further into the pond. She then stepped into the water in another effort to retrieve her hat and lost her footing on a slippery stone. She fell a couple of feet further and immediately began to panic. Frantically, she tried in vain to regain her footing and keep her head above the water's surface. Her younger sister, Patient, observing that she was in distress, immediately sprang to her rescue. Patient grabbed the same stick and handed it to her struggling sister so that she could get a grip and be pulled out of danger. That turned out to be hazardous as Agatha's pull on the stick was so forceful that Patient instantly lost her footing and fell into the water as well, where they both perished.

No one in the vicinity saw what had happened; hence, no one could help them. And because these two young females could not swim, they slowly sank to the bottom of the pond, where they, unfortunately, lost their lives. A local diver, and father of the two girls, Mr. Casey Black, hoisted them from their watery grave that same day. They both were buried at the same grave at Ashton Cemetery later that day. Shortly after that, Mr. Casey Black suffered a stroke and was unable to function effectively or do regular activities for the remainder of his life.

The ruins of Basin Pond (Basket). Built during the 1750s by a French man named Jean Augier. This pond was once a source of drinking water for animals and slaves.   Photo -Don Wiss.

It was a horrendous day, not just for the parents but also for the community as a whole. Many, many years later, kids were severely warned to exhibit care when extracting water from the eternally useful Basket. Stephen, a son of Ms. Siderlyn, who was born many years after the tragedy, said: "Boy, I couldn't even pass too close to Basket and make my mother know about it. Can you imagine how much licks I got just for being at the pond with my friend?"

Regrettably, Basket Pond is remembered mainly because of the two girls that lost their lives rather than it's many years of conveying water for the ancestors and residents of Ashton.

HURRICANE JANET

Mappish: "Is only by the grace of God why I'm still alive today."

The destructive Hurricane Janet of 1955 is seen here ravaging the Caribbean islands.

I t is widely reputed that the redoubtable Hurricane Janet may have been one of the most destructive force of nature that have grazed the region of the Caribbean, and more so, the soil of Union Island. It shared huge similarities with the formidable "Windward Island Hurricane of 1898," but none was as devastating as the Great Hurricane of 1831, whose impact on the region was unprecedented. Nevertheless, the effects of Hurricane Janet are still remembered by every elder throughout the little island. Is it because it had happened in recent years, only 60+ years ago? Janet's destruction on the islands of St. Vincent and Barbados was also astronomical, not to mention the effect on the rest of the Caribbean Islands that lay in the path of this redoubtable force of nature. For Unionites, Hurricane Janet was the most memorable hurricane to brave the soil of Union Island. Many older folks are familiar with the calypso below which was sung in 1955 by the late Lord Christo of Grenada. For many English-speaking islands of the

Caribbean, this song will conjure up a tremendous amount of memories of such time -the *Then*, as opposed to the *Now*.

Aye Jar...net, ah beg yo hard; Jar... net not Trinidad
Aye Jar...net, ah beg yo hard; Jar...net do not Trinidad
Yo blow down the whole ah Grenada,
Same fate, the Barbadian suffer.
And everyday we read the evening news,
Enough to make ah man jump out he shoes.

Janet hide in the mountain,
Janet lick-down ah million buildings.
Janet's sister was Kathy,
Janet blow way the whole ah Miami.

They had ah misprint, they published there
They say Jar...net had silky hair.
About six foot, the paper state,
September, the twenty-eight.
When Janet visit Grenada,
She blow down the place like ah pasture.
And everyday the monkey paper say,
"Kathy will move Janet from the area."

Janet hide in the mountain,
Janet lick-down ah million building.
Janet's sister was Kathy,
Janet blow way the whole ah Miami.

In St. Vincent, I was afraid,
So help me, when Janet raid.
She blow down a concrete wall,
and it fall down on the Town Hall.
When Janet start to ramajay,
if you see how Vincentians breakaway?
And everyday the Monkey Paper say,
"Kathy will move Janet from the area."

Janet hide in the mountain,
Janet lick-down ah million building.
Janet's sister was Kathy,
Janet blow way the whole ah Miami.

Aye Mex.e.co was bitter-ly damage, lord have mercy
Woman and children were left to roam,

Janet destroyed their home.
Death was their only companion
And so, they died from starvation
May their souls departed, rest in peace.
Thank heaven, this Janet business ceased.

She died in the mountain,
and leave them repairing house and kitchen.
Janet sister was Kathy,
Janet blow way the whole ah Miami.

On Thursday, September 22, 1955, Hurricane Janet, a category three (3) hurricane, packing a force of 115 miles per hour, slammed into the Caribbean region, causing extensive damage to the islands of Barbados, Grenada, St. Vincent & the Grenadines, and St. Lucia. It is believed that the island of Grenada suffered tremendously and endured much more damage than the other islands in the region. Known for its vast production of nutmeg and other spices, Grenada suffered a loss of approximately 75 percent of its nutmeg plants to this raging wind. The coastal areas of St. Lucia, another island in the neighborhood were devastated by this Atlantic hurricane. "St. Vincent was literally leveled," the news stated. "The destruction resulted in a major setback for the island's chief agricultural product -bananas." It is estimated that the entire region suffered upward of 160 deaths at the hands of this natural disaster. Some claimed that the number quietly surpassed 500 deaths. Fortunately, only two lives were reported lost on Union Island. Prior to the presence of hurricane Janet, leaflets were haphazardly dropped from an airplane that hovered over Union Island. These leaflets were meant to alert the residents of the imminent danger, and that no one should leave the shores of Union Island on a boat. Although many hastily received the information, others had no idea that leaflets were dispersed. One small boat from Clifton had left Union Island a little while before this information was disseminated. They had left for Palm Island, a hunting ground of crabs, and farmland for planting sand-potatoes. Residents also harvested salt there.

On that boat to Palm Island, was one of my late great-aunts, Janey Roache. She was also the sister of my grandmother Telina Roache (Tan Tillix) of Clifton. The late Mrs. Margaret Ovid and a few other people were said to be on that adventurous trip as well. They reached Palm Island safely, unaware of the imminent danger. Twenty minutes on their arrival on the little island, they had to abandon their task immediately and seek shelter under the same raft that had just brought them safely across the water. They turned their little boat upside down against the wind, leaving enough room for each one of them to crawl under to safety. They were packed like sardines in a can, but that was the least of their concerns; their primary objective was to remain alive.

The whistling sound of the sand coupled with the incoming rain made it rather impossible for them to sleep during that eventful night. I had the opportunity to listen to Aunty Janie on a rainy afternoon as she talked of Hurricane Janet. "It was like a sand-storm that refused to end," Aunty Janie whispered softly to me. She placed her hands over her ears as though she was hearing the horrifying sound of the sand against the little craft, and reacted to what had transpired some twenty-three years earlier. Then suddenly a huge smile surfaced on her previously melancholy face. "We used to get a lot of turtle eggs, whelks, and conch in Prune, even paddocks we used to reap by the bags. Those days were good days," she said, chuckling. "I could never forget that beautiful island." She shook her head and walked slowly into her bedroom.

On Union Island, the seemingly sheltered harbor of Clifton was not as fortuitous for the Seamang -a vessel owned by King Mitchell (entrepreneur) was also smashed to ruins. The Lady Sylvania, another vessel that was owned by the late Peter, and lives were reported lost in Union Island.

Samuel Wilson, another vessel was also moored in the harbor due to the might of the storm. Meanwhile, on land, numerous residents lost their thatches at the hands of this vicious storm. Even today, many residents talk about the events that transpired during Janet's reign of terror. "It was one of the most memorable disasters that Unionites have experienced within the last sixty years." One resident said. "One thing that stands out most conspicuously about the wrath of Janet was Mr. McKay John's wooden house which was physically moved from its location and deposited, intact, some three hundred yards away." She continued. Ironically, that place of inertia was among the countless tombstones of the Ashton Cemetery. One native of Canouan who once lived in Union Island mentioned that her son was born during the time of Hurricane Janet; she just could not remember the exact date and year.

Ms. Mappish, the mother of the most acclaimed tailor of

Union Island, the late Mr. McNeal Cox, had quite a bit to say about her misfortune at the hands of Janet. She was nicknamed Mappish, which was short for Ma Patient. Only older folks will remember that her name was Patient. This Ashton resident had lived opposite the building that was used as the dispensary; the edifice was once home to the late but well-known shopkeepers Joseph Alves (Daddy Alves) and his wife, Edith.

Remembering this hurricane, Mappish stretched her hands outward, pointing at her huge fallen plum tree, then shouted: "Is only by the grace ah God why I still alive today." Her younger sister, Ma Julies, had her say as well; she spoke passionately, as though it had happened only a couple of days ago. "You see all across here was water, the whole place flood!"

Still further inland at Ashton village, countless thatches lay feebly signifying the presence of this unprecedented reign of terror on the island. In Clifton, the situation was identical; some residents were fortunate enough to lose only the roofs of their houses. With the strength that Hurricane Janet possessed, they were at God's mercy. **Isabella Roach** (mentioned earlier) was among the countless residents that lost their wattle and daub houses to this reign of terror. She found refuge at her the home of her last son. His name was Johnathon.

As the horrendous sound of the raging wind preceded the presence of Hurricane Janet, one parent out of fear, placed her baby and toddler into a cabinet. She thought that the cabinet was the safest place for her young ones. Fear inundates the heart of every parent on the island; even the galvanized roofs that protected some of the sturdier houses reacted like paper.

For the residents of Union Island, Janet's destruction of the little isle was so pronounced that whenever there is a lesser storm in the region, the older folks are reminded of 1955, the year that Janet's presence was felt; in fact, they remember no other disaster that equates that of Hurricane Janet. Since the year, 1955, until today, the name *Janet* is seldom given to any female child in Union Island.

Other hurricanes of note were Hurricane Hugo of 1980, Hurricane Lenny of 1999, and Hurricane Tomas of 2010, whose presence was felt mainly in St. Vincent and St. Lucia, and the recent Hurricane Irma of 2017. Nevertheless, none of these other terrors of nature had been as memorable as that of Hurricane Janet; Janet's presence brought tremendous fear to the minds and hearts of Unionites.

LAND EROSION, EVOLUTION

Forty years ago, vehicles drove from Ashton Jetty through the salt pond to Big Tamarind. Today the Ashton Salt Pond is a complete marshland.

Look back at the Union island two generations ago, one can affirm with absolute certainty that the landmass has changed drastically along the shorelines. There was once a small rock that extended out of Basin Beach. There is no sign of it today, for it was completely eroded by the constantly incoming waves. The once huge expanses of land that make up Basin and its adjacent beaches have eroded considerably into a sharp V-shaped projection. This area was once called "Sand," and its projection along the coastline, Queensbury Point."

Earlier maps of Union Island clearly show the extent of the erosion caused by the encroaching sea. The coastline west of Basin Beach is another visible site of erosion; numerous boulders lies along the shoreline some three hundred feet, while the land immediately above, still bears a near sixty-degree drop. This is a clear indication that that portion of the land had faced erosion many years before. The coastal area that was easily accessible by foot some forty years ago has become almost impossible to walk because of the encroachment of the sea.

In "Sand," numerous local grape trees and coconut palms were once a major part of its lush vegetation. Today, a few rotten trunks mark the presence of a once-flourishing coconut plantation; some of them can now be seen in the sea. On the other hand, a few grape trees are still there, though sparse compared to earlier years. Among the coconuts palms formally in the region, residents of Ashton Village once occupied individual plots of land that they cultivated with sand-potatoes or Puddocks. The cultivation sand-potato in that locality of the island is a thing of the past. Today, in Union Island, only a miniscule few of the older generation can remember the name Puddocks, for such name is considered archaic. The potatoes are cultivated in Union Island, and maybe some of the other Grenadine islands.

Sand potatoes are primarily white and small, ½ the size of the regular sweet potatoes. They are very tasty, especially because of the high salt content in the sandy soil, as opposed to that of the lands of higher altitudes.

This 2009 photo of Basin Beach is overcome by the encroachment of the sea. Land erosion seemed to be dominant at several of Union Island's beaches. Only thirty years ago, the location where the person is standing was solid grassland.

Erosion, as alluded to earlier, has indeed proven its dominance over any natural accretion on the beaches. Everyone remembers the beautiful white sandy beach called Top Yonder Bay; this little harbor became the principal shipyard on the island dating back to the Mulzac's era. Unity, the last of the local vessels that was built and launch on that site in 1974. One notable vessel that was built and launched at this site was Princess Louise, which was owned by August King Mitchell. This location was also where some of the largest festival (boat building) took place; it was where the African culture came alive with the beat of the Big Drum (African Drum). Alas, Top Yonder Bay is now a thing of the past.

On any Sunday afternoon, the famous beach would have been filled to its capacity with residents enjoying a sea bath. The proximity of this beach to the Ashton Village makes it easily accessible for nearby residents.

The mangrove marshland that partially engulfs this beach has been moving inward for many years now. The marine project of Frigate Rock that was mentioned earlier may have contributed partially to this unfavorable outcome. For residents to get to this beach, the best practical route would be water transport.

Forty years ago, vehicles drove from Ashton Jetty through the salt pond and on to Big Tamarind (a significant landmark on Clifton Road) to get to Clifton. The salt pond was solid land, then, and void of the large expanse of mangrove vegetation that now exists. The Easter festival of 1979 marked one of the largest sporting events that had ever taken place on Union Island, and it happened on the Ashton Salt Pond. Cricket, a notable sport, was played there. The Union Island Secondary School had its Cricket team during the 1970s. In 1975-76, the team competed with the Hillsborough Secondary School of Carriacou at the Ashton Salt Pond. Two years earlier, it had competed with them at Hillsborough, Carriacou.

With the loss of the principal cricket field, playing ground, and a few beaches at the hands of the encroaching mangrove and sea, Union Island have regressed quite a bit. From a sporting perspective, surely the island is not in a better state today than it was forty years ago.

◆◆◆□*Chapter Seven*

IS THIS LAND YOUR LAND

Regrettably, the possessory title Act (38 of 2004) *has allowed many opportunistic land predators and thieves to relieve lands from those who should rightfully inherit them.*

Private Lands continue to change ownership.

In the beautiful islands of St. Vincent & the Grenadines, the enactment of the Possessory Title Act #38 of 2004 was made into law with the intent to benefit the nation as a whole, but instead, it has proven to be a disadvantage to many landowners in recent years. The salient question here is: why is this legislative undertaking a drawback in the public's opinion? Is it because we are found wanting in the way of Jurisprudence here in St. Vincent & the Grenadines? Some concerned citizens have referred to this legislative enactment as an absolute travesty to private landowners. They furthered indicated that it creates a fracture in the law and also encourages land theft in the region by a whopping 65%. Let's take a keen look.

Not too long ago in Union Island, the communal lifestyle and customs had enabled some residents to buy lands without any form of written documentation. *Word-of-Mouth* was all that was needed because people trusted each other. A man's *Word was his bond; it* had enormous clout, and hence was the final authority. However, *Word-of-Mouth* has proven to be an impediment in recent years because many landowners are unable to provide deeds for the lands that they had bought. Many of the ancestors died without having the palest idea that multiple problems would later arise from those verbal contracts that were once valid and binding. With no deed made out for a portion of the land that was bought during those earlier years, these owners were unable to transfer ownership of their lands to their offspring. The only alternative left is for these offspring to obtain these inherited properties through a lengthy process of legal administration.

With the above being a quandary for multiple years in St. Vincent & the Grenadines, lawmakers have been encouraged to enact an amicable system by which some form of administration could be initiated (Act 38 of 2004). This act allowed a person to own an estate that belonged to his/her ancestors, or property that he/she had occupied in good faith for 12 or more years without having a deed. As a result, it enabled some plots of lands to attain a deed for the first time.

The legal application process of the Possessory Title Act commences with a surveyed plan of the property; it must be no older than two years and must bear the applicant's name. Secondly, all landowners whose lands border the property in question must be adequately informed; hence, a bailiff must be employed for this purpose (Affidavits Of Service). Following that is the Affidavits Of Service that must be filed on time showing total compliance. Two postings of the application must be done on a newspaper over a three-month period. The above will be followed by the inevitable (the court hearing), which should bring closure in a short time. But if the application is contested, then it can result in a protracted trial. But after the entire process, the court should be able to present the possessory title to the worthy person.

But some of these thieves are daring, and believe it or not, they may take dishonesty to another level by seeking the help of false witnesses to testify in court to corroborate the abundant lies of their affiliation to these lands. These false witness-bearers are willing to take risks by making false oaths or bearing false witness to substantiate these false claims in court. Why are they taking these high risks? Because they are paid a substantial sum of money, but when money is not available, they are instead given a portion of that same land as their payments.

In every hearing in court, the quests of the judges are to extract the facts from each party. And the Truth can be revealed when these false witnesses are questioned and cross-questioned by judges that are adamant to get the truth during a hearing. This shouldn't be too complicated a task, for, A Liar Has No Memory; in most cases, he/she uses one lie to cover another lie until he/she leaves himself/herself vulnerable. Then ultimately caught. These false witnesses are just too cavalier and seemed not to understand the severity of bearing false witness, even at such high platforms. It is only when someone in a court of law is confounded by a myriad of piercing questions, then found guilty, and jailed for fabricating false statements will such a criminal act ever ceased.

In most cases, the application processes of Act #38 of 2004 are not followed as required by the law of the land. Thus, the landowners whose lands border the properties are never informed until they realized that they have new neighbors. After all, these culprits are making an effort to steal the property of another person. Therefore, they will use every clandestine effort to attain that land. But unfortunately, when the dust settled, it might be just too late, for someone, somewhere might have lost his or her property.

"The scary truth is that this enactment creates a gigantic opportunity for intruders to steal the properties of private landowners. You see, there were many unoccupied lands whose taxes haven't been paid for many years," said Kwame, a former resident of Ashton, Union Island. "These land arrears, unfortunately, gives many intruders the opportunity to pilfer lands surreptitiously, or by other means such as legerdemain. Many have falsely and maliciously declared that they had occupied those lands for more than twelve years as satisfactory to the Possessory Title Act (Act. 38 of 2004). The truth is, these unscrupulous intruders know only the location of the properties through research, but have never physically occupied these lands. There are also professionals who are privy to the law, and they too have capitalized on every opportunity necessary to get themselves the best real estates. Rather than apprising some of the less fortunate that have legitimate family ties to those lands, these so-called professionals, or White-Collar workers, instead, swindle-up these properties for their personal uses.

Each week, the local newspapers are inundated with a multitude of applications for the declaration of possessory titles. Although many of these applicants appear to be legitimate, there are times when these newspapers are honeycombed with applications from the unscrupulous, the unprincipled, the covetous and/or opportunist. The latter seize every opportunity and loopholes to attain the properties of their fellow citizens by any means necessary. What a shame!

"It is a few years now since my family has lost a significant portion of land here in Clifton, Union Island." Said Esther, another former resident of Union Island. "We have lost this property to a few who has no legal tie to our family land, and it is unfair to us, the descendants of the original owners of these lands. Today, my siblings feel threatened, even on this small plot of land where our family house is constructed. What can we do about this? Can we trust our neighbors, those that have declared to the nation and the world that they are Christians? The answer is an emphatic no! For they too have made up the number of thieves in Union Island.

"This vicious land-crave began during the 1990s," Esther further explained. "A group of savvy Land-Hounds discovered that the taxes for some private properties in Union Island that were once cultivated with the cotton crop now lies abandoned. Immediately, these Land-Hounds began to pay up the annual taxes for these plots of land while they patiently wait for the 12 years' period to end before they make their immoral moves."

Today there is a resurgence of land theft, and it is not exclusive to Union Island, but extends all through the Grenadines, as well as St. Vincent, the mainland. During the (1990s) wards of Crown Lands were gobbled up by these Opportunists. Thanks to the incumbent Government; I learned recently that they had retaken most of these lands, and now they are back to the rightful owner -The State."

Will land-theft ever stop? Should the Possessory Title Act #38 of 2004 be reversed because of the tremendous negative impact that private landowners have endured, and are prone to encounter in the near future? Many Vincentians that are living abroad are now obligated to peruse the local newspapers on a weekly basis to ensure that their lands aren't listed as an Application For A Declaration Of Possessory Title. To do otherwise, may result in a tragic loss of properties that may provoke hostility. The salient question has revisited us again, "Was the land of your forefathers and foremothers bequeathed with dignity?"

Thus, it is paramount that some landlords, whether they are civil servants, lawyers, politicians, or just ordinary citizens, need to be legally questioned as to how and when they have attained the lands for which they now hold a deed. I am quite sure that many of them will be unable to establish ANY form of family ties, legal proof of purchase, or verification that such lands have been bequeathed to them. Surely, the only scapegoat here might be the Possessory Title Act (Act #38 of 2004). In this case, it is deemed legal.

Regardless of where these legitimate landowners reside (North America, Europe, etc.); the burden of responsibility still lies with them to ensure that their properties are not listed in newspapers and are later taken over by unscrupulous predators.

It is because of the might of The Exodus Factor why there is a mass emigration of the younger generation? They have left Union Island to seek education advancement and employment abroad. As a result, lands and properties remained under the stewardship of their parents and relatives. Tactlessly, when their parents and relatives die, many properties are left abandoned for several years. Regrettably, this has allowed many opportunistic land predators and thieves to relieve the lands from those who should rightfully inherit them. It is the opinion of many that a legislative enactment must be made into law so as to preclude this unethical practice or bring it to a screeching halt.

It is important to note that this dastardly act of pilfering private lands in Union Island remains a public crime and not simply a private wrong. Stealing private properties is a felony that should be punishable by a considerable amount of years spent behind bars. This method might be one of the legitimate means to avert the machination of land theft in Union Island.

THE UNION ISLAND UPRISING

Cuban soldiers in Grenada escort one of Union Island Freedom Fighter, and an unknown assailant (1979).

"I Lennox V. Charles (aka) "Bumber" do hereby make this written statement of my lifetime sacrifice as the True Revolutionary Leader of the Union Island People Liberation Movement for, and in the sole benefit of the People's Ownership and control of the Land, Union I-land."

By the 1970s, Union Island was now in the last quarter of the 20th century, and surely one would expect that the residents should have been thoroughly desensitized by the legacy of disenfranchisement that has been levied upon them for well over 260 years. The Africans, during the 1750s, were brought in bondage from the west coast of Africa and were enslaved on this 3.54 sq. Miles landmass for approximately 160 years. Inevitably, the institution of slavery on the soil of Union Island represented privation, suffering, destitution, hardship, misuse, abuse, neglect, murder and death at the hands of their oppressors. With hardship being the status quo on Union island for so many years, the consensus may opine that these Africans should have been acclimated to that cruel way of life a long time ago. Such is not the case with these Africans who had become the burden bearers for their oppressors since they were brought in captivity. Understandably, these Africans were nothing short of defiant.

In 1909, the peasants of Union Island openly expressed their disapproval of the leadership of Mr. E. Richards, the last owner, and landlord of this southern Grenadine Island; his rulership represented one of the worst life experiences for the people of Union Island, post-slavery. His stringent demands from the farmers of that day made life a living hell for them. On the brink of rebellion, these farmers aggressively presented a petition to the government. Although the petition demanded several changes, it principally suggested that the Government should take immediate ownership of the island from the hands of the callous landlord; he was nothing but a ruthless tyrant. Sighting riot to be the alternative of the disgruntled residents, the government of that day acquiesced immediately. Regretfully, the legacy of oppression still remained overt on Union Island for multiple decades and had continued as the status quo. Sixty years later, the oppressed once again retaliated. This time, it was on December 7th, 1979, when a contingent of armed young men from the village of Ashton, under the leadership of Lenox *Bomba* Charles (seen on page 260) took the Island by storm and instantly unseated the sole protective force on the island -the police. With an atmosphere that was saturated with resentment from the residents, who had been ignored for centuries, this insurrection was not merely inevitable, but also markedly germane. From the outskirts, this seemed to have all of the ingredients for a better Union Island, but its premature nature has proved to be a major disadvantage to a community that was badly in need of change. Unfortunately, this insurrection came to a screeching halt in the afternoon of that day. With all of the adequate elements and ingredients clearly expressed in the subsequent pages, the tone for reprisal was fundamentally set in place for an insurrection.

You have read in previous chapters that palely expressed that Union Island has experienced severe water shortage since the mid 18th century or the beginning of European presence and history on Union Island; indeed, this statement is worth repeating and should be mainstreamed. This water shortage in Union Island is due in part to the low annual rainfall on this arid landmass. Yet, the dearth of this basic necessity has never been addressed by all of the governmental administrations that ran Union Island. Those administrations dated back to the presence of the Europeans in Union Island during the 1750 to this current day. Without adequate water supply coupled with the squalid conditions that the Africans were subjected to, multiple epidemic and diseases inundated their communities.

Samuel V. Morse, a commanding engineer, made a timely visit to Union Island on July 22, 1778; he immediately observed that the lack of water was a major problem on the little island. Appalled by the scarcity of water to supply both livestock and the slaves, he witnessed the deplorable health condition of the slaves and the squalor that they endured daily. He found that the Europeans, on the other hand, were well prepared for this condition; they used rainwater, which they conserved in earthen jars and well-built cisterns. This is what he had to say:

"There are no rivers in any of the Grenadines but springs in most of them, which by sinking wells supply the Negroes and stock most of the year. The water, in general, is not good, frequently brackish and disagrees with the Negroes... The white inhabitants principally depend upon rainwater, which they preserve in cisterns or earthen jars."

Don Carlos Verbeke, a Benedictine priest, was also appalled by the condition that he observed when he visited Union Island in 1928; approximately one hundred and sixty-five years after the Europeans laid foot on the island, yet there were no changes to address the extreme scarcity of water. He described briefly the grave shortage of water on these islands by indicating that there was scarcely anything to drink. He went on to say that the people had to scoop water from mud-filled ponds, and that the island was devoid of grass to feed livestock. Nevertheless, he was overwhelmed by the people's desire and will to overcome such impoverished state. Below is a short description of this letter:

"Those islands at the time of my visit were literally burnt, there being not a blade of green grass left. I have seen the sheep and cattle dying along the roadside. I have witnessed the people cutting the last leaf off banana trees to give to them. The people

have no water to drink. I have seen them gathering water from ponds, mud in the strictest sense of the word. How they manage to live, to tide over this appalling misery is a mystery to me."

As expressed above, water shortage was not the only problem that the Africans had to endure, for multiple diseased arise from the squalor, gross health conditions, and inadequacies. In 1891, Dr. H. N. Nichols, an American doctor was invited to visit Union island to address the ailing lepers on the island. On his arrival, he was astounded and felt compassion for the residents whom he observed were destitute and totally neglected by the Government of St. Vincent. These are his words, rueful of candor:

"They get nothing from the Government. People are ill and die on the island, and no doctor can be got. There is no protection for life or property; no road kept up by the Government, and it was really a wonder when we arrived that the good people of Union did not assemble to drive us off. We gave the people nothing, we added neither to their comfort nor their happiness, and we took away the money they had barely earned by carrying their produce in their crank boats to Barbados and Carriacou."

With all of the above said, there was still another major problem that was disheartening to the residents during the Metayage or Sharecropping system of 1850 to 1909. It may have been the major contributing factor, or the straw that broke the camels back on September 30th, 1909. For these hard-working peasants, the countless hours that they spent each day on their respective plantations to cultivate the cotton crop was rather meaningless; distressingly, their rewards were only a pittance, and that did not equate the tremendous hours that they spent in the plantations toiling in the hot sun. As a result, it takes away greatly the peasant's insensitive and enthusiasm to start work early each morning, from sunrise, all the way to sunset.

In 1978, only one year prior to the Union Island Uprising, Premier Robert Milton Cato of St. Vincent was quite aware that the constituents of the Grenadines were not in favor of his leadership; instead, they were long-lasting supporters of the opposition People Political Party (PPP) under the directorate of E.T Joshua. Mr. Cato's sentiment towards the people of the Grenadines, particularly Union Island, was not one of affection, but of disapproval. It is reputed that during one of Mr. Cato's political campaign in Union Island to garner votes, he made an irresponsible statement to the people.

Immediately, his statement went viral throughout St. Vincent & the Grenadines and ignited anger in the heart of Unionites. His statement to the people of Union Island was, **"If you don't vote for the St. Vincent Labor Party, you all will eat grass."** His statement was echoed in every nook and cranny of the Grenadines. Thus, as stated, the residents were very disturbed having been openly promised another term of neglect once again by another administration of St. Vincent. With over 260 years of marginalization from servitude to a so-called civilized community, the residents were once again victims. Fed-up, the residents, expressed openly that the government takes only from its thriving tourist industry, and also tax the residents, but never give back or addresses the infrastructure, well-being, nor hardship that the people endured daily. Finally, because of the burden of taxes that were levied on goods that were imported on Union Island, many shopkeepers reverted to the use of contraband to alleviate the enormity of the tariffs. The Government of St. Vincent, on the other hand, was privy to this legacy, and at times would alert the police force of such infraction. The armed force, in turn, will travel to Union Island by boat during the night, and at the dawn of the day, they would make strategic raids on the homes of all these small businesses and shopkeepers. Consequently, all goods and supplies that did not bare the resemblance to that of domestic goods were confiscated forthwith. These were the basic ingredients that engender the revolution. The residents had seen enough and were willing, able and ready to express their longstanding aversion in the streets. Let us now take a look, first hand, at the onset of the Union Island Uprising.

On a perky Friday morning (Revo-Fridee), December 7th, 1979, Unionites woke up to the overwhelming sounds of dynamites and gunshots that inundated the atmosphere. The vicinity of the Ashton Police station was darkened with thick clouds of smoke; some residents in the proximity of the Ashton neighborhood of Jerome were seen fleeing their respective homes to the nearby hillside of Mt. Olympus. The explosive sounds they recognized were coming from the single police station that was situated at Clifton Road. The young armed force, deemed the Union Island Freedom Fighters

(UIFF) had attacked the police station; simultaneously, two young policemen were seen fleeing the station on foot. They frantically ran across the nearby Ashton Salt Pond in desperation; they were in haste to reach the home of Mr. Cleve Mulrain, a civil servant that worked at the lone post office on the island. An hour later, several residents frantically gathered to the site of the damaged police station to investigate the commotion; on their journey they also witnessed that some walls and major streets of Ashton were stenciled with captions. The newly applied bright white paintings were still wet, even at sunrise; these captions read (I). Free Union Island (ii). Union Island is for Unionites. (iii). UIFF with the symbol of an AK 47 rifle; the acronym UIFF represents Union Island Freedom Fighters. But for all intents and purposes, one may ask, "Were these neatly painted captions relevant to the atmosphere that existed on this island during this sudden insurrection?" ideally, those captions that are mentioned above did embellish every major street on the island. The kinetic force, on the other hand, that saturated the atmosphere on that Friday morning clearly expressed the candor, dissatisfaction, disgust, and anger that the people have shouldered for several years under the then incumbent government of Premier Robert Milton Cato.

The UIFF fighters immediately made their way to Clifton, the capital, and Eastern corridor of the island; there they were greeted by many vibrant youngsters that were eager to bear arms in defense of the Island against the longstanding injustice that they themselves had been witnessing each day. The armed force in quick pursuit descended on the Union Island Airport and on arrival, they shut down the airport and expediently prohibited all air landing. Marine access to the island was at a standstill, and that also barred any boat that was scheduled to arrive on Union Island.

Because of the legacy of disenfranchisement that the people of Union Island had endured for centuries, coupled with the added neglect from the St. Vincent Government, understandably, the atmosphere was saturated with widespread resentment. And so, to look back at the event that transpired on Friday, December 7th, 1979, it was by no means a surprise to the older folks of Union Island; they were neither moved, timid, squeamish, nor dissuaded to see young men bear arms in hopes of effecting futuristic changes on Union island.

The details of the Union Island Uprising you will read in a book that will be released in the near future. The author will collaborate with the revolutionary Lenox "Bumber" Charles and other key elements to make this publication a reality. Mr. Charles, a novelist who currently resides in the United Kingdom is the spirit, the backbone, and nucleus of this revolt; In one of his deposition at St. Georges, Grenada, He stated unequivocally: *"I Lennox V. Charles (aka) "Bumber" do hereby make this written statement of my lifetime sacrifice as the True Revolutionary Leader of the Union Island People Liberation Movement, for, and in the sole benefit of the People's Ownership and control of the Land, Union I-land."*

In the upcoming publication, folks will read for the first time, the views, ideas, and perspective of a man whose blood, arteries, and veins are tethered to the sea, land, and ether of Union Island. Stay tune.

Dr. Kendall B. Stewart

Earlier in this book, mention was made of migrants, many Unionites that have sought other frontiers for greater employment opportunities, educational advancements, and various other reasons. Among the many that have departed the soil of Union Island, here is the success story of one of Union Island's native son, Dr. Kendall Basil Stewart.

Dr. Kendall Stewart is a descendant of the first owner of Union Island, Admiral O. Samuel Spann; he is also a descendant of Charles Henry Mulzac, a Kittitian and first man to introduce sharecropping on the soil of Union Island. Dr. Stewart is also the grandnephew of Captain Hugh Mulzac, the first black man to captain a ship in the United States Merchant Marine.

Deemed the Honorable Kendall Stewart for the vast contributions that he has made in the lives of New Yorkers in the New York metropolitan area, his name, life, and legacy are permanently etched into the cornerstone of the history of New York City. He is an esteemed visionary with fervent passion in humanism. His motto speaks for itself: "To hear him is to help him, to help him is to know him, to know him is to love him, to love him is to see his vision of community development and empowerment."

Dr. Kendall Stewart was born in Ashton, Union Island in the Grenadines. He is the son of the late Solomon and Millicent Stewart of Ashton, Union Island. Like this author, he too is the fourth-generation of the esteemed Mr. William McDowell Stewart and his wife, Mrs. Louisiana Stewart nee Wilson. They are the root and sole ancestors of Union Island's entire Stewart family, which at one point made up the largest segment of the island's population.

The former state committeeman of the 58th Assembly District and member of the Kings County State Democratic

Committee in Brooklyn, New York; Kendall Stewart served on the city council for eight consecutive years. He also held membership in many social and educational groups, and was the recipient of countless awards. Board certified in podiatric surgery, he is a member of the Podiatric Medical Association, American Podiatric Circulatory Society, American Institute of Foot Medicine, and also a medical panel member of Local 1199 and many other local organizations.

From the Ashton's primary school on Union Island, Kendall Stewart migrated to St. Vincent to better his education. Then later, he traveled to Trinidad, West Indies, where he attended the Caribbean Union College. Several years later, he graduated. His penchant for a better life coupled with his passion for learning propelled him to migrate to the United States of America; he then became a graduate of Albert Merrill School of Computer Science and later earned his Bachelor of Science degree from City College of New York. From there he went on to earn his doctoral degree in podiatric medicine from New York City College of Podiatric Medicine.

At his office at 4016 Church Avenue, this is what the ebullient Dr. Kendall Stewart had to say: "When I was a boy, my parents told me that my hands were very important tools, and whatever I touched turns to gold."

This Midas-like philosophy that this humanitarian possesses is what bolstered him and gave him that extra impetus to take on all of life's challenges and success with renewed energy and cheerful readiness.

As an entrepreneur and practicing physician in the heart of Brooklyn, New York, this humble surgeon (Podiatrist) remains patriotic in his service to the multiethnic communities that witness, facilitated, and benefited tremendously from his growth and development over the last 30 plus years.

The letter below, which was drafted in 1940, depicts the racially hostile atmosphere that overtly existed in America during the time of World War II.

Auburn, Ala, Oct. 14, 1940

Hon. Pete Jarman
House of Representative
Washington D.C.

Dear Pete:

I wish you would lodge a serious protest to the President against the announced policy of the present administration to issue commission to a bunch of Negro army officers.

You know, from experience and observation during the First World War that the Negro private does not respect the Negro officers placed in command over him. No Negro likes to take orders from another Negro. This is especially true in military organizations.

You know and I know that our boys detest the very thought of having to render a military salute to some "burr-head" who is his inferior racially, intellectually, etc.

Even Abraham Lincoln refused to commission Negroes; the same was true under the administration of William McKinley during the Spanish-American War. They were republicans, but they recognized the limitations of the Negro by placing white officers over them.

I wrote a letter to the late Hugh Dent at the beginning of the other great war and begged him to block or protest against the then announced policy to commission Negroes. He kept silent. His silence led to his defeat at the hands of Judge Tyson in the Second District.

We had race riots in several American Cities following the muster-out of the Negro officers and soldiers. Lynching broke out all over the South, the Klu-Klux Klan was born amid that welter of racial fires, all caused by the attitude of the Negro officers who had been elevated to a plane of military superiority in rank and grade over thousands of fine upstanding white Americans. We don't want this sort of history to repeat itself.

Our British cousins never commission Negro army officers. Their Negro troops are always commanded by white officers. Why should we sow the wind and reap the whirlwind? Negro officers can't stop Hitler – it will take the best white brains and white man's courage in America to stop the "Wizard" of Berlin.

Your Friend

Emmett P. Smith

Emmett P. Smith

As I am about to conclude this book, I would like to share with you one of my personal conviction concerning my willingness and desire to learn the history of St. Vincent & the Grenadines, but particularly Union Island -the land of my birth. I earnestly believe that if we desire anything morally, that adds value to our lives and the lives of others, we must endeavor to acquire it regardless of the risks or rewards it brings. "For the person who risks nothing, does nothing, has nothing, is nothing, and becomes nothing. He may avoid suffering and sorrow, but he simply cannot learn, and feel, and change, and grow, and love, and live." The latter are the esteem words of Leo F. Buscaglia Ph.D., an American author, motivational speaker, and professor at the University of Southern California.

Folks, if you have been reading Union Island's History – Servitude, Metayage and Civilization (UIHSMC) from the onset and have gotten to this point, chances are, you have acquired a complete or thorough understanding of this text. And with the same token, you have attained a command of the history of a tiny island of the Grenadines, Union Island. Well, now that you are approaching the leisurely segment (section II) of this book, you can again relax, but in an even more comfortable mode; prepare yourself for the raised eyebrows, laughter, the Oh no! Is that so? Really? As you enjoy the final pages of yet another intriguing read. And feel obligated to share the contents of this book with another human being.

Section II♦ ♦ ♦ ☐*Chapter Eight*

ALL FOOLS' DAY

Ambo: "Deliver this to Cayenne Waist for me quickly; don't open it, yo hear."

Though this book may chronicle a few challenging times of my life, there were indeed many times of joy and humor as well as intriguing events that will definitely raise a few eyebrows. Many folks that once lived in Union Island may be able to empathize with me; their miseries or woes, bliss or glee may escalate into a hearty well-deserved laughter, or even tears after many, many years of suppressed memories. But before I get to what I really want you to know, let me share with you what my good friend had to say. She shared the "Then and Now" opinion as she touched on the subject of April 1st, All Fools Day:

"April 1st, known as 'All Fools Day,' was an age-old tradition from the days of colonialism and may have started sometime during the late sixteenth century. The Caribbean later embraced this particular day from the British settlers and passionately made it their own.

"April 1st in the Caribbean was a day that everyone would try to remember because it could prove costly and embarrassing if you were oblivious when that day rolled around. On April Fool's Day, the young and old alike played mischiefs on their friends, neighbors, strangers, and other villagers. These mischiefs were designed to fool each individual with the intent of having a good laugh when discovered hours, days or years later for that matter.

"Sadly, it is clear that the disappearance of many of our treasured cultures and traditions has resulted from the modernization of our societies. That once significant day of the year now comes and goes without the slightest bit of acknowledgment. With the advent of the cell phone, iPod, and other electronic devices, the possibility of playing a well-organized prank on another person is simply a thing of the past."

Sadly, the best description is to refer to it as archaic. Today, even the youngest among us would question why they should have to take a note to another person—a district away—when "they can quickly make a phone call or send a text, an email, WhatsApp, etc.

"Suffice it to say that modernization, like everything else, has its advantages and disadvantages. One of the disadvantages is the loss of our rich heritage—the customs and traditions of the ancestors on Union Island. Inability to manage the cultural transition because of evolution, it has resulted in the loss of the baby and the bathtub as it is said proverbially."

"Generation X and Y will never know the true meaning of April Fool's Day in Union Island because they have not experienced the creative ways that our friends and neighbors once played those tricks on us. They will never hear the loud bursts of laughter across the street when the tricks were discovered or witness the embarrassment on the faces of those who were tricked. Gone are those good old days!"

Yes, my friend is quite on point with her keen observation; I could not agree more. So now, let us focus a bit on one of my personal experiences on Union Island.

I was eight years old in 1970. I was sent to do some shopping at Mr. Robert Wilson's shop, located approximately half a mile from my home at Bottom Campbell. Groceries during those early days encompassed rice, sugar, flour, cooking oil, butter, baking powder, black pepper, and other basic necessities and condiments for everyday use. Unfortunately for me, that day was All Fool's Day (April Fool's Day).

I did most of my shopping at Mr. Robert's shop. His nickname was "Toe Joe," but on that day, Toe Joe did not have any cooking oil, so my next bet was Mr. Wilton Wilson's shop, or so I thought, and there the old fiasco began. Everyone knew him as "Wash Brain," a nickname that he had inherited earlier in his life; I have no knowledge of its origin. But I can take solace in referring to him as "Brain Wash" a couple of times here.

Well, in Mr. Brain Wash's shop, I meant Wash Brain, I got

one bottle of cooking oil, paid for it and was just about to leave when he said to me, "Boy can you deliver this note to Mr. uh... Ambo for me?" I nodded affirmatively as he grabbed an old cement bag, tore off a piece of brown paper, scribble a few words, and then wrapped the paper in an unkempt manner and handed it to me. "Don't open this paper eh, just give it to Ambo fo me. You could leave your groceries here until you come back. Do quick."

I was harmless as a dove and obedient as a rented mule, so there was no way that I could have made an excuse or refused to go; that was not in keeping with the culture of Union Island; if an elder sent you out, you go. That's it! So, I took the rumpled brown paper from Mr. Wash Brain, but before I could leave the shop, he warned me, "Do not give it to Teacher Mary, yo hear?" I replied yes in a very soft voice and took off to deliver the note to Mr. Ambo, who was another shopkeeper.

Now, Teacher Mary was Mr. Ambo's wife, and surely Mr. Wilton did not want that paper to get into her hands because she was a mother herself and might be more ethical and compassionate, and that could have subverted his clandestine plans. "Good morning Mr. Ambo," I bellowed as I walked quietly into his shop. "Good morning," he replied. Then immediately I handed him the note and informed him of its origin. He unwrapped the paper and stared at me for a few seconds, and then a cunning smile emanated from his previously straight face. My eyes were now fixated on him as he summoned me not to leave just yet. I did not have the slightest idea of what was going on or what to make of the note or his hefty laughter. Soon after, he too tore a piece of brown paper from a cement bag, jotted down a few lines, and told me to deliver his note to Mr. Hudson Mulzac. "Deliver this to Cayenne Waist for me quick; don't open it, yo hear." And off I went to a sprint to get his note to its destination as quickly as I can. It is presumed that Mr. Hudson Mulzac (another shopkeeper) got his nickname, Cayenne Waist, from the city of Cayenne, the capital of French Guiana.

"Good morning, Mr. Hudson," I recited, breathing heavily when I walked into his shop. Mr. Hudson was fully attired. His shirt was in his pants, and his pants were well above his waistline. That morning I thought he was using his huge belly to keep his pants up because his pants appeared to be a bit too big. He took the note and read it without exhibiting a smile; he was as serious as a beast as he stared at me from head to toe. One of his eyes was a bit off target, and at one moment I could not determine whether he was staring at me or something nearby. This is a condition of the eyes that is referred to as strabismus. Although shaken, I was staring at his pants that were pulled well above his waistline. "Who you boy? Who your parents?" he asked. "Mr. Garfield's son," I replied, while I was still a bit shaken. "You could go by Cleve Mulrain for me?" He forcefully asked.

I was in a daze at that time, totally taken aback by his question because Mr. Mulrain lived almost halfway between Clifton and Ashton, and that wasn't anything less than 45 minutes of brisk walking for my small feet. But, on the other hand, I started to think reward. If he sent me that far, obviously, he would reward me monetarily though I did not have the boldness to say it. At that moment, I could hardly stand upright in front of that man without trembling slightly.

But fortunately, he never forced the issue, so I did not have to walk such a long distance in the hot sun. Honestly, I believed that he was cold-hearted enough that on my return he would not have the faintest idea that I could have been thirsty after such a long walk, much less give me 25 cents. So, I was exempted from going to Mr. Mulrain's residence, and I thought he would tell me to go home. Instead, Mr. Hudson or Cayenne Waist, as he was called went to the back of his shop and got a clean piece of brown paper on which he scribbled something. "You went to Russell yet? What about Meldon?" He asked me.

I told him that Mr. Meldon's shop was closed, but he refrained from sending me to Mr. Russell's. Even now I still wonder why he did not send me to Mr. Russell's shop, for he did not appear compassionate in any form or fashion. He pondered in displeasure and then handed me the note, "Take this back to Mr. Ambo for me."

So again, I was on my way to Mr. Ambo's shop to deliver Mr. Hudson's brown paper note. But before I could get inside Mr. Ambo's shop, he again burst into laughter as he looked at my worried face and folded palm. I began to laugh too, for I was happy to see him laugh without restraint; his laughter was healthy and pure. That is the kind of laughter that I refer to as contagious and therapeutic, in retrospect. He took out his pen, wrote something on that same paper, and then whispered, "Take this back to Cayenne Waist just one more time, just one more time."

Now it had been a while since I had left home, and if Mr. Robert's shop was the only shop I had visited, I should have been back home almost twenty minutes ago. So, I knew that my parents had to be wondering why it was taking me so long. But how could I say no to an adult? I was concerned about returning to Mr. Hudson's shop with that brown paper, for I did not know what to expect from that man. He was as serious as a bull and looked so wild-eyed when he stared at me. As a kid, I used to wonder if something was wrong with one of his eyes. I later learned that his seriousness was just a front that he was putting up to ward off uncontrollable folly among kids. He had a small notice board situated on the outside of his shop with the following caption: *Post no bills, park no bicycles.*

Mr. Hudson stretched out his hand to receive the brown paper once again from Mr. Ambo, and then he proceeded to the back of his shop again, his face bearing a slight smirk. "O God, not again," I muttered under the breath, but this man was adamant that I should be sent to yet another location. "You went by Jonah yet?" he asked me in a bold, commanding voice, as though I should have been sent there a long time ago. "No, Mr. Hudson" I replied in humility, and out came the brown paper once again. "Take this to Jonah; walk straight." I acquiesced immediately.

I nodded and set off to Mr. Jonah's shop with yet another folded brown paper. It did not take me two minutes to get to Brother Jonah's shop, for he lived very close to the Gospel Hall Church and was an elder of that church; my parents also attended that church. I was happy to be there because my friend and cousin Curtis Stewart was his son, and we had gotten along well since we know each other —and to make things better, we were classmates as well. Brother Jonah immediately took the paper, opened it on the counter of his shop, read it to himself, looked at me for almost half of a minute, and then said to me with a smile, "Boy, go and meet yo mother." It was only at that moment that I suspected that something was out of the ordinary, yet my innocence and naivety still would not allow me to understand fully what was taking place.

A customer stepped into the shop during the time he was exhorting me to go home to meet my mother, and immediately his attention turned towards her, as he left his note unattended on the counter. Then suddenly, the brown paper fell to the floor, and as I bend to fetch it, I saw a couple of words that read: "FURTHER ALONG."

I took up the brown paper immediately and though no one was paying any attention to me, but Mr. Jonah stretched out his hand to receive the note, and I obliged. That day I felt totally embarrassed and uncomfortable, walking all the way back to collect my groceries. I kept my face straight ahead and walked quietly to Mr. Wilton's shop to get my groceries. I met his wife, whom we usually call Mom or Ms. Look-Sin. She handed me my groceries, and off I went all the way back to Campbell, where I took a verbal whipping for spending excess time up the village. I did not tell my parents that I had been sent out to deliver some notes. Yet, I never figured out what the complementary words on that brown piece of paper were. Although this had a negative impact on me for many years, I treated this incident with personal care, and like other things that have transpired in my presence, I did not view them as issues to be shared with anyone. But in my later years, I surmised that the preceding words on that paper might have read: "Send that fool a little..." Well indeed, those folks had a field day with me that morning but should have chosen someone that was much older than me. Nevertheless, the true essence of All Fool's Day was exhibited in raw form.

Can this, or similar prank be done today with this current generation? You better believe otherwise. I already heard an emphatic "Hell's No!" from a generation whose social life is circumscribed to the cell phone, computers, iPod, and other modern-day gadgets. Unfortunately, devices like these in the hands of Generation X, Y, and Z have engendered the growth of individualism to unprecedented levels.

AN OLD YEAR'S NIGHT COOKOUT

"Terry, you in it too!" the old man asked. "No, Mr. McKay," Terrence replied, "I did not steal the fowl, but I eat some of the food."

It was on a Friday night, December 31st, 1971. Three youngsters from the village of Ashton were eager to put the final pieces together on a cookout that they had planned one week earlier. Four other members from the district of Campbell were to provide the pots, dishes, rice, cooking oil, butter, sugar, and other condiments to cook a huge pot of Pelau that night. The only missing part of the puzzle was the chicken, and these chaps had no intention of spending a dime for this product. The three chaps had suggested earlier that week they would have one of Mr. McKay's biggest roosters. They planned to the old man's foul as soon as he left his home that night for a walk in the village. Mr. McKay was an old farmer who lived very close to the road at Campbell Village. In his garden were a wide variety of fruits and vegetables. As kids, it was always a boon to pass his way; one could always count on getting a handful of peanuts, a slice of watermelon, or even a roasted coconut bake—a specialty of Union Island.

Many folks were afraid of Mr. McKay; they believe that this old man does a lot of supernatural things. And to make matters worse, he had a Calabash tree very close to his home. In Union Island, it is reputed that the calabash tree is home the zombie. Mr. McKay's huge calabash tree (Boulie) was located close to Campbell Road, and all of his chickens slept on that tree. With the night's activities thoroughly planned out, these young chaps had already decided how they were going to catch the birds. The birds were to be stolen before the clock struck 12:00 midnight for fear of encountering zombies on that Calabash tree. The three youngsters were: Garnett, Urias, and Stephen. Garnett, the designated climber, was to climb the tree, catch the bird, and hand it to Stephen, who would be a few feet below. Urias, who was to stand at the base of the tree, was the lookout person, as well as the final person to receive the rooster.

The three youngsters hid among the pea plants of Mr. Adrian Simmons' garden, (neighbor) and waited patiently for the old man to leave his home. Within a few minutes, the old man, with his permanent limp was out of his house and heading in the vicinity of Mr. Meldon's House. (Mr. Meldon lived a couple of hundred yards away from Mr. McKay's house.) The boys were safe now and had no intention of wasting a minute. Garnett, being lanky and agile, had climbed the tree in a matter of seconds and was closely followed by Stephen. Quietly, he grabbed one of the biggest birds and held its head tightly so that it could not make a sound. He immediately handed it to Stephen who further muted the bird before it got to Urias, who placed it into his bag. Sighting another huge fowl nearby, Garnett decided to take advantage of the opportunity and have a second. He grabbed the bird by its head and quickly handed it to Stephen, and they both descended quietly from the huge Boulie tree. Everything seemed to be going fine thus far.

The three young men quickly headed for the village, unnoticed by any of the neighbors. They then joined the other four members of the crew and decided to cook their food under another Boulie tree that was located next to Mr. Gifted Wilson's home. Mr. Gifted Wilson was a resident of Ashton Village. With two flambeaus ablaze, everyone went to work. They plucked the two fowls, cut up the meat, and had it seasoned in a short period of time. It was about 11:00 P.M., when Stephen placed the pot on a three-stoned fireplace that was fueled by wood for energy. Every so often, passersby would stop to take a glance at the noisy crowd of youngsters, who were busy being chefs. They were really having a good time.

Finally, the cooking came to a close. The smell of the Pelau was all over the area. All, but one of the members of the crew was eager to enjoy the fruits of their labor. While six youngsters, namely Stephen, Garnett, Terrence, Junior, Urias, and Henry, all sat down to eat, Sylvan refused; he was not satisfied with the way they had attained the meat.

"I ain't eating because I don't want no fowl to crow in my belly," he said. The other chaps tried to cajole him to eat some of the food with them, but he was unyielding. "No fowl ain't crowing in my belly," he said again and again. He remained adamant not to put a single spoonful of the food into his mouth. Meanwhile, four members had finished eating and, still hungry, they went back for seconds. The food was now down to the bottom of the pot, and Stephen began scraping the last bit (Bun- Bun). Seeing that the Pelau was about to be finished, Sylvan became uneasy that he might not get a taste of the food. He held on to the pot and bellowed, "I go eat some ah the Bun-Bun; I don't want no chicken, just give me some ah de Bun-Bun, that's all."

Sylvan took the pot, scraped the remainder of the food, and quickly devoured it. Everyone was basically filled except Sylvan. By that time, it was well past 2:00 A.M., and the crew of seven was having a great time. They remained under the tree for another two hours chatting and laughing and were later accompanied by other youngsters who came on the scene to hangout.

The following day was New Year's Day. It was a very quiet day, and it went by quickly. Sunday was yet another quiet day, a regular church day, and that, too, went by quickly, with lots of youngsters attending their respective churches.

On Monday morning, Stephen woke up very early and left his home to attend to his animals at Ms. Irene's. When he reached Mr. McKay John's house, the old man greeted him. "Ah Stephen, I miss two ah meh biggest cock fowl. Do you know anything about that?"

"True, Mr. John? That is real wickedness; I don't know anything about that, but that is real wickedness. That is real wickedness."

The savvy old man stepped closer to Stephen and asked, "You sure?" Stephen had thought that McKay would ask him the question and leave it at that, but he was wrong. Feeling a bit nervous, Stephen was about to leave when McKay said to him, "Anyway, whoever took my f@#*$% fowl has nine more days to live."

Stephen panicked upon hearing those words, and his heart quickened. Feeling fearful that he was going to die in nine days' time, Stephen stared at the old man for almost a minute and then whispered, "It was n-n-not me Mr. John, not me." Then he sadly left for his journey to Ms. Irene's.

Stephen hurriedly attended to his animals at Ms. Irene's without uttering a word to anyone he met. On his return, he quietly walked by McKay's house as though he did not know the old man. He immediately visited each one of his friends who had been part of the old year's night cookout; He told them that Mr. McKay had missed his fowls and that they had only nine more days to live. Instantly, they all became worried, and no one wanted to speak on that subject, fearing that they had messed with the wrong person. But no one seemed to be as concerned as Stephen and Sylvan. "I don't think I will die because I did not eat any fowl; just the Bun-Bun," Sylvan said sadly. "McKay say everybody go dead, everybody," Stephen retorted sharply. "We only have nine days left." The youngsters really needed help, but did not know what to do, and they could not tell their parents of this ordeal because their backsides would have paid the cost. However, folks in the little district began to sense that something was wrong with these young men. They were uncharacteristically reclusive.

While at home that afternoon, Stephen sat for a while and pondered where he could get help. Then suddenly, he came up with an idea. "I am going to visit Porcho (Mrs. Pricilla John). I think she knows something about Obeah," he said softly to himself. Porcho was an old lady who lived opposite of the Ashton Cemetery. "I think she could help me out." Within ten minutes, he was at the old woman's house.

"Good evening, Ms. Porcho," he greeted her. "Good evening, son," she replied. But before she could utter another word, he again said to her, "Ms. Porcho, I have a complaint to make. Mr. McKay says we have nine days to live." "Nine days?" she echoed as Stephen hesitantly described in detail what they had done. "Boy, I don't think Sido (Stephen's mother) will like to hear that," she replied. "Boy, who and you do that?" She questioned the nervous lad. He answered again with tears in his eyes. "Anyway, don't pay that *no mind.* Don't bother with McKay John. Nothing going to happen to you." She said. Well, that surely did not appease the troubled youngster, for he had just revealed in detail to the old lady what had transpired without receiving solace. "O right, Stephen, tell Siderlyn good night for me, yo hear," said the old lady. "Okay, Ms. Porcho," he replied and left immediately.

Still dissatisfied, Stephen decided that he must get some help, and the only way he could get that help was through an old person, he thought. His other target was Daddy Mac (McCauley), an old fisherman from Carriacou whom he assumed might know his way around the compartment of superstition. He wasted no time revealing what had happened on that Old Year's night and mentioned all his accomplices. He reminded Daddy Mac that they had only nine days to live and that he must quickly do something about it. Daddy Mac sat for a while and then laughed uncontrollably, wiping his teary eyes. The old man replied, "I don't think anything going to happen to you, but to be on the safe side, go under the Boulie tree where you cook the food and pray early each morning for nine days before the sun come up, okay. All, all-yo." The old man again burst out in laughter and shook his head, amused. "So we wouldn't dead?" Stephen asked pitifully. "No," said the old man, and the lad left quietly.

Stephen was very contented to hear Daddy Mac's remedy; it was the first time for the entire day that he felt at ease. The young lad immediately relayed the information to all of his friends and told them what they had to do to keep from dying within the next nine days. Unfortunately, anxiety got the better of him that night, and he was unable to sleep soundly.

Early Tuesday morning before six o' clock, the group of seven teenagers gathered under the Boulie Tree to start their first morning of prayer. Sylvan, realizing that he had been given another opportunity to live, took the state of affairs very seriously and brought with him a bell. He rang the bell during the prayers. The other six members made use of their turns by praying meaningfully.

Later that morning, Terrence was on his way to Ms. Irene's and was greeted by Mr. McKay. "Terry, you in it, too!" the old man shouted. "No, Mr. McKay," Terrence replied, "I did not steal the fowl, but I eat some of the food. Yo cud forgive me, please?" he begged the old man pitifully.

Mr. McKay assured him that he would forgive him. On hearing that, Terrence begged the old man to forgive his cousin, who was also part of the plot, but Mr. McKay refused. "No one else," he yelled. Although Terrence left feeling somewhat relieved, his relief did not prevent him from joining the crew under the Boulie tree to pray for the remaining days. They did it consecutively until the ninth day, and after no one had died, they were so remorseful that they all decided to do an extra three days of preying.

◆◆◆ □*Chapter Nine*

FRED HEMCEED

Mr. Fred was a loner who was not hesitant to have a drink or two, but he liked the company of young boys.

I n the little village of Campbell lived a middle-aged man named Frederick Hempseed. His neighbors called him Fred. Fred lived alone in a white stone house with a dog he called Ned. Stones are bountiful on Union Island, especially in the district of Campbell. Fred's house was built during the 1960s when concrete houses supplanted the previously wattle & daub and board houses that had been pervasive throughout the Grenadines. The natives sometimes referred to them as thatch houses.

Wattle & daub houses on Union Island were built of a mesh of woven sticks and vines chiefly acquired from the rich mangrove vegetation that lies endlessly along the coastline. These meticulously woven sticks and vines are skillfully smeared with mud—a combination of cattle dung and a special type of dirt that is proportionately mixed into a dough-like paste that possesses great bonding capability. One location of Union Island where the most suitable soil was found for building these houses was in the vicinity of the late Mrs. Mo and Kent Hutchinson at Clifton Road. In essence, the wattle supplies the mesh, and of course, the daub is the mud. The roofs of these villas were made primarily of grass, making these small shelters amazingly attractive (page 42). Again, these were the first dwellings on Union Island, and of course, they speak well of the ancestors' skills in creating stuff of astonishing complexity.

Now, Mr. Fred was a loner, a white man who was not hesitant to have a drink or two, but he liked the company of young boys. He was one of those cunning, deceptive recluses who really enjoyed and took advantage of the liberty that existed on this pristine and unspoiled cay. He never wore a hat; he thought it was too hot to cover his head in a hot, tropical island such as Union. He walked along the beach early each morning and looked up at the clouds. Once I heard him say, "Rainbow in the morning is fishermen's warning, but rainbow in the night is shepherd's delight." He was staring at a rainbow that morning.

Many times, he mentioned that his homeland was Ireland, but he said nothing in detail. He did not speak with an Irish accent, which makes me now wonder where this short white man was really from. "Row, row, row your boat gently down the street, merely, merely, merely, merely life is but a dream," he would sing under his breath. He never talked about his friends and family back in Ireland, but he mentioned he had a daughter or a niece; I cannot quite remember exactly which it was. I can remember clearly these two words that he repeatedly uttered: *Sapoo Fay* and *Gadiloo*. That's exactly how they were pronounced, but they were foreign words. I did not know what language it was. *Sapoo Fay*, he said, meant "What to do?" I would sometimes listen to what he had to say while my father would so often engage him in conversation while we were on our journey to take care of our animals. We reared a lot of animals deep in the bushes of Ms. Irene's, and we had more than one hundred of goats. We were proud farmers, and although I was relatively small then, being the second son of my family, I was deemed the principal caretaker of our large herd.

I was a part of almost all the activities and decision making at home. I had multiple responsibilities. They trusted me very much, and I felt I was obligated to perform way above the abilities of my siblings, and I was expected not to make the kind of mistakes that my siblings made. This perception was a disadvantage, as I began to look at my life very seriously, and would later rebel in my early twenties. I would exhibit high levels of defiance when I thought that my rights were challenged.

The onus of responsibility was squarely on my shoulders, and the weight of accountability affected me both positively and negatively; I am now a perfectionist and can spend painstaking amounts of time to get a job done, even if it may be daunting and extremely challenging. The negative is that I may expect total commitment from others who, by today's standards, may not possess that level of tenacity. I later learned from the renowned English author Dr. Samuel Johnson, who wrote, "As I know more of mankind I expect less of them. I am ready now to call a man a good man upon easier terms than I was formerly." That surely mitigates the stress of expecting too much from others; it renders a bit of solace.

But who was this man called Mr. Fred Hempseed? Was that really his name? What would cause someone—a foreigner, for that matter, to leave the comfort of his country or origin to make the most southerly island of St. Vincent and the Grenadines his home? A third-world country at that. An island that was deficient of nightlife, void of electricity, telephones, and even the hope of having a television to connect with the outside world. Transistor radios at that time ware the sole method of communication with the outside world, yet, amazingly, this man never looked back at his country, not even for a vacation.

There were neither proper medical facilities nor hospitals to handle the sick. Hence, anyone who succumbed to a serious illness was transported by boat to the mainland (St. Vincent) for medical attention. Fred did not have a wife or children, and he surely did not have a woman or a girlfriend. He did not come to Union Island as an entrepreneur, nor was he a part of any philanthropic or altruistic organizations. He did not possess any of the qualities that would have rendered him productive at his new abode.

Because he was not personable, no one expected him to be community oriented, for he was never a part of any social gathering and was seldom seen as a spectator of any of the local sports on the island. He really kept a low profile. He was abnormally reticent, and that may have been the best thing for him to be. He was totally out of sight, for lack of a better word. Being a recluse kept him from being under any possible surveillance if anyone was out to get him.

No one knew enough about him to speak of Mr. Fred Hempseed at length, so they did not. Hence, this question must be asked again and again. Who was this man? A stranger he was in the legal sense, yet the government of that day did not question his presence and could not care less for that matter. It is believed that he was not a resident of St. Vincent and the Grenadines, but was amicably accepted by the people of Union Island, who were overly humanistic by nature. To the older folks, he was their neighbor. They treated him as their own, and he exhibited neighborly responsibilities as well. He had a huge water tank, a cistern, and he was never hesitant to give a couple of buckets of water to his immediate neighbors during the almost ubiquitous dry season that has plagued Union Island from the time of the ancestors even until now.

Mr. Fred has been deceased some thirty years, buried at Ashton Cemetery on May December 7, 1981. He occupies a space among the graves of the ancestors. His tombstone states that he was born on May 2, 1902. Unfortunately, we may never know who Mr. Fred Hempseed really was; whether he was a fugitive—as was said of John Donaldson (mentioned later) by two white couples, a mercenary, or just another peaceful and humble resident who choose the serenity of the Little Tahiti to spend the remainder of his life. Many are a bit dubious about the latter, for the scars of his sealed left ear spoke voluminously of his former life outside of Union Island somewhere on another frontier. Only heaven knows.

WHO WAS JOHN DONALDSON?

Shortly after Ms. Hunt became Mrs. Donaldson, Mr. Carville left his teaching job at the school to work at the Ministry of Finance in St. Vincent. Did he really work at that ministry?

It was on a quiet Sunday afternoon at Basin Beach. Usually on a day like that, one would expect the Baptist church to be loudly singing "Tell me, how you did feel when your sins were washed away," as they prepare to baptize another convert. That afternoon I was walking the beach alone when two white couples, gracious in their approach, asked me my name, age, where I lived, the whole nine yards. I eagerly acceded to their request and even divulged more information than they requested. Immediately, they became fond of me, and I was comfortable, too, so I asked them if they had sailed all the way from America to Union with a yacht. They did not tell me that they were from America; I just surmised that most white folks were from America.

At the secondary school that I was attending, we had an American teacher by the name of Ms. Helen E. Hunt, so I went on to talk about her because she, too, was from America. Now I should have been at Sunday school by then, but much time had already passed, and if I'd had any intention of going to Sunday school, I should have been home at least two hours earlier. But I had already planned out my afternoon, and Sunday school at Gospel Hall Church was surely out of my roster. To make matters worse, I was enjoying the company of those white folks. It was much better than listening to Brother Lenox (Sunday-school teacher) for two Sundays in a row.

But as the hours passed, I began to feel on edge. I felt it was time to go home, but at least I had a worthwhile excuse to give my parents as to why I was not at home in time for Sunday school. Just before I left their company, one female asked me, "Do you know John Donaldson?" Yes, I replied, once again I was engaged and ready to spew the contents of my guts. "He has a goat that eats money—a big goat," I continued in elation. "His name is not John Donaldson," she replied as she fixed her stare on me. "He is a fugitive." She was rather contemplative.

"What is his name?" I asked. They all smiled but never responded to my question. "What is his name?" I bellowed in excitement again and again but to no avail. At this time, I guessed that I had outstayed my welcome, but in fact, they were enjoying every moment of my presence and my dialect as much as I enjoyed their company. "He is a fugitive," the other female replied again as I prepared to leave. I bid farewell and left immediately as the sun crept its way toward the horizon.

It was not a bad day at all I thought, as I got closer to home. "His name is not John Donaldson, and he is a fugitive?" I continued asking myself repeatedly.

These two statements aroused curiosity in my mind, but I did not know what to make of them. I did not know what the word fugitive meant, either, but the little old Oxford Concise Dictionary, being the only dictionary at home, became the final authority. I was not in the mood to discuss with my parents what those white folks had told me, nor was I in any hurry to relate to my friends or siblings what I had heard. I thought that Mr. John Donaldson was still living in Union Island at that time and did not know what all of this meant. Little did I know that those two statements I'd heard would give rise to unanswered questions that would puzzle me for many years to come. Still today, after almost forty years, the best I can do is to make conjectures.

Helen Hunt, as I mentioned earlier, was one of two teachers sent to us from Canada as a humanitarian gesture; this information came through the grapevine of informal communication. Later, we were told that these two teachers were from the United States of America.

Ms. Helen Hunt and Mr. Mike G. Carville were excellent teachers. They started as teachers at the Union Island Junior Secondary School on June 5, 1973. My classmates and I later learned that they were Peace Corps volunteers. Whatever that was, it surely did not mean too much to us then, for we were wrapped up in the art of learning. Ms. Hunt taught language arts while Mr. Carville was responsible for mathematics. The discipline that Ms. Hunt taught us in class has influenced me so profoundly that it has stayed with me even until today. Mr. Carville was subtle and less imposing.

Mr. Mike G. Carville was well versed in teaching mathematics, and the method that he employed was well received. The name of our class was Form 2A, and by now we were doing extremely well, but as the saying goes, "All good things must come to an end." Indeed, the end was closer than any of us had anticipated. Ms. Hunt married the aforementioned John Donaldson after a short time—maybe less than one year. Mr. Donaldson established a construction company, bought land, and built houses that provided off-and-on employment for some of our local contractors. I had seen Mr. Donaldson but once, and that afternoon he appeared drunk. That afternoon he came to Crossroad with a huge ram goat. Some of the kids at the time were saying that the goat ate money, and that was appealing to me as a youngster. He had two daughters, Elizabeth and Kate (Katharine). Kate was the younger sister. We attended the same school during her stay on Union Island; she was my classmate.

Shortly after Ms. Hunt became Mrs. Donaldson, Mr. Carville left his teaching job at the school to work at the Ministry of Finance in St. Vincent, or, so we thought. He never returned to Union Island after that and was never seen by his students again.

Although there are many charitable organizations that welcome people who truly desire to reach out to the less fortunate, and many good people do volunteer to devote a year, several years, or even their entire life to work overseas among the needy; it must be questioned whether it was the true intention of these two people to volunteer their services in a third-world country? Again, some of the same questions raised about Mr. Fred Hempseed (mentioned before) might be asked about these two people. Why would they confine themselves to a lesser standard of living than what they could attain in the great US of A? During such time, they were not offered housing and living conditions that commensurate with the life that they were accustomed to in their homeland. This is not to speak disparagingly about Union Island in any way, fashion, or form. This is just the unadulterated truth. Being candid and ingenuous is just in good keeping with integrity.

Ms. Hunt's stay in Union Island from that point on was short-lived; she, too, left quietly. Her husband also disappeared.

It was reputed that a yacht came near where he had built his house in the Richmond area and abducted him. This is an area where he was said to be living quietly, if not peacefully. If Mr. Donaldson was indeed abducted or forcefully removed from his residence, then we must question by whom? Was the government of St. Vincent and the Grenadines aware of what was taking place in the Little Tahiti at that time? Unfortunately, Mr. Donaldson was never heard of or seen again. The vast acreage of land where Mr. Donaldson once lived in the vicinity of the Richmond, Union Island, now bears his name, with no negative connotations attached to it.

Some folks said that after spending many years in her homeland, the USA, Mrs. Helen E. Hunt-Donaldson finally returned to visit Union Island one last time.

Although Unionites have known and referred to John as Mr. Donaldson during his stay on Union island, and acreage of land on the map of Union Island now bears the name, Donaldson's Estate. It is said that the spelling of this man's name is in error. His name is now understood to be *JOHN DANIELSON*, as opposed to the name that Unionites are accustomed to 40 plus years ago.

PERPLEXED

A massantow or Flambeau is a bottle with a narrow mouth, (a wine bottle) half filled with kerosene...Lit to provide light.

It was now in the 1970's, and the roads of Union Island were still in dilapidated conditions. My family and I have been living in Campbell since 1968, and it was common knowledge that one day there would be a paved road that leads from Campbell to the pastures of Ms. Irene. We were also told that this road would eventually extend all the way around Union Island. We were accustomed to the use of numerous tracks to take us almost everywhere we wanted to go, and our legs were our principal and only means of transportation. These tracks were rocky, thorny, and unfriendly to our bare feet. We had to contend with the irritating leaves of the Burn Bush, Stinger Nettle, and the notorious Red Man Blood (Thorny plant). The leaves of the latter may lay camouflaged amongst the numerous dry leaves during the severe dry season. The thorns of the Burn Bush are clear crystal, so when one is pricked with this notorious plant, there is no need to make an effort to extract those seemingly colorless needles; it is best to leave the needles where they are. The needles from the Burn Bush plant exude not only a burning sensation but also a highly agitating itch that irritates for a long period of time.

So yes, we were excited about hearing our parents and other natives talk about the paved road coming to fruition; we now had something to hope for, a dream. This proposed new road would be a replica of the existing roads, which consisted of two-lane tracks or wheel strips that ran parallel to each other. That was the most economical means for the government to provide viable roads on the island during those early years. These lanes were meant for the tires of motor vehicles, most notably the jeep, which was the first means of vehicular transportation on the island during the early 1960s. So, this proposed new road would have been a boon, enabling us to use a vehicle when necessary, but more importantly, to ride our bicycles from our homes all the way to the pastures of Ms. Irene where our goats were tied and kept.

We had quite a few animals to take care of: goats, sheep, cow, pigs, chickens, and ducks were a few of the many. Taking care of many animals was a huge part of our daily responsibilities. The latter three were reared at home. In fact, we were involved in the largest animal husbandry on the island during those earlier years; hence, we were never buyers of fresh meat, poultry, or even fish.

Being a kid and expecting a road in rural areas did engender a bit of excitement. I had my plan concocted and in place, for I had been looking at my father's old bicycle for a very long time. I intended to use it as soon as the road was put into place. Unfortunately, this road never materialized as anticipated, but surprisingly, what transpired two years later was so baffling that it left me confounded for many, many years to come. The idea of writing this book had been on my mind for quite a long time—since I was nineteen years old. However, the drive it took to get on my computer and make (UITN) and *"Union Island's History –Servitude, Metayage, and Civilization,"* a reality, essentially stemmed from this imprisoned story that I am about to set free.

It was a beautiful day; the clouds were high in the sky. I guess they were cumulonimbus if my memory serves me correctly. Change was in the air -something seemed to be happening. At 4:30 P.M., my brother Urias and I were on our journey to the bushes of Ms. Irene to take care of the numerous goats and cows. We had just come in sight of Mr. Fred Hempseed's house when we saw two small jeeps parked with their keys still in their ignitions. That drew our attention, but we had to hasten our travel to Ms. Irene's pastures before darkness set in.

On Union Island, and on all the Caribbean islands for that matter, the sun always set early. Six o' clock and it would be pitch-black. Nevertheless, we were on our way when we observed that work was being done on the road. Excavation, tree removal, boulders, and so on were in progress. We were tempted to stop and look, but the sun's haste to get to the horizon was enough to deter our puerile affinity for folly. So, we went by hastily, took care of the animals, and returned quickly. It was evident in our minds that we were not going to be thorough in taking care of the animals that afternoon. We glanced at each other, and that tacit message was fully communicated. We returned to the worksite, and there were three white men still working. But they did not stay much longer, for they had done quite a bit earlier that day and were just about ready to retire after a hard day's work.

The following day, two others accompanied the three white men. They cleared the road rather quickly, almost to the Devi-Devi tree that overlooked Basin's beach. It would take another two days to get to Basket, a local pond that we used to supply drinking water for our animals. Wells were pervasive throughout the island, but none were available at such an altitude.

The clearing of the much-anticipated road continued, but instead of continuing in the path where the old track existed, it made a sudden ninety-degree turn just before it got to the pond. That raised concern for my brother and me, for this road, did not appear to be going where the old road existed, which was where we reared our animals. This road ran another 120 meters through the dense bushes east of Basket Pond and then took a sudden right turn 140 meters up to a small hill. This hill overlooks Basin Beach and the entire coastal area, which encompassed Queensbury Point, Frigate Rock, Carriacou, Petit Martinique, Petit St. Vincent, and Palm Island (Prune); it offered a clear but partial view of the Clifton Harbor. From there, one can remain in seclusion and observe almost every marine activity at a distant.

Though there were limited manpower and minimal machinery for such a gigantic task, the clearing of the road went quickly. Vehicles were driven all the way to the top of the hill now; the hill is known as Fort Basin. It is situated near a plot of land owned by Ms. Izolyn, Zennie's mother (mentioned earlier). By then, she was an old woman who lived up the Village of Muddy Street, or Pauper-Land as it was called during the earlier years. Rumor had it that those white folks were going to build a house at the top of the hill. The hill was cut clear of its vegetation, giving more reason to believe that a structure was imminent on that particular site. What was a bit intriguing in retrospect is that I have never observed any person of authority from Union Island or St. Vincent visiting that site or giving it any form of approval.

In my observation, not one adult engaged those folks in any conversation. Every adult I knew who was present during that time acted as though they were consumed with other social issues that did not allow them time to do anything else. Most were rather standoffish, as though it were out of bounds to even venture near those guys. It was a tacit feeling of acquiescence that we, the natives, exhibited toward most foreign folks. It always made me feel out of place. But this attitude was so pervasive in the community that any action or inaction contrary to the folkways or customs would have stood out negatively like a sore thumb. To look back now at this and other similar experiences, I can genuinely say that the institution of slavery had its profound impact on us then, and even to this day. These folks did not say too much to us despite the fact that we were kids who could not resist the temptation of satisfying our probing eyes.

That new road provided easier access to other grazing pastures. We sometimes rotated from pasture to pasture, giving one exhausted area ample time to replenish itself with fresh grass. On the new concrete road, the logical step to follow would have been placing a layer of well-orchestrated concrete capped with a layer of pitch. After all, it was in the hands of white folks, and in our minds, much was expected of them. If anyone could have done the best job, it would have been white folks. Or so we thought.

In the late afternoon and into the night, these white men remained in the bushes with backpacks but never gave the impression that they were strangers. They knew exactly what they were doing. They were on a mission and were accomplishing their mission quickly. Then suddenly, two local masons built a small concrete shed with a galvanized roof. It was located close to the coastline of Basin Beach but in an inconspicuous area. The sand for building the structure was collected at the nearby beach. Those were the years when residents had the privilege of using bayside sand for all their construction. That privilege has since been taken away because it only harms to the land that is already susceptible to sea erosion.

Basin Beach is an almost isolated, beautiful beach of Campbell where lots of boats and small vessels came in unnoticed from other islands with foodstuffs, liquor, and other valuable commodities without having to pay tariffs or excise duties. These boats would come in late in the evening laden with products, spend approximately two hours there, and then disappear to another location. This was a long-time custom that helped many shop owners to escape the enormous taxes that the government charges.

This form of illegal trade was not exclusive to Union Island. Nevertheless, it is believed that this method of evading customs with contraband escalated into drug trafficking on a large scale.

About a week later (1973), after the construction of the shed, my brother Urias and I left home on a Saturday night at 8:00 PM. with a flambeau / massantow and caucus bag, to catch crabs in the lower area of Campbell. A massantow is a bottle with a narrow mouth, (a wine bottle) half filled with kerosene, and plugged tightly with a cloth extending approximately four inches into the bottle while another inch and a half protrude out of the bottle to be lit by fire. While the fire is lighting, the bottle is tilted every ten minutes so that the kerosene can provide fuel to the fire. Though this may be considered primitive by today's standards, it was an effective method of providing a sustainable glow of light during those dark nights when electricity was only a figment of the imagination. It efficiently provided light for us during crab catching, opossum (Manicou) hunting, and turtle catching—and even for our fishermen who desired a well-lit massantow in the early morning after a hard night on the sea.

We were excited to leave home that night; finally able to flex our muscles and enjoy doing some manly things. We were not up to visiting some of the regular crab-catching spots, so we went to a couple of other areas where we sighted only two crabs but were fortunate to catch them. Now two crabs were not enough, so we decided to journey all the way to the bottom of Ms. Irene's where we could catch some bigger crabs. I carried the caucus bag while Urias had the massantow blazing high above his head. The shoreline was always the shortest distance, so we continued nonchalantly through the still of the night. In my mind, I always viewed my brother Urias as a very coward chap, and for that reason, I never felt totally protected in his presence.

One particular time while we were walking, I had a leery feeling and wanted to turn back, but I did not disclose it to him. We continued walking until we were just about to pass the last part of Basin beach. Then all of a sudden, the massantow fell and broke, and without delay, Urias darted toward the shoreline. "I see somebody, I see somebody," he exclaimed softly, again and again. Immediately that triggered my nervous system, and big beads of sweat began running down my forehead. I had to make a split-second decision, so I started to follow him in quick pursuit with all the energy I had.

There was not enough time to think; I could not tell whether he had seen or heard something. I held the bag tightly and was able to close the gap between us. Our quest was to distant ourselves from the location of the sighting. We were approximately ninety yards away when we looked back and saw that the wick from the massantow was still burning, and the grass around it was on fire. I was not surprised; I had enough experience with my brother in the past to know that he could literally run off and leave anyone behind if he ever felt the least bit threatened.

Though we had been somewhat shaken, we still had a bit of courage left in us, so we decided to return to the area of his sighting. Some time had passed, and we were curious to look at the grass that was on fire. We walked the beach a few feet before converging on the blaze. There we found ourselves just a few feet away from two men with bags, walking toward the shed that I mentioned earlier. We froze there for a few seconds, and these seconds escalated into a minute or two. Suddenly, four more guys appeared walking by to a red dingy where they were offloading some merchandise. "These are faces that we had seen before," I whispered under my breath. The sighting of these familiar faces allowed my beating heart to slow down, and somehow I was at peace with myself. Then unexpectedly, a bottle from one of those guys fell into the water. Urias grabbed it immediately and handed it to one of the men, but the bag-like box that the man was carrying was so unwieldy that he could not receive it at the time. He returned a minute later and began to ask us, in a very friendly manner, our names and what we were doing alone in the dark of the night.

Eventually, I found myself helping to hold the dingy steady on the shore from the raging waves. Urias, on the other hand, was busy helping to tote those box-like bags to the shed. We ended up with a few dollars in our pockets and a new flashlight that we eventually used on our destiny to Ms. Irene's. We were so excited that we never discussed what might have been the contents of those bag-like boxes.

We were elated to use our well-earned flashlight to get to Ms. Irene's, where we could catch some big crabs. We took a cursory glance at the grass on fire, but it did not appear to be escalating into anything out of control, so we did not try to put it out. We left the site immediately for our journey to Ms. Irene's. Our crab-catching venture was more than successful; there would have been enough crabs for another half bag, but we had only one bag. Within an hour, we were on our way back home, with the legs and claws of the crabs protruding from the bag; that was rather uncomfortable against our bodies. We wanted to carry the bag on our backs, but we would have had to risk getting clawed if we were not careful. So, we took turns carrying the bag all the way home. On reaching home, we put the contents of the laden bag into a drum. We had enough crabs to last us for approximately three weeks after we had given some to our grandmother Telina Roach and her best friend Rosanna; they both lived at Point Lookout, Clifton.

A few months later as the rainy season made its approach; grass and shrubs began to grow profusely on the newly excavated road. Because of a lack of proper drainage, the unmanned water eroded the road so badly that vehicular transportation was no longer possible. Maintenance was never done on the road, especially the part that turned at a right angle from Basket all the way to the hill at Mr. Izolyn. This continual growth of trees and shrubs, as well as the improper drainage of water on this road, caused it to look like a forest in only a couple of years.

The remains of a safe-haven at Basin beach. This was once a valuable repository. As seen here, it was well built then and is still structurally intact today, after forty years.

As quickly as these men had come, they disappeared. They

left an unfinished road that turned to a track and later to a forest. The holding house or safe house used to house their dingy and the numerous box-like containers were left at the mercy of the weather. Looters later removed the galvanized roof and wooden door, but as the picture above shows, this fortress was well built to provide service at a time when they needed it. It can be seen at the western end of Basin Beach. It still is far from conspicuous, as it lies hidden by the evergreen Manchineel trees that provide shade at the beach.

Based on what has transpired, one can only surmise that the intention of these folks was never to build a house at Fort Basin. The cutting of the trees and the clearing of the site were to provide a proper lookout for the valued commodity that they had expected on that particular night. Many have seen the above structure I am sure, but never knew when it was built and why. The next time you visit Basin Beach, be sure to take with you a camera or your cell phone; you might be tempted to take a picture.

ABBOTT MANURE

"Where is Verrette?" the white man asked, then reluctantly he left the shop without uttering another word. He was never seen again.

The name Abbott Manure was a familiar name to the residents of Ashton Harbor, Campbell, and later, the entire island during the latter quarter of the 20th century. One may ask, what was Abbott Manure? Was it just a conveniently manufactured name, or was it a plant's food as some had thought? And if it was deemed a plant food, then where did such large quantity of this product came? This may sound a bit puzzling, but surely, all of the above questions and concerns will be answered in the multitude of paragraphs that follow.

In 1975, the sheltered Bay of Chatham became extremely busy when a yacht laden with merchandise was eager to offload its cargo so as to stay afloat and sail another day. That was what Mr. Phillip Mondazie Thomas, a caretaker of a private property at Chatham Bay, Union Island was told. Three white men he said, boarded and coerced him into providing storage for their valued cargo; a cargo that they referred to as Abbott Manure."

Mr. Thomas, a short, burly man, was born in the neighboring island of Dominica in the year, 1905. Almost everyone in Union Island had an alias, and there was no exception with Mr. Thomas, he was known throughout the island as Mr. Verrette. In fact, only a few people on the island had known his correct name. Mr. Verrette found love on Union Island and became the mate of one of the native daughters of Ashton Valley. Being a paid watchman at Chatham, he subsequently had to make that secluded part of the island his home. His function was to take care of two houses on that plot of land that was owned by a foreigner named Mr. Ray.

One afternoon, while the sun was swiftly making its way to the horizon Mr. Verrette was confronted by a group of white men who wanted to use his home as a storehouse for their cargo,

"Abbott Manure. "Although he had been breathless when they confronted him, he still felt a sense of status in that he had been privileged to grant his bequeathed superiors a favor. Huge bales of fully packed manure were at his doorstep before he could accede to their demands. He directed them to the two houses that he had been watching over for several years. His little shack was just too small for the bulk of merchandise that they brought to him. Hastily, the merchandise was packed tightly into some rooms of the two houses that he was looking over. Mr. Verrette was paid a small sum and cautioned in no uncertain term to keep what he knew out of the public's domain.

A still tongue was all that was needed to avert the dissemination of this information and avoid alerting the frail authority (police) on Union Island. But Union Island is a place where everybody knows each other's business, and so, to keep a secret in Union Island is almost impossible. Just as these white men had arrived without notice, they likewise disappeared almost instantaneously, but not before cautioning him again that they were going to be back pretty soon for their prized commodity. Mr. Verrette really thought it was plant food, and he was sure he had the privilege to use a bit of it. After all, he had a garden too, so he made use of some of the plant food at the roots of his pigeon peas. This resulted in a drastic turn of events; many are still confounded even until today.

"A still tongue keeps a wise head" is a meaningful verse in the book of Proverbs, but in general, it is more rhetorical than practical these days. Residents of Union Island believed in the mass dissemination of news—and any form of information, for that matter. If something major were to happen at Point Lookout, Clifton, within a few minutes the entire island will be notified. In Union Island, it is customary that people tell their neighbors where they were going, even if they were to leave their homes for just a few minutes. "Nabe, I am going to Clifton to see Cousin Mabel; I hear she's not feeling well." And after that, one could be questioned at any time in that community about the trip to Clifton and how Cousin Mabel was doing. In short, everyone communicated everything mouth to mouth, for there were no telephones on the island.

Mr. Verrette was no different. If he had been reticent when he first visited Union Island; he evidently had succumbed to the rigorous demand of assimilation. No one holds a secret on Union

Island; no one. Well...maybe a few, but Mr. Verrette was not one of those few; it was just a matter of time before a strong drink would have loosened his tongue.

Some weeks had passed since those white folks from the yacht had visited his home at Chatham Bay, and he could not resist the temptation of talking to some old friends about what had mysteriously happened at his home. Mr. Verrette had a small boat, and he usually left Chatham to visit his former home at Valley to see some of his old friends, and to take care of some of his personal needs. Whatever that is? Among these friends, Verrette was truly in his comfort zone; evidently, his demeanor and actions clearly evinced the level of excitement that he felt among them. In the company of his friends, the old man would reminisce, drink, laugh, and have a good time. He also did his grocery-shopping there as well. One Sunday afternoon at a local rum shop, Mr. Verrette kept repeating haughtily, "I big," but no one knew what Mr. Verrette was talking about. He would command the shopkeeper to serve him and his friends beers and liquor, and then before the table was empty, he would call for another round. Without giving too much away in words, he would repeat the expression, "I big." He felt burdened and obligated to share his news bulletin. He wanted to "spill his guts" as the saying goes. He was exhibiting lots of hints, but he wanted someone to literally dig it out of him. "I big," he shouted again as he poured himself a drink into a glass. Because he was under the influence of alcohol, it was clear that the appropriate scenario was created whereby he could relieve himself of his burden. That evening he spoke in depth about his affiliation with his newfound white friends and the bulk of plant food that he was left in charge of. Unfortunately, that was the beginning of the end; no one knew exactly what he was referring to, but soon everyone became eager to find out. A week later, he offered samples of the fine manure to his close friend and another friend in the Campbell area. Mistake! That is all that was needed for this product to get into the hands of a couple of savvy people who knew just enough to take advantage of the situation.

As news gets around, some youngsters, decided to travel on foot, all the way to Chatham Bay to the caretaker's watch-house. They wanted to break into the properties to get the product, and they knew it could only be possible when Mr. Verrette was not at home. The first invasion of the houses at Chatham began on a Sunday while Mr. Verrette was out at the Ashton Harbor having a great time with his so-called friends.

On that same Sunday afternoon, Urias, one of my siblings was on his way to the pastures of Ms. Irene to get one of the milking cows. On his way, he was skylarking, picking seaside grapes, and taking his sweet time cruising along when he came up to the famous Divi-Divi tree that overlooks Basin Beach. At that location, he could clearly see everything on that beach all the way up to Palm Island. On Basin Beach was a small fishing boat with some of the local fishermen, and they were offloading huge, boxlike cargo. "There was one female inside of that boat whom I knew very well, he said, she was very compassionate but cunning as a fox; I waved to her, but she never waved back." That woman, whom he described, has been deceased well over two decades ago. At the time, there was nothing that Urias could have made out of what he had seen except to think that it was just another case of contraband, which was the norm. In fact, every shopkeeper engaged in that form of trade. It was until a few weeks later that he learned what the shipment was really about. But by the time he had found out what had been happening on Union Island, everyone else had already been informed. Remember now, the island was very small, and the news did get around quickly.

So, where did these guys get the box-like bags that they were offloading? One key thing was missing. He did not see a huge boat anchored in the deep where this small boat would have gotten its cargo. But the bags sure reminded him of the ones we had seen many months earlier when we met those white folks on Basin beach while on our journey to catch crabs.

Now, returning to the subject of this episode: Where was Mr. Verrette while his house was being looted? He had already shared his secret while under the influence of alcohol, and that was just about the end of that, or so he thought. How careless can a man be in the distribution of something that does not belong to him—and worse yet, making himself a target in such a secluded area? The product that was deemed to be Abbott Manure was now in every nook and cranny in Union Island. This was a result of numerous timely raids on Mr. Verrette's home when he left Chatham Bay to visit his friends at Ashton Bay. Some took boats to Chatham Bay, took the goods, and journeyed directly to Basin Beach, where the goods were offloaded and transported via vehicles to their diverse locations. In addition, lots of young men went to Chatham Beach on foot. Bales of this product were found in many remote areas of the bushes of Colon Campbell, where they were hidden and protected for safekeeping.

Almost immediately, it was discovered that "Abbott Manure" was really marijuana. "Oh, drugs are on the land," was the cry of the righteously indignant. Yet this product can be found at almost every home on the island. In the meantime, the protective authority on the mainland of St. Vincent received circumstantial information about the influx of this product on the island. This resulted in another form of influx—policemen whose physical presence was viewed by the people of Union Island as adventurous rather than investigative.

The deluge of marijuana on Union Island was a novelty not only to Mr. Verrette, an innocent citizen, but also to the majority of older folks. They literally had never seen a sample of this product in their entire lives and could not differentiate it from any regular bush or herb. And they knew nothing about its constructive or destructive use. However, the word was out that it had value and was rather expensive. Every adult male then tried to get possession of this illicit product to make some money. But as occurs in the world of business, when there is a large influx of any product on the market, it can force demand and supply out of balance, lowering its worth. And Union Island being so small was just an added disadvantage to the "wannabe" pusher. A few took to the sea to sell their freebies to other regional islands for whatever prices they could attain just to get the product off their hands. Then there were a minuscule few that was really savvy; they did make good on their trade.

Meanwhile, the protective force was able to get possession of a large quantity of the ubiquitous marijuana that surfaced from time to time, but without making any physical arrests.

One afternoon at the junior secondary school playground, the students were playing cricket, then suddenly, two policemen came out of the nearby police station with three large containers of marijuana. They emptied the containers, heaped the contents into one large bulk, and then lit it on fire while students were still playing their game. The students stopped the game immediately and circled the fire in curiosity; the scent escalated as the fire grew larger. That pungent scent caught the attention of the whole village, and soon many people began coming toward the burning pot. The officers tried to keep the students at bay from time to time, but there were just too many onlookers. Some older folks were disgruntled and were voicing their opinion on how wrong it was to burn drugs in front of students, but these officers did not respond. The dried herbs were completely burned in approximately one hour, and then the officers took a couple of buckets of water and put the fire out.

Realizing that his properties had been entirely relieved of the valued commodity -Abbott Manure, Mr. Verrette became disappointed, deflated and depressed when he realized that he could not trust anyone, even his best friend. He did not know who had stolen the manure and hence could not ascribe the blame to anyone in particular. His spirit was dampened, but he still had the will to live. He began to spend longer periods at his recluse in Chatham Bay. Unfortunately, loneliness would prompt him to retake his small engine boat back to Ashton Harbor, where he would again exhibit his generosity by spending a few dollars and having a couple of drinks with his so-called friends. It was the only form of recreation that he had, and he found solace in it. The two words that he had been using incessantly with authority (I big) were no more; it appeared as thought they had gone into seclusion.

After about eight months, all developments surrounding Mr. Verrette had become "stale news." Most people thought it had all concluded and that those white folks would not return to Union Island anymore.

One Sunday afternoon, after having a drink or two at a local rum shop at Ashton Harbor, Mr. Verrette left. The shop was rife with activity when suddenly a tall white man with blond hair and blue eyes showed up. In a calm voice, the gentleman asked about the whereabouts of Mr. Verrette, having been alerted of Mr. Verrette's weekly itinerary. The shop was instantly silent. The lanky fellow finally asked again in a calm voice, "Where is Verrette?" Hesitantly, they told him that they did not know who Mr. Verrette was. Reluctantly he left the shop without uttering another word and was never seen again.

What was quite surprising was, that after Mr. Verrette had his fill with his friends, and as drunk as he often was, he would get into his boat all by himself, start up the engine, and head all the way back to his home in Chatham. And despite his state of drunken stupor, his friends never saw fit to accompany him to the lonely destination he called home. This he had done on many occasions; his final trip was on a Sunday afternoon in the month of December. Many residents of Campbell can still remember seeing this little engine boat as it passed Frigate Rock on its way to Chatham Bay. It was the last time that I saw Mr. Verrette and his boat as he eagerly made his way beyond Queensbury Point into oblivion. Permanent oblivion, that was.

One day later, Mr. Verrette's little engine boat was found at Long Rock, an area at Chatham Bay. It appeared as though the engine had been powering the boat continuously without direction until it ran out of fuel. As a result, the exterior of this unmanned craft was harshly battered and bruised. But there was no sign of Mr. Verrette; remains of foodstuffs were found inside of the boat when it was retrieved. The dwellings of this old man at Chatham Bay were quite intact, and there were no signs of foul play or a break-in.

The tomb of Phillip Mondazie (Verrette) at the Ashton Cemetery

Two days later, the old man's body was found floating some 200 meters off the shore of Chatham Bay, in the vicinity of Long Rock. His body was immediately towed to the Ashton Harbor later that evening, where it remained until the following day. He was buried early that day at the Ashton Cemetery, a burial ground that bordered the seashore. To date, no autopsy was conducted on the remains of Mr. Verrette's body. It was reputed that fish to some degree had eaten his body.

To this day, no one can be certain how Mr. Verrette spent the final minutes of his life, whether he met his doom at the fate of his drunkenness or at the hands of a skillfully revengeful predator.

Everyone seems to agree it was the latter.

Rumor had it that the crew from this mysterious yacht that approached Mr. Verrette at Chatham Bay had narrowly escaped the surveillance of a marine drug enforcement agent.

EPILOGUE

I have come to the point where I must again close this book; it is the unabridged version of UITN. My passion is still coercing me to continue writing, but there is a time for everything. And as I have expressed before, there will always be another day to write or tell another story. In the words of Aristotle, he said. "Tell them what you are going to tell them; tell it to them, then tell them what you told them." I did. And I do hope that I have conveyed successfully all of the key points on the history of Union Island in this book. Again, this book is the extended version of *Union Island Then & Now*. I know that there are much more that I still want to share –the little things, and they too have their places. During my literary journey, on "*Union Island's History –Servitude, Metayage & Civilization*" my greatest motivation was to write the complete history of Union Island. I also wanted to share some of my experiences on the island –the subtle things that had been pent up in me for almost my entire life. Because of this, I still spend sleepless nights on my computer pecking away at the keyboard. The italicized phrase below which I coined several years ago has become more relevant today than ever: *"While many are comfortably asleep, I am wide-awake and tediously at work."* I do hope that one-day I will be relieved of the copious information that saturates my brain.

On some occasions, it appeared that I was living for one reason, and one reason only, and that was to eat sleep and drink in the history of Union Island. I did it ravenously because it was never made available to be read, not even in the classroom. Well, it is done. Amen! And this I observed is the existing state of the Now on this still unblemished landmass –A Paradise!

Throughout the entire 20th century, though various elements in part have contributed to the current state of Union island's culture, the principal underlying part must be ascribed to the ever-present Exodus Factor. With the age of social transformation reaping havoc worldwide, the people of Union Island though without mass institutions of change, are awakening to a new dawn. The once vibrant agricultural sector is now at the mercy of a technologically advanced demographic that assumes the title, "knowledge workers." Today, as the quest for academic advancements becomes even greater, so too does the quest to venture abroad to pursue a better life. This, however, has resulted in a mass exodus of natives to several developed countries to satisfy those needs.

History has taught us enough about the formally ubiquitous cotton crop that literally was the systemic lifeline of Union's economy during the period of Slavery and Metayage. The drastic declination of this industry during the mid 19th century represented a loss of wealth for the investors. Later cotton has given way to the corn/pea crops during the turn of the 20th century. Although the latter is currently at its lowest, no significant crop has supplanted them thus far. Hence, the subsistent factor that was considered dominant for the better part of the 20th century is now archaic as its compatriot -the old bartering system. The absence of exports of the island's resources such as Tamarind, Divi-Divi, sugar apples, crabs, and by-products of farming and fishing have disappeared over the years. The numerous vessels that have been an integral part of the import/export trade for a period of eight decades have taken a significant nosedive, unfortunately. The Fishing industry too is impacted negatively since those principal fishermen have transitioned to the ancestors without effectively imparting their knowledge to the youngsters. Regrettably but true, it should be questioned whether there is a legacy of fishing in Union Island. Again, the Exodus Factor is partial to be blamed for this.

The Maroon, Vessel Launching, Maypole dance, Fisherman's Party, Harvest, Regatta, Woman's Police Day, Dancing of the Cake & Flag of the traditional marriage, and many other customary practices over the past 50 years have practically gone by the wayside, resulting in a declination of the island's culture, and some of its invaluable virtues. And regrettably, the Wake, Lightning Up (All Saints Night) and Christmas Carol serenading are struggling to stay alive. The Easter gala that has evolved into the noted Easterval celebration is currently gaining momentum and has supplanted the age-old communal spirit of Christmas.

Back in January of 1968, when I returned to Union Island,

our first night at Campbell Village was spent without a television. Gone were the days of looking at the show, *Batman & Robin* –a TV show that we once enjoyed in Laventille, Trinidad. As kids, we had to adjust quickly, and somehow, we did. During those earlier years, I observed that Union Island did not have electricity, telephones, gas stoves, secondary school, banks, airport, and proper roads. Several years later, some of the above became available. Later, with technological advancement, the computer, Internet, Cable TV, phones lines, and many other gadgets have surfaced, and so were the tablet, and the ubiquitous Cell Phones.

In a poverty-stricken island as Union, the residents depended heavily on the corn & pea crops, and the rearing of animals as a source of food. The latter may generate a meager to nondescript income. And although fishing has been an integral part of the island's livelihood for centuries, it too generated very little in the way of revenue. With only a pittance in their pockets to spend, the residents buy food and clothes –the chief areas where their monies were expended. Today, still with a smidgeon in the way of an income, the residents are now encumbered with the expense of cell phone, cable, Internet, electricity, and prodigious gas bills. The latter can be substituted with the use of firewood as a source of fuel. But in an evolving culture where everyone is inclined to keep up with the Joneses, it appears that societal pressure is far too overwhelming to avert. Nevertheless, to do otherwise is a clear demonstration of socioeconomic or cultural inferiority.

In my estimation, I do not think that it is wise to abandon all of the old customs and tradition that make up the culture of Union Island; for although people need to understand new ways of life, it is senseless to forget the olden days –the past. In all honesty, it grieves me badly and makes me sad to see that the old ways are forgotten, and all of the old skills have been eroded and lost.

Folks, you have read this time and several times before, but perhaps it bears repeating: The occasion has arrived, and we, the sons and daughters of Union must accept the inevitable as the current state of affair. History has shown us clearly without any shadow of doubt that the ever-present *Exodus Factor* is here to stay. Amazingly! A population of approximately 3.5 thousand that occupies a landmass of 3.5 sq. miles remained constant, amidst one century of incessant farewells.

Bibliography

Ancestry.co.uk © 2002-2013 Ancestry.com

Ancestry.Com © 1997-2013 Ancestry.com

Ancestry/Genealogy-Family tree & Family Historical Records

Bill Cosby (2013) Negro History lost, stolen or strayed –Great Documentary.

BlackPast.Org -Remembered & Reclaimed, an online Reference GUIDE TO AFRICAN AMERICAN HISTORY.

Columbus Sally & Ronald Behm. (1995) What Color is Your God?

David Freeman Hawke (1971) Benjamin Rush: Revolutionary Gadfly.

Douglas A. Blackmon – Slavery by Another name: The Re-enslavement of Black Americans from the Civil War to World War II

E. Carolyn Graglia (2016) Domestic Tranquility –Summit Ministries

Fender Frederick Abildgaard. (1915) Alone in the Caribbean – Outing Publishing -University of California, U.S.A.

Frazier Adrian Dr. (1980). Development of peasantry in St. Vincent 1846-1912. Thesis presented at U. W. I., Barbados.

Forward Susan Ph.D. (1997) Emotional Blackmail. Harper Collins publishers, Inc., USA.

Hai Matsu (2015 Publication) -Slavery by Another Name.

History of the British Colonies. *Internet Archive.*

Jacques Daudin (2010) A Socio-Political history of Union Island.

Kings James Authorized Version. The Holy Bible.

Library of Congress Unchanged Memories -Reading from the Slaves Narratives.

Morse. (1778) Report on the Grenadines to Lord Mac Carthney.

Mulzac H. N. Captain (1963) A star to Steer by. International Publishers, Co., Inc. USA.

National Archives of St. Vincent & the Grenadines (Government).

Nichols H. Dr. (1891) Diary of a trip through Grenada, the Grenadines and St. Vincent.

Richard Newman, James Mueller (2011) Antislavery and Abolition in Philadelphia. EMANCIPATION AND THE LONG STRUGGLE FOR RACIAL JUSTICE IN THE CITY OF BROTHERLY LOVE.

Scrubb-Kirby, Cleo. (1975-1976) The Unionite Magazine.

St. Vincent Gazette (Government).

Tcmuseum.org/culture-history/salt-industry.

THE ENCYCLOPEDIA OF CARIBBEAN RELIGIONS (2013) UNIVERSITY OF ILLINOIS PRESS *Urbana, Chicago, and Springfield.*

The Gilder Lehrman Collection © **2012** The Gilder Lehrman
Institute of America History **www.gilderlehrman.org**

Josiah Stewart (2013 Publication) Union Island 'Caribbean
Paradise' Then & Now.

Zinn Howard. (1980) A People's History of the United States.

Born on Union Island to **Sheila** Roache and Garfield Stewart, a young Josiah only three months old was taken to Trinidad, an island where his parents were able to get work to provide food for three young children. Already a student of the Piccadilly Government School, Port-of–Spain, in 1968, Josiah now six years of age, was brought back to the land of his birth -a place where his umbilical cord had been carefully severed from his mother's placenta. To Josiah, Union Island was a new world, and instantly he fell in love with it. This little island represented freedom -the kind that he has never experienced anywhere else.

Author & historian: Josiah Stewart Sr.

Even today! Amazingly, he immersed himself fully into the island's lifestyle and quietly drank his full of its dialect, customs, mores, folkways, and norms. He reared a multitude of goats, sheep, cattle, and pigs on almost every pasture of Campbell. Fully engrossed in the garden that provided plentifully, the young man played a significant role there too.

He attended the fame "Small School" and the larger Ashton Primary School, both at Ashton Village. Then in September of 1972, he was enrolled into the Union Island Junior Secondary School, also located at Ashton. This school was timely built to elevate the then horrific educational level that existed for a long period of time on the island. Despite attaining some favorable grades throughout his school life, assimilating into the educational system of that day was exceedingly daunting.

Youthful, vibrant, energetic, and strong, a teenaged Josiah

left the confines of the beautiful little island to perpetuate "The Exodus Factor," a system that had already been an integral part of Union island's culture for approximately one hundred years. Fortunately, he was already impacted sturdily by the island's culture and an unquenchable desire to grow -an asset that he held on to tenaciously. In his quest to excel on foreign soils, the young man learned firsthand that the importance of food, clothes, and shelter supersedes everything else –Abraham Maslow Hierarchy of Needs (1943). "These are the fundamentals of life and existence," he said. "Hence, it was paramount that I gave priority to these basic necessities of life during the many trying years and experiences in America."

"Like the late Hugh Nathaniel Mulzac and the multitude of hardships that he encountered in America, I will be derelict not to reference the numerous challenges that I too have experienced here. Markedly, for most Caribbean people, where the status of residence may be unfriendly to them in foreign environments, the ability to advance in life is often met with fierce, sustained challenges. As a result, countless educational dreams and aspirations were reluctantly sidelined." He further indicated that this plight might not be exclusive to him, or Caribbean people per say, but an experience that many dark-skinned people from all walks of life have endured on frontiers thousands of miles away from their natural habitats.

"As a Unionite, the source of countless obstacles and hindrances that have negatively impacted my educational advancement have begun during my formative years," he said. He then continues. "Mine started at the famed Small School at Ashton, where vital resources were exceedingly limited or nonexistent, to begin with. It is out of this state of lacking, or being without, that I attained a modicum of patience, humility, and a fervent yearning to strive for a better life. And although that innate hunger hasn't been waned over the years, I do understand clearly, that Nature - that redoubtable force that engulfs, protects, and sometimes harm us, has no predators, but countless preys. And as we grow older as human beings, we are confronted with myriads of impedimental health issues that are deemed inevitable. The likes of Hypertension, Diabetes, Prostate enlargement, Arthritis, Myopia or Presbyopia, Dementia, cancers and other diseases, are only a few of the many conditions that determine our abilities and inabilities to continue life's journey; but at what pace? Not to mention the quandary or opportunity of attaining the stature of Old-Age."

"The above question has rightfully brought my writing to a conclusion. Working in the capacity as a Health Care professional in New York City for the past few years, I felt blessed and opportune to deliver love, empathy, compassion and hope to the sick. For the Will-Less, aspiration, enthusiasm, excitement and a newfound purpose for life. And for the strong, a smirk, a smile, and then another that inexorably escalates into a hearty laughter."

"With meaningful transformation, my life has just begun," he stated. "And as Caribbean people, we all have a testimony of a similar nature to share." He continued, "For me, perseverance is the key, but one's character is the litmus test." Ase!

THE ANCESTORS

Below are the names, of the ancestors, our ancestors of Union Island: The mothers, fathers, aunts, uncles, sisters, brothers, sons, daughters, grandmothers, grandfathers, great grandmothers, great grandfathers, cousins, in-laws, and relatives. Ninety percent of which the author has known personally; the other 10%, he has seen and may have spoken with at least once.

The names of the beloved ancestors are now alphabetized for easier access. If by chance the author has missed, failed to include or record the name of anyone that have transitioned during recent years, it is only by error. Nevertheless, Unionites must take into consideration that none of their beloved deceased have transitioned before the year 1967. Peruse carefully with an unavoidable feeling of nostalgia. The End.

Aaron Douglas (*Doug*)
Ada Scrubb
Advira & Irvin Adams
Agatha & Harold Dennis (*Jap*)
Agatha Simmons
Agnes Roache-James
Alban Alexander
Alcina & Lawrence Wilson (*Larry*)
Alfred Cox
Alice & Allan Scrubb (*Ba Allan*)
Alston Charles
Amelia Scrubb (*Ms. Popo*)
Amos Stewart
Amuthel & Conrad Adams
Anella & Garnet Stewart
Anella Harvey

Anesta Harvey
Angelic Saxon
Ann Jane (*Baby*) & Joseph Coils
Annie Adams
Arabella Cyrus (Brown Best)
Audley Alexander (*Sugar in the boots*)
August King Mitchell
Augustine Cox
Aubin McKenzie
Avis Mills & Casey Abraham
Baby Hutchinson
Baby Douglas
Beatrice Samuel (*Day-Tay*)
Benita Thomas
Benjamin Adams
Bentley Stewart

Bernadette Noel
Betty Haynes
Blossom & Adrian Simmons (Burn Man, *Mammam Mueh*)
Boysie Scrubb
Branford Saxon & Louquisha
Canny Ambrose (*Brother Can*)
Caroline (*Anto*) & Augustus Ramage
Caroline & Gransul Joseph (*Lab*)
Caroline Roache (*Telina, Tan Tillix*)
Celestine Saxon
Ceretha
Civil & Abraham Snagg (*Bram*)
Civil Ackie

Claire Ackie-Friday
Claude Ambrose
Clement Noel
Clem Stewart
Cleve Mulrain
Conscience Scrubb
Constant Allen
(*Corn-do-doo*)
Cosmus Joseph
Crystal Clouden
Cynthia & Ewirth Cox
Daphne Ackie
David James
David John (*Gayman,
Lally*)
Denty Jones
Denzil Stewart
Dogma Mulzac
Dolly & James Selby
Donna Dallas
Dora (*Maa-ta*) & James
Stewart (*Chiquita*)
Dora Campbell (*One
hand Dora*)
Edmond John
Edmond Wilson
Elaine Simmons (*Ta
Lain)*
Elaine Wills (*Mother
Lyn*)
Euine & Elbert Jones
(*Chammer*)
Eldon Thomas
Elitha Scrubb (*Mamma
Lee*)
Elizabeth Cox (*Dee-
Dee*)
Elizabeth Simmons (*Liz*)
Ellen & Jonathan
Alexander (*Lixy*)
Elma & Russell Wilson
(*Russ*)
Elmina and Gilbert Cox
Elvin Burton Joseph
Elvis Ambrose-Prince
Emelda & Milton John
Enna Ramage
Eny & Efford Joseph
Eris Samuel
Ernest McTair
Essie Stewart & Charles
Jones
Esther & Theopolis
James
Ethneil Mitchell
Etty Scrubb (*Tettie*)
Euthrice Warner
Evelyn & Caser Room

Ezekiel Roache
Faith Ambrose
Faith Coban
Faithful Bibby (*Jitterbug*)
Federica & Shem Room
Fegina & Gordon
Hutchinson
Felix Cox
Fena Alexander
Flora Ambrose
Florence Charles
Florence & Buckley
Forde
Florence Wilson
Fred & Zena John
Fred Hutchinson
(*Caldo*)
Garfield Stewart (*Daddy
Gaf*)
George Hutchinson
(*King George*)
Girvin Thomas
Gifted Wilson
Gladys Simmons
Gloria Saxon / Mitchell
Gussy Hutchinson
Harriet & Theopolis
Longdon
Helena & Joseph
Wilson
Henny & Theopolis
Regis (*Toffee*)
Henrietta Ambrose
Henry M. Stewart
Henry Stewart (*Soft
Walks*)
Herbert Thomas
(*Thomas*)
Hudson Mulzac
(Cayenne Waist)
Icy & Leacock John
Ida Alexander
Princess & Ifield Pope
Ina & Son Allot
Incoman & Millicent
Stewart
Inez & Ewing Alexander
Iola & Norris Harvey
(*Zuggy*)
Iris & Persival John
(*Bus*)
Isabella Harvey (*Bella*)
Isabella Roache (*Ta
Muggy*)
Ivan Quashie
Izolyn Bibby
Jacqueline Stewart
James Cudjoe

Jane Ann Daniel (*Tan
Jane*)
Jane Ann
Richards/Morgan (*Ce
Margin*)
James Isaac (*Brother
McKie*)
Janey Roache
Janey Stewart
Janie & Goldstein
Alexander
Jean Frederick
Jestina Alexander
(*Jesso*)
Jestina Clouden (*Ms.
Costy*)
John Roache
Johnnie Joseph
Joycelyn & Johnson
Thomas (*JT*)
Jonah Stewart
Joseph James (*Yagga*)
Joseph Roberson
(*Jiggery*)
Joycelyn Quashie
Julia Joseph (*Momma*)
Julie Wilson (*Ma-Jules*)
Kelvin Selby
Kenny Ambrose
Leah & Robert Wilson
(*Togo*)
Lemuel Ambrose (Lem)
Lenie Joseph (*Dema,
Auntie Mearl*)
Leonard Stewart
(*Sandman*)
Leonie Mills
Lettuce & Pentland
Selby (*Ah-who way*)
Lillian Robinson & Ellie
Andrew (*Woopsin*)
Linda & Jerrus Stewart
Lorna John
Lucita Joseph
Lucille Simon-Small
Lucy & Wilfred Daniel
(Santas)
Luther Bibby (*Bronson*)
Lydian & Conrad
Ramage
Lyn Room
Lynette James
Mable George
Margaret Ovid
Mariah Clouden
Mariam James
Mary & Mano
Hutchinson

Mary & Wycliffe Hutchinson

Madeleine Ramage

Mary Edward (*Ce Mary*)

Mary (*Tall-away*) & Norbert Stewart

Masson Wilson (*Tanty Ma*)

Mattie Thomas

Matthew Jones

Maudlin Polson,

Mavis Ambrose

Maybe & George Clouden

Maybe Ambrose (*Tan-Tan*)

McKay John

McNeal Cox (*WDM Cox*)

Medford Blencoe

Meldon & Emelda John

Mercy & Isaac Hutchinson

Methrina Scrubb

Mie (*Ta Mie*) & McCauley Vesprey

Mildred & Festus Hutchinson (*Esso*)

Mildred Alexander (Ce Mildrey)

Mildred Simeon

Milford McIntosh

Millicent & Solomon Stewart (*Ball a-Fire*)

Millicent Alexis

Mona Jones (*Ma Mone*)

Morgan Snagg (*Uncle Morgie*)

Ms. Brownie

Ms. Mo & Kent Hutchinson

Muriel Hutchinson

Nathaniel Alexander

Nathaniel Stewart (Natty)

Neta

Noreen Alexander

Nurse Celina Clouden

Olive Clowden

Ony Scrubb

Oscar John

Patience (*Lena*) and Royal Noel

Patient & Bertram Stewart (*Big city*)

Patient Wilson (Ma-Phish)

Patricia & Ozias Paul

Percival Thomas (*Brother Tom*)

Peter Alexander

Peter Mitchell (*Shuvvy, Poo-Pa*)

Peter Wilson (*Father Priece*)

Presaul Ambrose (*Presey*)

Preston Ramage (*Kayber*)

Pricilla (*Mom, Look-Sin*) & Wilton Wilson (Wash brain)

Pricilla & Leo Gellizeau

Pricilla John (Porcho)

Princess & George Samuel

Princess Alexander

Princess Ambrose-Bernadine

Purgin Wilson (*Ba Purgin*)

Rachel Simmons

Ralph Joseph

Rebecca Noel (*Faithful*) & Mc Lawrence Noel

Ritiann & Claude Scrubb

Ronald Mulzac

Rosa & Pablo Scrubb

Rosalyn Jones

Rosanna Hall

Rosetta Ambrose (*Ta hn*)

Rubina & Carlton Lucas

Ruthven Alexander

Safety Hypolite

Samuel Regis (*Sweet Rose*)

Samuel Saxon

Sara Hutchinson (*Miss Tony*)

Selwyn & Pauline Stowe

Siderlyn Wilson,

Simeon Stewart (*Daddy Stroad*)

Sonny Wilson

Stella & Fen Badnock

Susanna Hall

Susanna Hall

Sydney Alexander

Sydney Roache

Tantoo Wilson

Tensy Ambrose

Terrence Scrubb (*Blow Way*)

Theopolis Stewart

Titus Hutchinson

Tyrell Harvey (*City*)

Tyrell Wilson

Una & Joseph Hutchinson

Uncle Bus

Veda & Thomas Coy

Venetta & Almond Mitchell (*Cat Balloon*)

Verna & Sylvan Hutchinson

Victoria Hutchinson (*Miss Vic*)

Victoria Hypolite (*Tanty Vic*)

Vileria McTair

Vincent Brown (*Biggest*)

Viola & Joseph Alexander (*Uncle Joe*)

Violet & Johnathon Roache

Virginia & Sylvester Alexander (*Sylves*)

Walton Bubb

Wap-Wap Stewart

William Stewart (*William Toast*)

William Thomas

Willimina Adams

Wilma Hutchinson

Winston Douglas (*Sky-Lay*).

Winston Longdon -Tano

Made in the USA
Columbia, SC
06 June 2018